Hands-on Azure Pipelines

Understanding Continuous Integration and Deployment in Azure DevOps

Chaminda Chandrasekara
Pushpa Herath

Apress®

Hands-on Azure Pipelines: Understanding Continuous Integration and Deployment in Azure DevOps

Chaminda Chandrasekara
Dedigamuwa, Sri Lanka

Pushpa Herath
Hanguranketha, Sri Lanka

ISBN-13 (pbk): 978-1-4842-5901-6
https://doi.org/10.1007/978-1-4842-5902-3

ISBN-13 (electronic): 978-1-4842-5902-3

Managing Director, Apress Media LLC: Welmoed Spahr
Acquisitions Editor: Smriti Srivastava
Development Editor: Matthew Moodie
Coordinating Editor: Shrikant Vishwakarma

Cover designed by eStudioCalamar

Cover image designed by Freepik (www.freepik.com)

Distributed to the book trade worldwide by Springer Science+Business Media New York, 233 Spring Street, 6th Floor, New York, NY 10013. Phone 1-800-SPRINGER, fax (201) 348-4505, e-mail orders-ny@springer-sbm.com, or visit www.springeronline.com. Apress Media, LLC is a California LLC and the sole member (owner) is Springer Science + Business Media Finance Inc (SSBM Finance Inc). SSBM Finance Inc is a **Delaware** corporation.

For information on translations, please e-mail rights@apress.com, or visit http://www.apress.com/rights-permissions.

Apress titles may be purchased in bulk for academic, corporate, or promotional use. eBook versions and licenses are also available for most titles. For more information, reference our Print and eBook Bulk Sales web page at http://www.apress.com/bulk-sales.

Any source code or other supplementary material referenced by the author in this book is available to readers on GitHub via the book's product page, located at www.apress.com/978-1-4842-5901-6. For more detailed information, please visit http://www.apress.com/source-code.

Printed on acid-free paper

Let this book be a daily reference guide for all the teams who use Azure Pipelines.

Table of Contents

About the Authors

Chaminda Chandrasekara is a Microsoft Most Valuable Professional (MVP) for Visual Studio ALM and Scrum Alliance Certified ScrumMaster®, and he focuses on and believes in continuous improvement of the software development life cycle. He works as a senior engineer - DevOps at Xamariners, Singapore. Chaminda is an active Microsoft Community Contributor (MCC) who is well recognized for his contributions in Microsoft forums, TechNet galleries, wikis, and Stack Overflow; and he contributes extensions to Azure DevOps Server and Services (former VSTS/TFS) in the Microsoft Visual Studio Marketplace. He also contributes to other open source projects in GitHub. Chaminda has published five books with Apress.

Pushpa Herath is a DevOps engineer at Xamariners. She has many years of experience in Azure DevOps Server and Services (formerly VSTS/TFS), Azure Cloud Platform, and QA Automation. She is an expert in DevOps currently leading the DevOps community in Sri Lanka, and she has shown in-depth knowledge in Azure Cloud Platform tools in her community activities. Pushpa has published three books with Apress and spoken at community events as well as in the YouTube channel of her Sri Lanka DevOps community.

About the Technical Reviewer

Mittal Mehta has a total of fifteen years of IT experience. Currently, he is working as a configuration manager. He also has experience working in TFS, C#, Navision, build-release, Azure DevOps, and in the automation and configuration area of Microsoft Technologies for the last eight years.

Acknowledgments

We are thankful for all the mentors who have encouraged and helped us during our careers and who have provided us with so many opportunities to gain the maturity and the courage we needed to write this book.

We would also like to thank our friends and colleagues who have helped and encouraged us in so many ways.

Last, but in no way least, we owe a huge debt to our families. Not only because they have put up with late-night typing, research, and our permanent air of distraction, but also because they have had the grace to read what we have written. Our heartfelt gratitude is offered to them for helping us make this dream come true.

Introduction

Demand for automation in the software delivery process has gone from an optional standpoint to a mandatory, essential, and integral requirement. To keep up with Agility in software development teams, there needs to be rapid and consistent software deployment methodology for development and operations teams to work together to ensure successful and fail-safe delivery of a software product to each target environment. It is essential to even provision infrastructure with automated code before deploying a software on a new environment to guarantee that all the required dependencies are set up before deploying software applications.

Azure Pipelines, which is the Continuous Integration and Deployment (CI/CD) tool in Azure DevOps, supports building, packaging, and deployment of software projects, developed with any language targeting any platform. It comes with a rich feature set that can be extended with various extensions, developed by Microsoft as well as third-party vendors and also community experts. If one cannot find an extension to do the job with Azure Pipelines, he or she can extend Azure Pipeline capabilities easily, due to its extensibility as well as readily available samples and templates for implementing such extensions.

Hands-on Azure Pipelines will take you through a journey with concepts of CI/CD and Azure Pipeline features and capabilities, while giving you a complete explanation of using each feature to implement the automation of your software project delivery using a consistent and robust approach. The book will highlight the capabilities in Azure Pipelines to build software developed in any platform and language, using Microsoft-hosted Windows, Linux, and MacOS agents, as well as giving you guidance on how to set up your own build environments with all three platforms. You will find hands-on guidance lessons to understand how almost each and every feature works in Azure Pipelines, including the latest YAML-based configuration and pipeline as code examples.

In addition to the exploration of existing features, the book will take you through the steps of extending Azure Pipelines, with additional tasks from the marketplace as well as implementing your own feature extensions, utilizing the Azure DevOps REST API. *Hands-on Azure Pipelines* will provide you with recommended build and release patterns to implement with Azure Pipelines and give you guidance on setting up artifacts and versioning for your release packages.

CHAPTER 1

Understanding the Importance of Software Delivery Automation

Modern software development heavily relies on agility as the key factor of success in a project or product development. Fast-paced technology growth and growing business trends require software to be delivered on time and with high quality. Such a rapid phase of development and delivery needs of software demand automations of the software delivery aspect to ensure quick, frequent deployments with a higher quality of production.

From setting up an environment to deploying a piece of software to that environment, software development should be codified and automated as much as possible to avoid human errors as well as to support a rapid release cadence, while maintaining the quality of the delivered software at the highest possible level. Automating the setting up of infrastructure as well as deployment and testing aspects of software reduces costs dramatically over the time of a given project or product, as it requires less human resource interventions. Adding to that, automation further prevents human errors as the same set of scripts or tasks utilized in each target environment enables consistency in deployments.

In this chapter, a quick introduction to automation of the software delivery process is provided, which is critical in Application Lifecycle Management (ALM) for software projects/products. Understanding the concepts of continuous integration (CI) and continuous deployment (CD) as well as discussing the importance of introducing automation of the deployment of infrastructure, configurations, applications, components, and enabling automation of testing after deployment will lay the foundation for the reader to comprehend and utilize the rest of the chapters in this book.

C. Chandrasekara and P. Herath, *Hands-on Azure Pipelines*, https://doi.org/10.1007/978-1-4842-5902-3_1

Lesson 1.01: DevOps

DevOps (software **Dev**elopment and information technology **Op**eration**s**) is the buzzword that you hear in the software development industry today. It defines the culture and practice of a software development organization. The aim of DevOps is to establish an environment where defining, building, testing, and releasing software happens rapidly, more frequently, and with a higher degree of quality and reliability. This requires an organization to adopt a collaborative culture where automation is a key belief. A company needs a significant amount of infrastructure changes or upgrades to support the new DevOps practices. In a DevOps culture, developers and IT pros are encouraged to collaborate and communicate more often with one another, which emphasizes the concept of teamwork. See Figure 1-1.

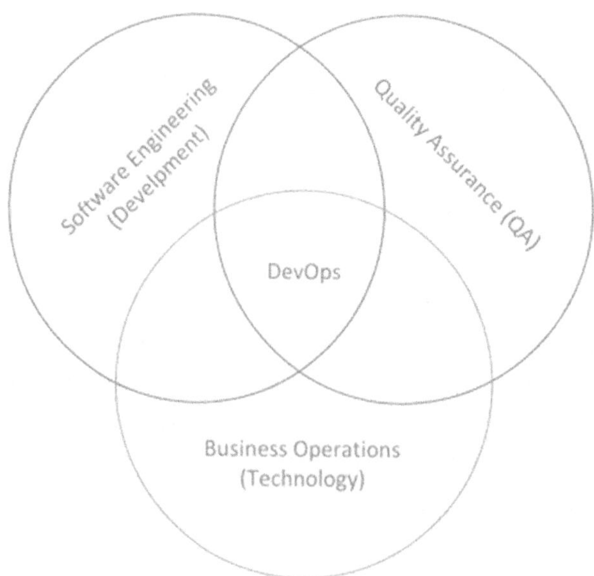

Figure 1-1. *DevOps at a glance*

Donovan Brown from Microsoft has provided a more meaningful definition for DevOps: "DevOps is the union of people, process, and products to enable continuous delivery of value to our end users." This highlights the fact that the people are the most important aspect of DevOps. People need to adapt practices and processes that help them to collaborate and contribute to the team's goals and create a culture where automation plays a significant role in delivering value to software users.

As mentioned, automation of software delivery is vital for delivering software with a higher quality and that takes less time to get to market. Hence, it is worth looking at deployment automation capabilities in Azure DevOps as a comprehensive suite of tools for DevOps. Let's try to understand the concepts of software building and deployment in the next few sections of this chapter.

Lesson 1.02: Continuous Integration (CI)

In a software development team, multiple team members develop code and contribute to create software functionality. While multiple people are contributing to a code base, keeping the integrity of the code base is important to ensure any member of the team can retrieve the latest code base, build and run it locally, and start contributing. To ensure the stability of the code base, two factors can be used. The first one is making sure the code compiles without errors. The second factor is making sure all unit tests are passed, with the latest code changes and code coverage of unit tests being at a very high percentage. A build can be defined to compile each check-in/commit to the code base and then execute all unit tests to validate the code base to ensure stability of the code base, which is generally known as a CI build. Depending on successful compilation and passing of all unit tests, the build can generate and publish output, which is deployable to a target environment. See Figure 1-2.

In addition to the unit tests, validation for code security vulnerabilities can be integrated into the build pipelines to improve the security aspects of a project/product. Further scanning for quality of code is also an aspect that can be validated in the build pipelines. Early detection of security vulnerabilities and code quality issues with such a shift-left approach would reduce costs in the long run, as a vulnerability detected in production would be costly to fix.

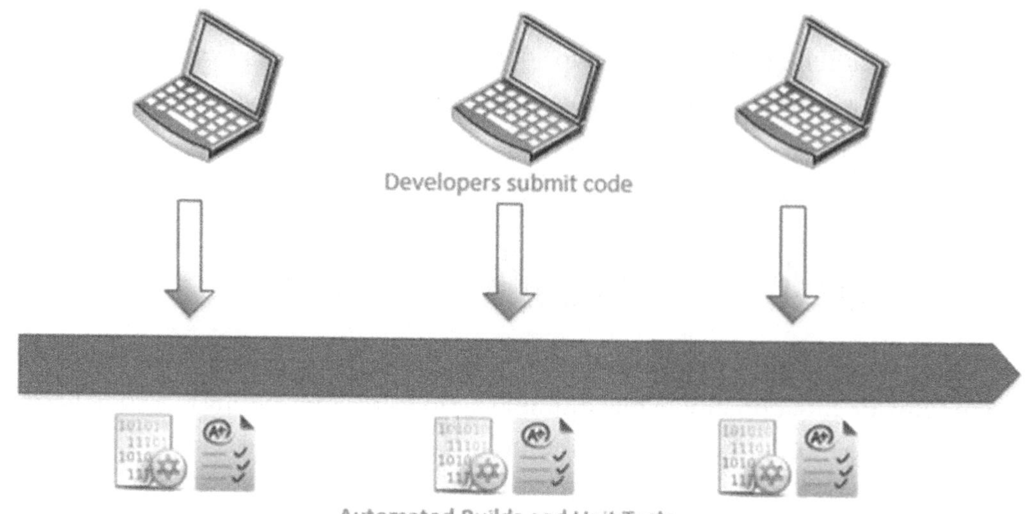

Figure 1-2. *Continuous Integration*

Lesson 1.03: Continuous Delivery (CD)

Development teams produce software in short cycles in modern-day software development approaches. One of the biggest challenges is ensuring the reliability of software releases to the target environments at any given time. A straightforward and reusable deployment process is essential to reduce the cost, time, and risk of delivering software changes. These could be incremental updates to the application in production. In a nutshell, CD is delivering software changes more frequently and reliably, and DevOps can be considered a product of continuous delivery.

Lesson 1.04: Continuous Deployment

Continuous delivery, on one hand, ensures every change can be deployed to production, while having the option to hold the production deployment until manual approval is given. On the other hand, Continuous deployment lets every change be automatically deployed to production. To implement continuous deployment, one must have continuous delivery in place, since continuous deployment is created by automating the approval steps of continuous delivery. See Figure 1-3.

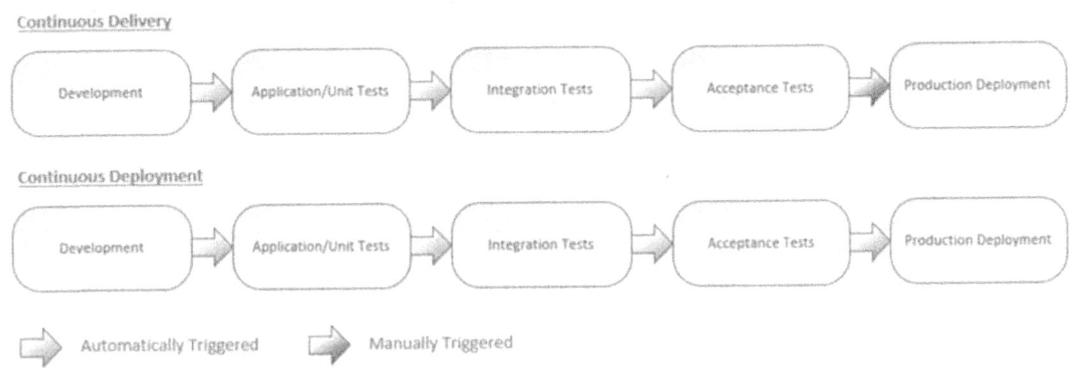

***Figure 1-3.** Continues delivery vs. continuous deployment*

Lesson 1.05: Release/Deployment Pipeline

A release pipeline delineates the sequence of actions from retrieving completed work from a source control to delivering software to the end user. The software retrieved from the version control has to be built, tested, and deployed to several stages before reaching the production environment in a release pipeline. The process involves many individuals, teams, various tools, and components based on the software development practice being used. A successful deployment pipeline should provide the visibility, control, and flexibility of the deployment flow to the teams/individuals using it. There can be multiple gates as well as approval levels to increase the reliability of software versions released via the pipelines. See Figure 1-4.

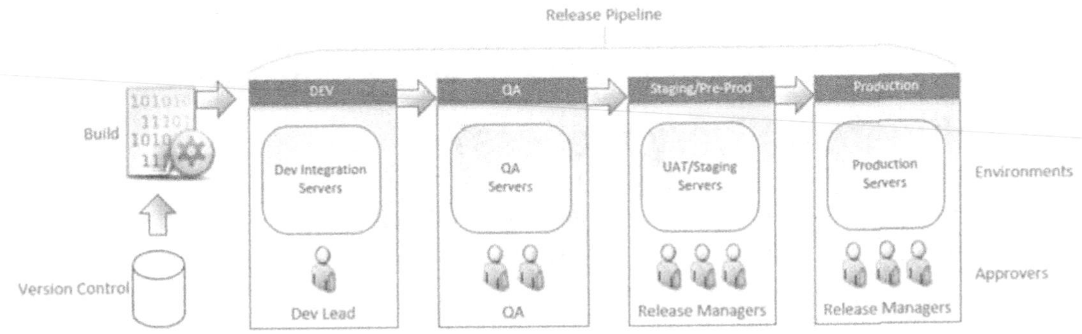

***Figure 1-4.** Release/deployment pipeline Release/Deployment Pipeline*

Lesson 1.06: Infrastructure as Code (IaC)

With the high demand of rapid deployments, setting up new environments to deploy software manually might possibly be a challenge and error prone. Hence, scripting the creation of the environment from scratch makes spinning up of the new environment faster and more reliable. Especially when targeting cloud platforms, setting up new environments with code gives faster, reliable results. Such code developed for setting up infrastructure is known as Infrastructure as Code (IaC). Having IaC allows even the version controlling the target environment setup in a given project, adding more traceability and visibility to how we set up environments. There are several tools and technologies we can use to implement IaC, and in this book we will be discussing them in more detail in later chapters.

Lesson 1.07: Test Automation Integration

As we have already discussed in continuous integration, the unit tests written to validate an application code should be executed in the build pipeline. However, there are other tests, such as functional UI tests, API tests, integration tests, and load and performance tests, which cannot be run at the build pipeline. The reason for the impossibility to run tests other than unit tests in build pipelines is that they are all required to be run against a deployed target environment. So, these types of tests other than unit tests should be integrated to the deployment pipelines to be executed, after deploying the project/product to the target environment. We will discuss more on test automation integration with pipelines in the Hands-On Test Automations book of this book series on Azure DevOps.

Lesson 1.08: Why Do We Need to Automate the Software Delivery Process?

We have discussed several aspects of software delivery process automation in the previous sections of this chapter. Without such software process automation, deploying software more often will be a challenging task. The Ops teams may have to spend a lot of time manually setting up and deploying new environments. There is a high possibility of missing steps in the setup, causing unexpected issues in new environments and causing the deployed software to not be usable or to have critical issues. All these would cost time and money to resolve. Further, setting up and deploying environments each time requires investing additional human resources for the tasks, costing more money. See Figure 1-5.

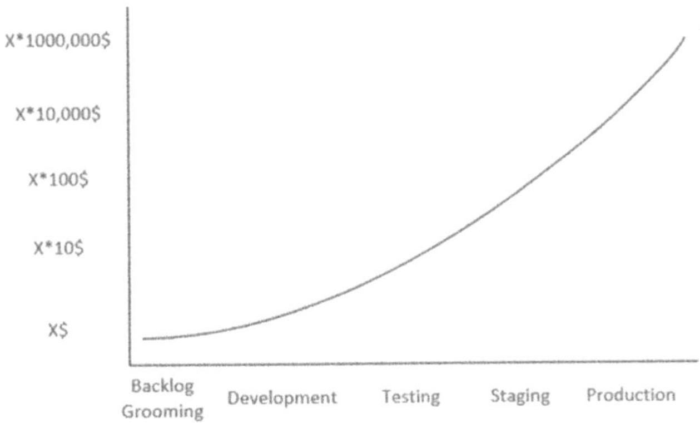

Figure 1-5. *Cost of bugs*

Without test automation to run regression and smoke tests on deploying applications, it would be impossible to perform full manual tests on each delivery, considering the time and human resources required to perform full testing. This may affect applications in two ways. One is skipping the tests because costs in testing may result in bugs creeping into production, which would cost more money or even cause clients to be totally dissatisfied. Sometimes such dissatisfaction causes legal action against software providers, which will sometimes cost the entire business and their reputation. The other option is trying to do all tests all the time manually to ensure quality, but that would cost money for human resources and delay the deliveries, causing the team to be unable to deliver on time. This shows the critical need of automation as much as possible to avoid costs and issues in software delivery testing. See Figure 1-6.

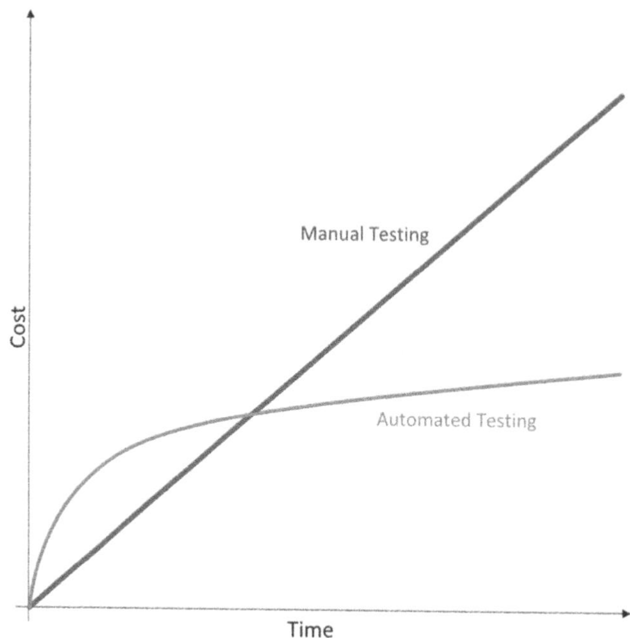

Figure 1-6. *Automated testing vs. manual testing*

To prevent all these costs, automating the deployment and testing combined with identifying security and other vulnerabilities in software, with a shift-left approach, is vital. Detecting these vulnerabilities as early as possible (on the left side of process flow as much as possible) will cost less money to fix them.

Summary

This chapter has taken you through the concepts of software delivery automation. We have explored the concepts of CI and CD, as well as the needs and benefits of using IaC and test automation to enhance the software delivery process. With this understanding of concepts around software delivery automation, we are equipped with enough background to explore the rest of the book's chapters, which are going to focus on Azure pipelines to implement the concepts discussed.

In the next chapter, we will discuss the overview of Azure Pipeline features that will support you in following the rest of the chapters, discussing each feature and its usage in detail.

CHAPTER 2

Overview of Azure Pipelines

Continuous delivery and deployment have become vital aspects of from the Detailed instructions link software development industry. As we discussed in Chapter 1, continuous integration and delivery pipelines instantly bring your software development process to a high performing and reliable level. Azure DevOps provides us with good features to create CI/CD pipelines according to our project requirements. This chapter will help you get an idea of Azure DevOps pipelines by providing a basic introduction to various areas of the Azure DevOps pipeline features.

Lesson 2.01: Introducing Pools and Agents

As you already know, CI/CD improves your delivery speed by automating the build and deployment process. When it comes to automation, you need a machine to do it for you without any human interaction. Azure DevOps provides agents to do CI/CD work for you. This lesson will help you to learn about these agents and where you can find them in Azure DevOps.

In Azure DevOps, you can find the Agent pool section under project settings. You will find all the agent details from the pool section. There are two types of agent pools:

Azure Pipelines: Microsoft-hosted agent pool containing machines with all platforms, Windows, Linux, and MacOS with many software tools installed in them.

Private /self-hosted Agent Pools: A default private pool is available and you can create more private agent pools as per your requirements. Then you can register machines in these private pools to be used as build or deployment machines.

Go to project settings and select the Agent pools under the pipelines section in a team project to let you view the agent pools. See Figure 2-1.

C. Chandrasekara and P. Herath, *Hands-on Azure Pipelines*, https://doi.org/10.1007/978-1-4842-5902-3_2

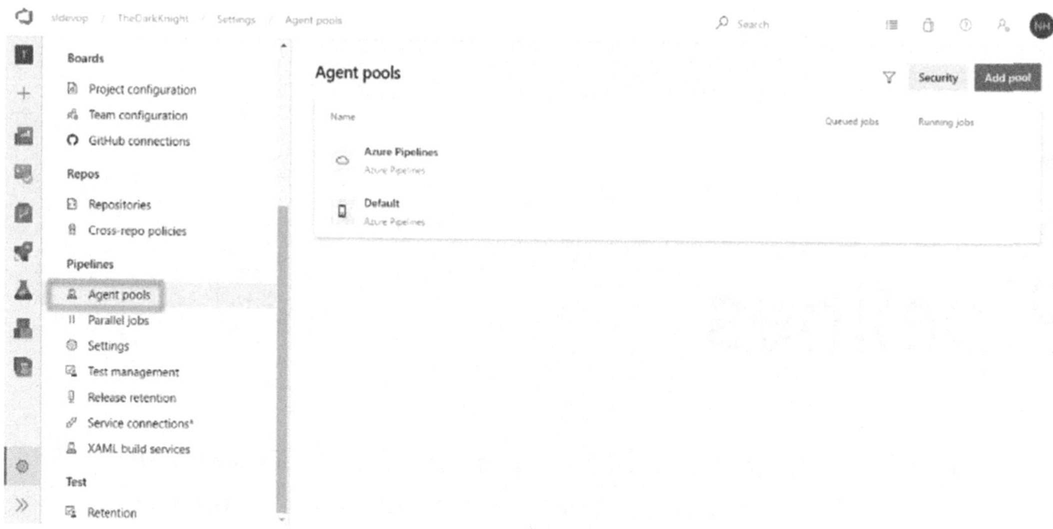

Figure 2-1. *Agent pool*

Azure DevOps allows you to use a number of hosted agents pipelines based on your project accessibility type such as private or public. Public projects let you use ten parallel executions on hosted pipelines at a time while private projects (where your source code or other project details are hidden from public access) only let you use one execution of a build or deployment at a given time. See Figure 2-2.

Azure Pipelines
Jobs Agents Details Security

Name	Last run	Current status	Enabled
Hosted Agent Online		Idle	On

Figure 2-2. *Azure DevOps agents*

As mentioned already, we can configure our own agents in private pools, which will be explained in detail in future chapters. After configuring a self-hosted agent, it will be added to the agent pool with all the information of that agent. As an example, the summary will give the details of the software installed in the agent with those versions.

Azure DevOps is well known for its multiplatform support. You are able to experience this multiplatform support of Azure DevOps once you check the agent collection in the hosted agent pool. Following are the different hosted agents available in the version we use for this book. It supports Mac, Ubuntu, and Windows. See Figure 2-3.

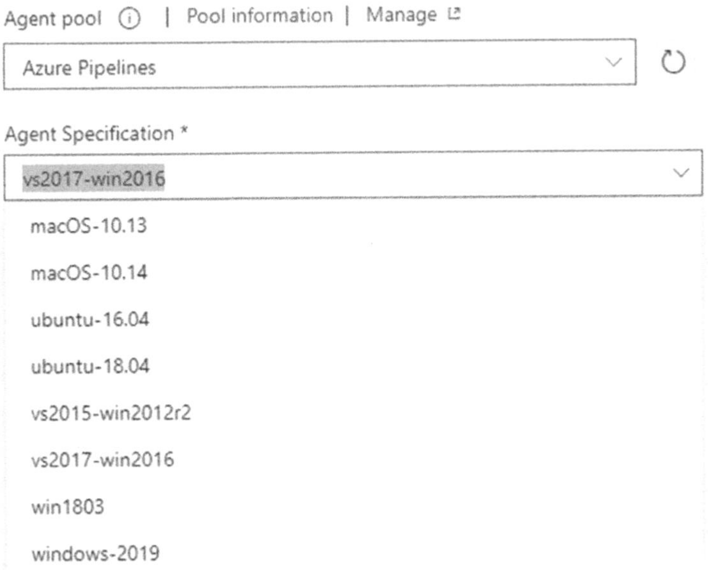

Figure 2-3. *Agents available in hosted agent pool*

Also, agent pool permission can be controlled to provide secure access. It has three main permission levels. See Figure 2-4.

- Reader - Can only view the agent pools
- User - Can view and use pools but cannot manage or create agent pools
- Administrator - Can administer, manage, view, and use agent pools

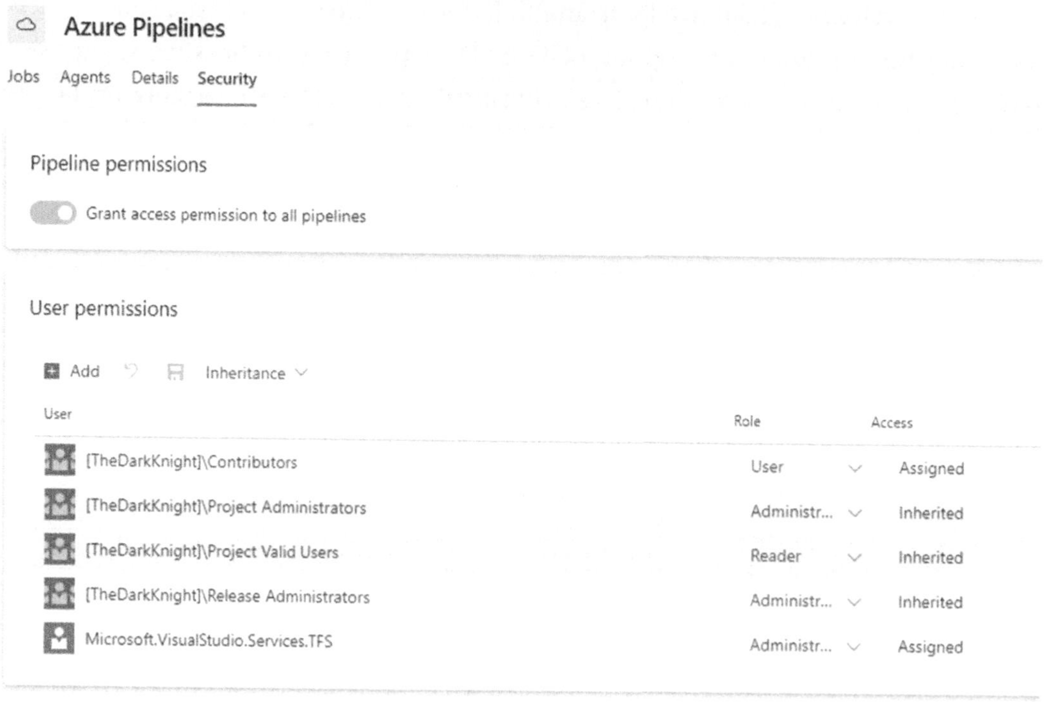

Figure 2-4. *Agent pool security and permission*

Even a single agent pool can be applied with individual permissions set similar to the one above.

This lesson explained what an agent pool is and what the types of agents available are. Further, we discussed that self-hosted agents' capabilities can be monitored using an agent pool capability section. Finally, we were able to understand how to control access and administer capabilities of agent pools using permission levels available in the pools' security section. We will discuss more details on agents in future chapters of this book.

Lesson 2.02: Deployment Groups

We have discussed agents and pools in the first lesson of this chapter. As we already know, an agent is a dedicated machine that helps to perform build or deployment. Deployment groups are also similar to agent pools. A deployment group is a set of machines set up with agents. The specialty of the deployment group is that each machine is an actual deployment target dedicated to each deployment environment with a role. As an example, a deployment group can have a machine with dev as the target and role as the webserver, which are used only to do deployments to dev environment web applications. Likewise, a deployment group has a dedicated machine for each deployment target and a role.

Go to the Organization settings of Azure DevOps. You will be able to find deployment pools under the pipelines section. From this section, you can create and manage deployment groups. See Figure 2-5.

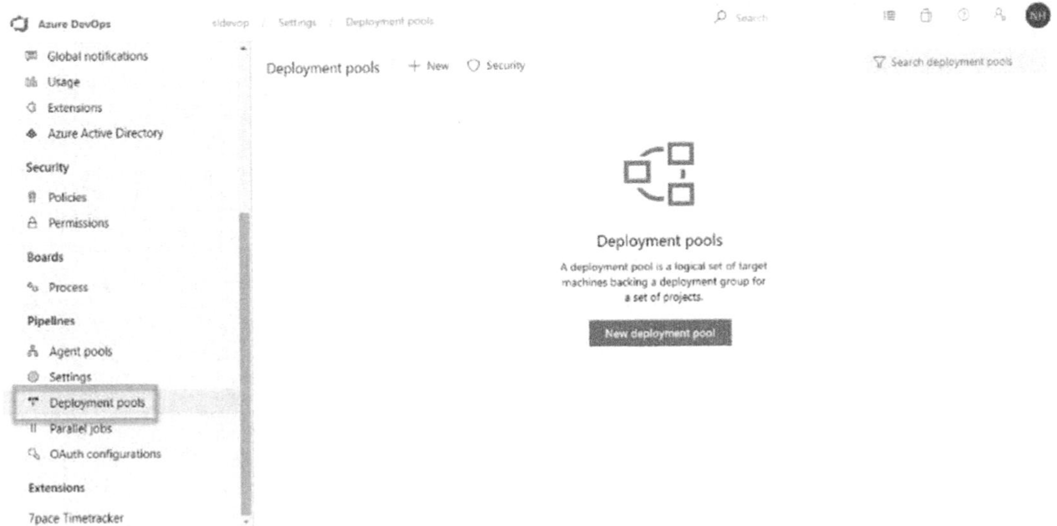

Figure 2-5. *Deployment pool*

While configuring a deployment group, we can provide the projects with which we are going to use the group. Once we create a deployment pool, it allows us to select the projects and target the server platform we need to work with. According to your requirements, Azure DevOps provides a registration script that can be used to configure a deployment group. See Figure 2-6.

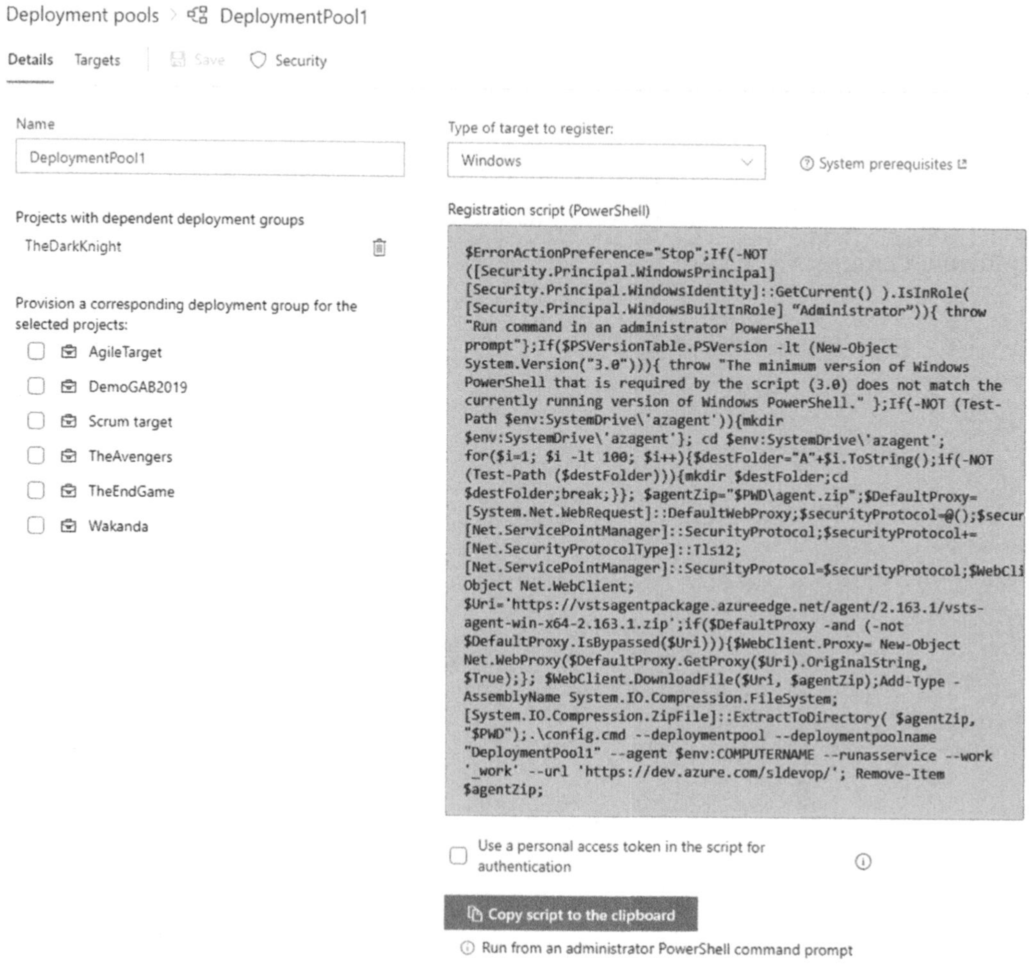

Deployment pools > DeploymentPool1

Details Targets Save Security

Name

DeploymentPool1

Projects with dependent deployment groups

TheDarkKnight

Provision a corresponding deployment group for the selected projects:

- AgileTarget
- DemoGAB2019
- Scrum target
- TheAvengers
- TheEndGame
- Wakanda

Type of target to register:

Windows

System prerequisites

Registration script (PowerShell)

```
$ErrorActionPreference="Stop";If(-NOT
([Security.Principal.WindowsPrincipal]
[Security.Principal.WindowsIdentity]::GetCurrent() ).IsInRole(
[Security.Principal.WindowsBuiltInRole] "Administrator")){ throw
"Run command in an administrator PowerShell
prompt"};If($PSVersionTable.PSVersion -lt (New-Object
System.Version("3.0"))){ throw "The minimum version of Windows
PowerShell that is required by the script (3.0) does not match the
currently running version of Windows PowerShell." };If(-NOT (Test-
Path $env:SystemDrive\'azagent')){mkdir
$env:SystemDrive\'azagent'}; cd $env:SystemDrive\'azagent';
for($i=1; $i -lt 100; $i++){$destFolder="A"+$i.ToString();if(-NOT
(Test-Path ($destFolder))){mkdir $destFolder;cd
$destFolder;break;}}; $agentZip="$PWD\agent.zip";$DefaultProxy=
[System.Net.WebRequest]::DefaultWebProxy;$securityProtocol=@();$secur
[Net.ServicePointManager]::SecurityProtocol;$securityProtocol+=
[Net.SecurityProtocolType]::Tls12;
[Net.ServicePointManager]::SecurityProtocol=$securityProtocol;$WebCli
Object Net.WebClient;
$Uri='https://vstsagentpackage.azureedge.net/agent/2.163.1/vsts-
agent-win-x64-2.163.1.zip';if($DefaultProxy -and (-not
$DefaultProxy.IsBypassed($Uri))){$WebClient.Proxy= New-Object
Net.WebProxy($DefaultProxy.GetProxy($Uri).OriginalString,
$True);}; $WebClient.DownloadFile($Uri, $agentZip);Add-Type -
AssemblyName System.IO.Compression.FileSystem;
[System.IO.Compression.ZipFile]::ExtractToDirectory( $agentZip,
"$PWD");.\config.cmd --deploymentpool --deploymentpoolname
"DeploymentPool1" --agent $env:COMPUTERNAME --runasservice --work
'_work' --url 'https://dev.azure.com/sldevop/'; Remove-Item
$agentZip;
```

Use a personal access token in the script for authentication

Copy script to the clipboard

Run from an administrator PowerShell command prompt

Figure 2-6. *Deployment group creation*

While configuring the deployment group, using a registration script allows you to add tags for each server of the deployment group to denote the role of the machine. As an example, if you create a server with a tag called "Webserver," you can use this server to do web application deployments. So, while working with deployment pipelines, it is possible to group deployment tasks by selecting a deployment group at the agent phase, which we will discuss in more detail in a future lesson, which will help you to understand well the deployment group concept.

In this lesson we were able to get a basic idea about the deployment groups and uses of them. You will be able to learn more about deployment groups in future chapters.

Lesson 2.03: Build Pipelines

In this lesson, you will be able to get a basic idea of how to build a pipeline. You will also get an idea on what a build pipeline is and why it is used.

Azure DevOps build pipelines can be used to build your source code to identify issues with the code early by using a continuous integration option. You can build, test, and create deployable packages of your code using Azure DevOps build pipelines. Further, builds can be used to assign version numbers to the output packages.

Go to the Azure DevOps project and select pipelines from the left pane menu. You are able to see the pipelines section where you can create your build pipelines. See Figure 2-7.

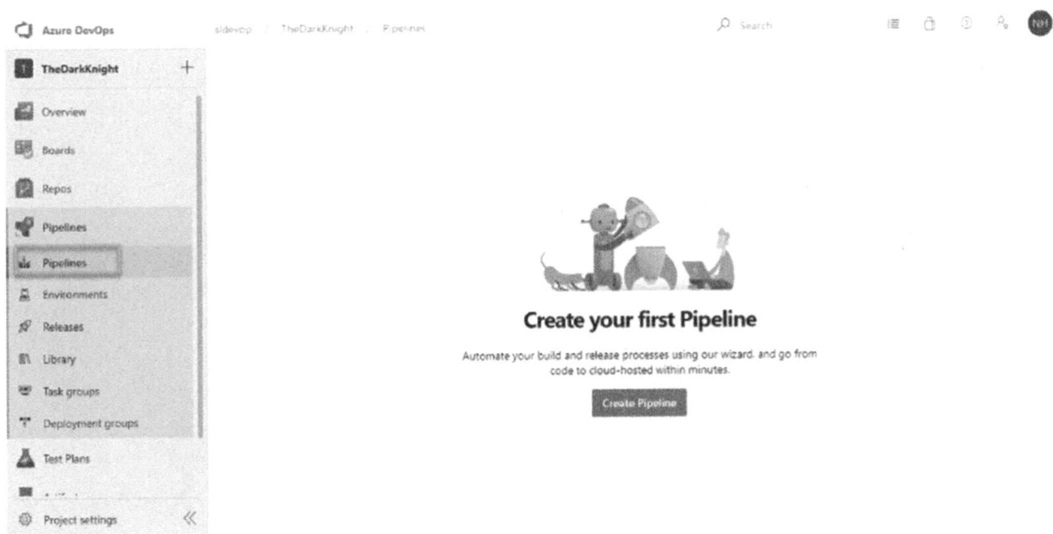

Figure 2-7. *Build pipeline*

Azure DevOps supports two types of builds: namely, classic builds and YAML Ain't Markup Language (YAML) builds. Classic editor allows you to use a graphical view and create build pipelines according to your requirements. But when it comes to a YAML build, you need to have a good understanding of YAML syntax to write declarative scripts to define the build pipelines as a code.

One of the main purposes of a build pipeline is to create deployable packages from the source code. But it is not mandatory to keep your code in Azure DevOps repos in order to use the Azure builds. Azure DevOps allows you to work with several source control systems. As an example, if you have your source code in Bitbucket, you can build Bitbucket code in Azure DevOps build pipelines. Azure Pipelines supports a wide range of repositories such as Azure Repos, GitHub and GitHub Enterprise, Bitbucket, Subversion, and other Git repos.

In classic editor, it allows you to select templates to create builds or use empty jobs, which are suitable for creating all steps accustomed to your needs. Classic build with an empty job will look as follows in Figure 2-8.

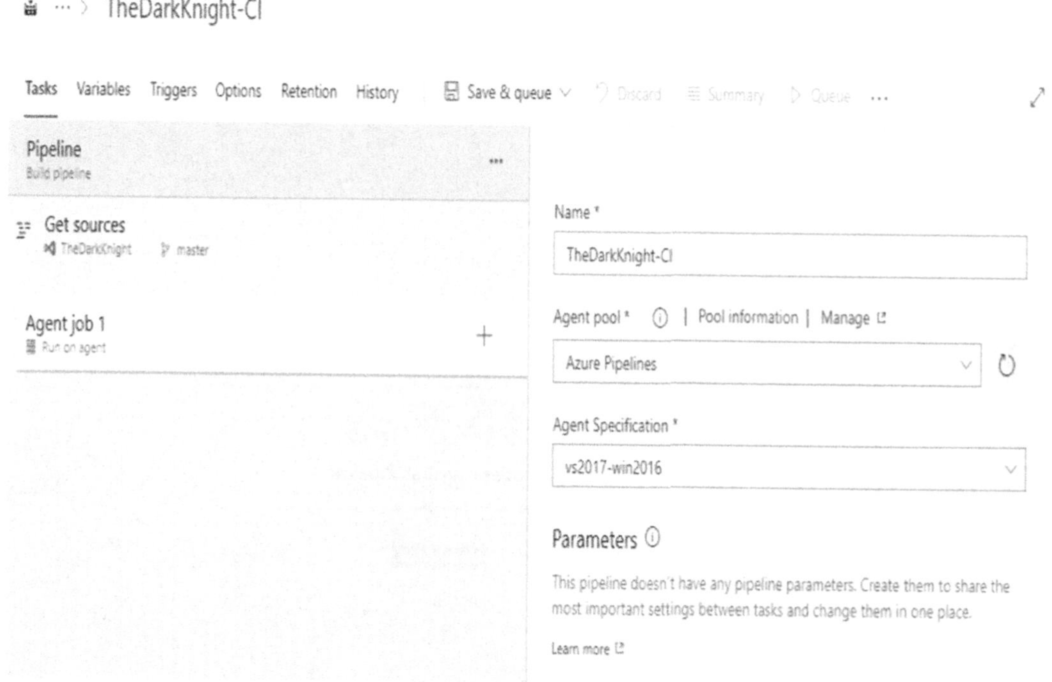

***Figure 2-8.** Classic editor build pipeline with empty job*

In build pipelines, there are agent phases that allow you to group agents' tasks under each phase. Azure DevOps has two phases:

Agent phase – It is connected with the agent in the agent pool and uses the agent pool agent to execute the tasks.

Agentless phase – It doesn't have the capability to connect with an agent in an agent pool. All the tasks under this phase will execute in Azure DevOps server itself.

The main purpose of the build pipeline is building the code, testing it, and generating an output package. When generating a build output, we can publish the package on a server or file share. Also, we can generate packages and push those packages to Azure DevOps artifact feeds using build pipelines.

Another important feature available in Azure DevOps pipelines is a trigger, which allows us to decide when to start a build. Triggers can be used to decide when a new build should start. Further, we can define it if the change comes from a specific branch and then only trigger a build. Also, we can control the triggers using folder paths as filters so that if something is committed to a given path, a build would be triggered. Another option is to set up the builds to run on a given schedule. We will be discussing these build triggers in later chapters.

Security is a very important feature of any type of tool. Azure DevOps uses several security mechanisms to protect the entire deployment process. Also, it allows you to secure each build pipeline individually by restricting access permissions for each user or user groups.

As discussed in this lesson, build can be used mainly to build, test, and package the source code as deployable output. We now have a brief idea of the capabilities of the Azure DevOps build pipelines. We will discuss more details in future chapters.

Lesson 2.04: Release Pipelines

This lesson will give an introduction to release pipelines. Release pipelines, a.k.a. deployment pipelines, are used to deploy the versions to a selected deployment platform. As an example, Azure DevOps releases pipelines that can be used to deploy web apps, function apps, logic apps, and various types of artifacts to the Azure platform.

Go to the Azure DevOps project and select releases under the pipelines section. From this section, you can create and manage all the release pipelines of the selected project. See Figure 2-9.

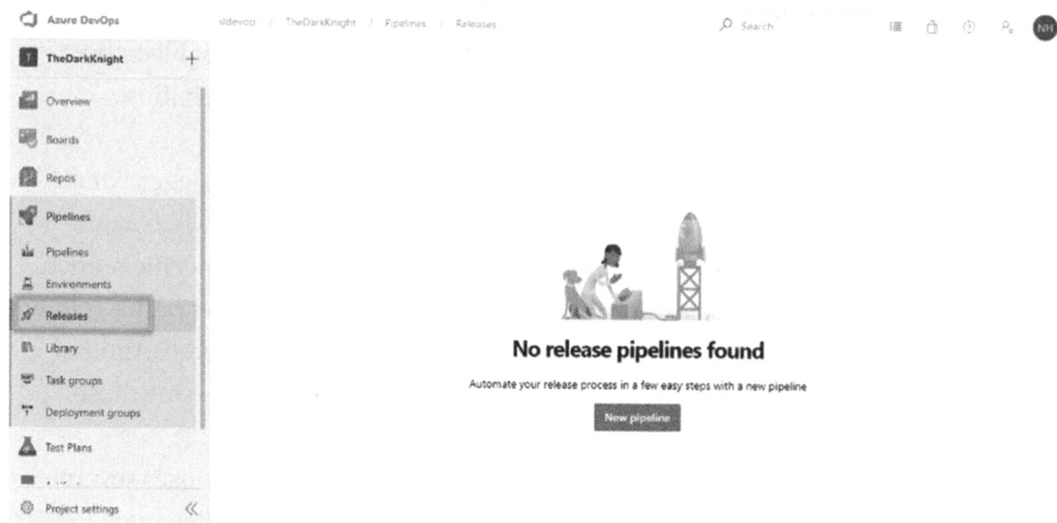

Figure 2-9. *Release pipeline*

The main purpose of a release pipeline is to deploy the deployable packages created to the target hosting platform.

The Azure DevOps pipeline has an artifacts section and stage section. The artifact is the starting point of a release pipeline and can be used for setting up a continuous deployment trigger. It is required to add a type of artifact to enable the deployment. The artifact section allows you to select different types of artifacts such as build output, a package from artifact feed, and third-party artifacts like Jenkins. We will explore all artifact types supported by Azure release pipelines in the next chapters. Once you enable continuous deployment, it is possible to control this continuous deployment using build branch filters. You can say deploy if the build is triggered due to the change that occurred in the given branch. Also, you can enable pull request triggers that allow you to decide whether to deploy the artifacts generated from a pull request to a given target branch.

In the stages of the deployment pipeline, you can define pre-deployment and post-deployment conditions that allow you to control the deployment. In pre-deployment conditions, Azure DevOps has three main triggers: manual trigger, start deployment after creating a new release, and trigger the deployment of the given stage if the deployment of the previous stages of pipeline have succeeded. Also, pre- and post-deployment approval let you control deployment flow based on manual approvals. It is possible to add artifact filters that allow you to add different conditions. So, deployment will continue only if these conditions are met. Further, you are allowed to add conditions to control pull- or request-based deployments. Azure DevOps has the gates feature that can control the deployment according to the result of the return value from the gate condition. Gates allow you to set various conditions based on Azure functions, REST API, work items queries, and several other gates. Also, schedule deployments can be controlled with pre-deployment conditions.

While working with deployment pipelines, you need to pause the deployment at several stages. As an example, once you deploy to a QA environment, if automated test cases don't test a reasonable area of the application as coverage, we need to wait until manual testing is completed to continue the deployment to production. So, we can set manual approvals in pre-deployment and post-deployment steps.

As with any deployment tool, Azure DevOps also introduces several options to secure the tool. When it comes to deployment pipelines, it is important to control these deployment permissions. Otherwise it will give you a lot of trouble if deployment happens at the wrong time and is out of control. So, we can secure each deployment pipeline individually by giving admin permission to only the selected users or selected user groups, allowing only designated people to approve deployments to important targets such as production.

This lesson gave a basic introduction to release pipelines. You will learn more capabilities of release pipelines in future chapters.

Lesson 2.05: Task Groups

You will be introduced to task groups though this lesson. As you already know, we can create Azure DevOps build pipelines for building, executing unit tests, and creating deployable packages. To deploy versions of your applications to target platforms, you can use deployment pipelines. Each type of pipeline uses tasks/steps to perform build and deployment steps. Sometimes while we work on a project, we create more than one pipeline and it might have the same steps used in both pipelines. If we have to create a hundred pipelines, we need to create the same pipeline a hundred times. But Azure DevOps provides us with a task group feature where we can create a group of tasks that can be used in multiple pipelines and send parameter values relevant to each pipeline. A task group facilitates implementable, reusable steps as a single block in multiple pipelines.

Go to the Azure DevOps project and select task groups under the Pipelines section. See Figure 2-10.

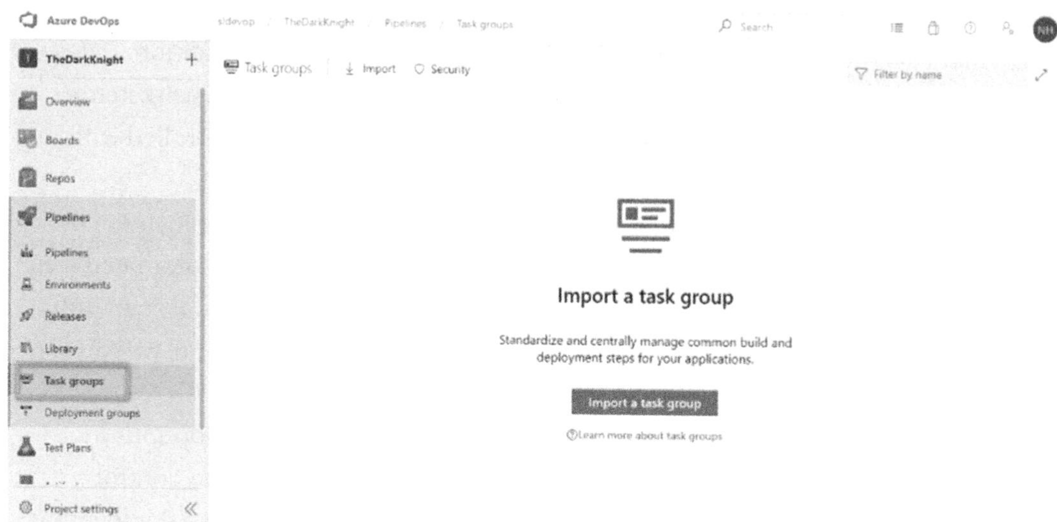

Figure 2-10. *Task groups*

The Azure DevOps task group also ensures task group security by introducing security mechanisms that we can use to control the access and administer capabilities for project users. We discuss the details of tasks groups and their uses with examples in the next chapters.

We were able to get a basic idea of what a task group is in this lesson. We discussed the purpose of a task group in brief, which will help you to continue prepared for the rest of this book's chapters.

Lesson 2.06: Library

This lesson gives you a basic introduction to the Library of the Azure DevOps. The library can be used to keep variable values of pipelines as variable groups and to store files as secure files. While you work with pipelines, you need to define variables for pipeline tasks. Sometimes there are variables that are shared between multiple pipelines. When there is such a need, we can keep shared variables in a variable group under Library.

Go to Azure DevOps project and select the library section under pipelines. You can add variable groups and manage shared variables here. See Figure 2-11.

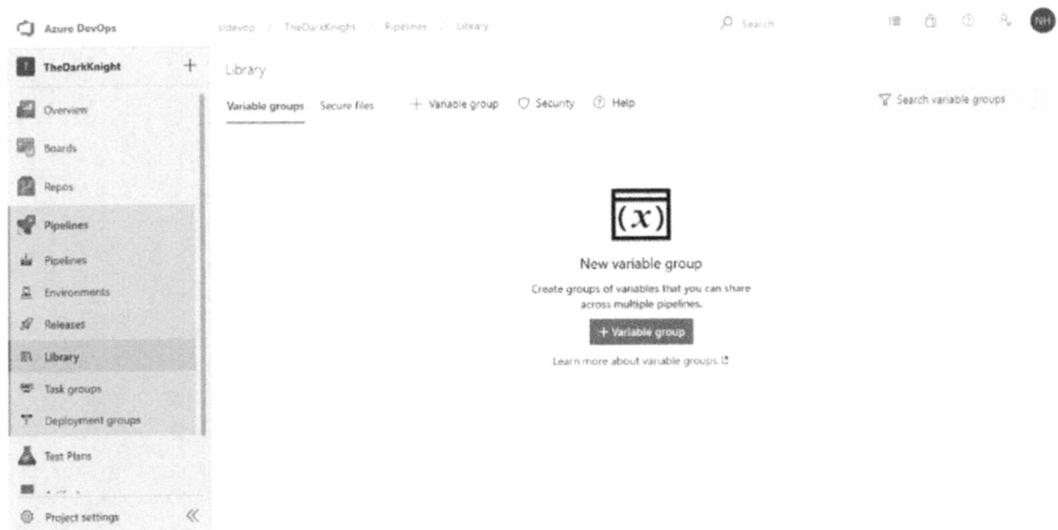

Figure 2-11. *Library*

Other than shared variables, the Azure DevOps Library allows you to keep secured files like certificates and keys that can be used in pipelines. So, you can keep all secured files in the library section. But if we keep the secured files here, we need to control the access permission for each of these files. Azure DevOps confirms the security of these files by allowing us to decide which pipeline can use the secured file and which project users can manage these secured files.

We discussed the basic use of the Azure DevOps Library in this lesson. You will learn more about how to create and use variable groups and secure files in future chapters.

Lesson 2.07: Service Connection

Service connection is one of the most important features required for deployment pipelines. While we do deployments, we need to create connections between our Azure DevOps organization and external resources such as platform services like Azure, source control providers, or other external services like NuGet feeds, etc. You may even want to connect to third-party build and deployment platforms or code quality checking or code security validation tools. A few examples are Jenkins, Octopus, or to deploy Sonar Cloud. Simple cloud deployment targets, as well, are supportive tools for builds and deployments that are connected to Azure DevOps organizations via Service Connections.

Go to the Azure DevOps project settings and under the pipelines section, you are able to navigate to the service connections section. See Figure 2-12.

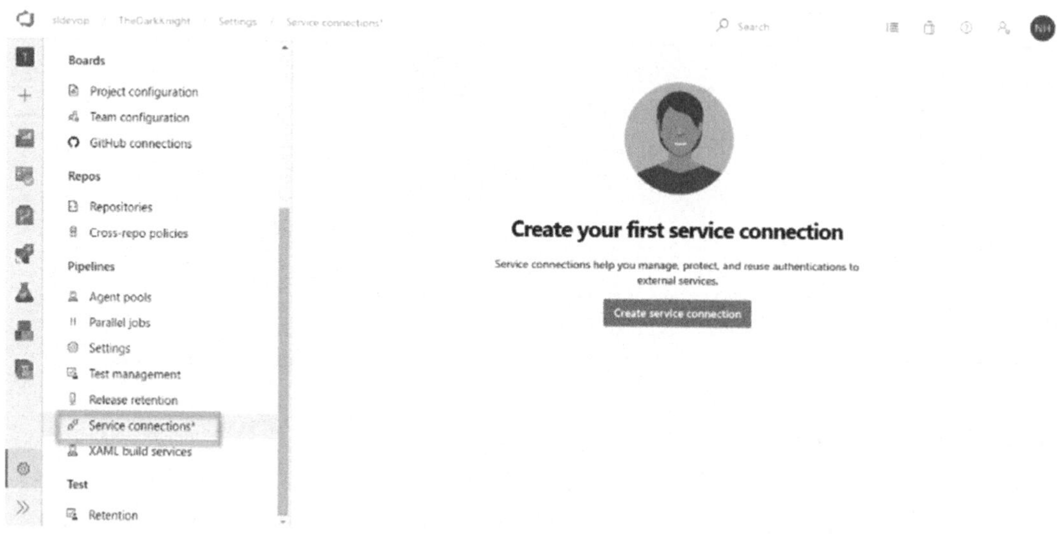

Figure 2-12. *Service connection*

Azure DevOps allows you to connect with a number of tools and external services. You can create service connections to connect with deployment platforms like Azure. Also, you can connect with external source control tools like Bitbucket and GitHub using a service connection. In some situations, we try to use multiple deployment tools. So Azure DevOps allows you to create service connections with servers like Jenkins and Octopus. There are a lot of tools you can connect with using a service connection.

After adding a service connection, it should not be controllable by all the users of the project. You can secure the service connections using the permission levels. We can have two user permissions for a service connection:

User - Can use the service connection but can't administrate it

Administrator - Can create, administer, and use the service connection

This lesson has given you a brief introduction on what a service connection is and how important it is for Azure DevOps pipelines. Also, we learned about a few external tools and services that we can connect with service connection. We will discuss how to create service connections and how to use those in pipelines in future chapters.

Lesson 2.08: Environments

Azure DevOps deployment/release pipelines can be used to do various kinds of deployments. We mostly do web app deployments, DB deployments, AKS deployments, function app deployments, etc. If Azure is the deployment target, it is required to go log in to the Azure portal to monitor each of these deployment targets. Azure DevOps introduces a new feature that can be used to monitor deployment targets from the Azure DevOps Server without logging in to the Azure portal.

The Azure DevOps environment section is available under pipelines. See Figure 2-13.

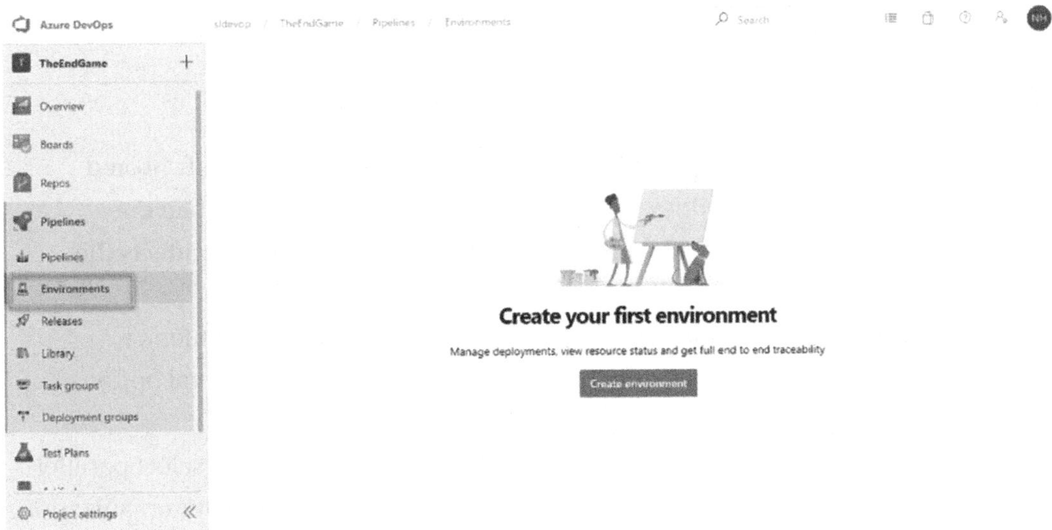

Figure 2-13. *Azure DevOps environment*

The Azure DevOps Environment represents a collection of resources that can be targeted by deployment pipelines. As examples, we can use namespaces of Azure Kubernetes services, which are databases in the Azure DevOps environments, at the time of writing of this book.

The Azure DevOps environment provides the capability of tracking the deployment pipeline history with deployment resource details. Also, you can track which change set deployed to each deployment environment, which is very helpful to identify which feature or bug fix was deployed. Further, the Azure DevOps environment has a very important feature that provides health details of the deployment resources. So, it allows users to track whether a deployed application is functioning in the desired state or it needs more attention.

The Azure DevOps environment security section allows you to control the environment administer capabilities using three different permission levels:

Creator - Can administer, create, and manage the environment

Reader – Can see the environments

User – Can create environments

Other than these user permissions, the environment can be used with only the permitted pipelines.

As we have discussed in this lesson, environments can be used to track performance of the resources related with deployment pipelines, which is very useful and helpful in tracking all the changes deployed to each target environment.

Lesson 2.09: Parallel Pipelines and Billing

As we discussed, Azure DevOps has two primary types of agents: Microsoft-hosted agents and self-hosted agents. But while we do deployment using more than one pipeline, we need the capability to do parallel deployments. Otherwise it affects the efficiency of the project.

If we use more and more self-hosted agents to do the parallel deployment, it will have a huge negative impact on the project budget. So, there are several options available with the Azure DevOps server.

In Azure DevOps, go to the project or organization settings page and select parallel jobs under the pipeline section to view the parallel job capabilities for your organization. See Figure 2-14.

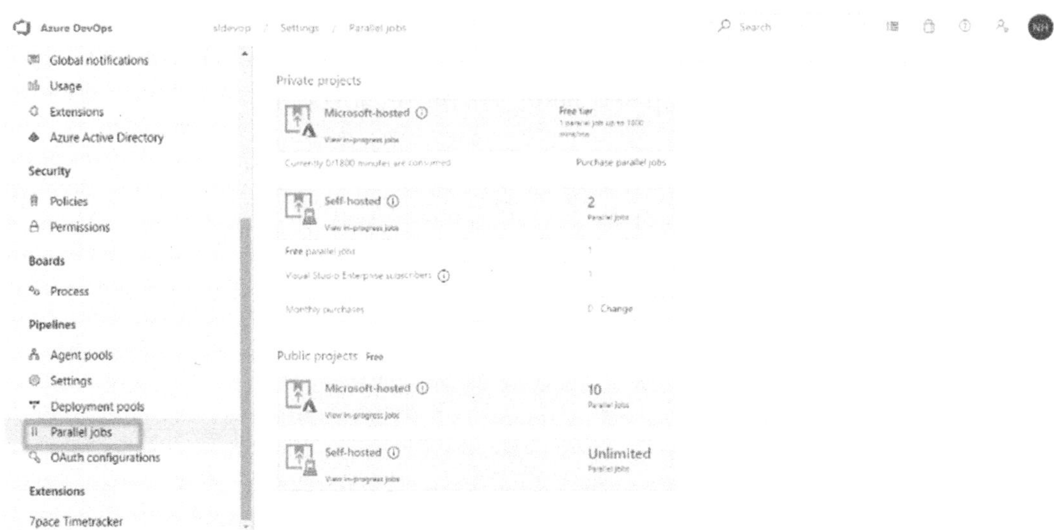

Figure 2-14. *Parallel jobs*

When creating Azure DevOps projects, there are two options as public and private projects. If the project is created as a public project, it can use the Microsoft-hosted agents, which support ten parallel jobs. Further, if you create a self-hosted agent for a public project, it has unlimited parallel jobs. So, it is very important to do deployments without hanging or keeping in the queue. So, Azure DevOps provides multiple parallel job execution capabilities to public projects.

If the project was created as a private project, the Microsoft-hosted agent provides 1,800 mins for month. Also, it has one parallel job, which means only one pipeline can be deployed at once. When it comes to self-hosted agents, it also has one parallel job. But if the organization has Visual Studio Enterprise subscriptions, one parallel job is added to the self-hosted agent. If the organization has more and more subscriptions, it will add more parallel jobs to the pipeline as one additional parallel job per each subscription.

When it comes to Azure DevOps billing, it provides most features for free. As we discussed before, it provides the Microsoft-hosted agent one parallel job and the self-hosted agent one parallel job for free. Boards and Repo are free for up to five users. Also, it provides up to 2GB artifact storage for free.

Testing also plays more importantly in the part of the build and deployment cycle. So, Azure DevOps provides a thirty-day free trial for test plan creation. After the trial period, you can purchase it.

Go to the Azure DevOps organization settings page and select Billing under the General section. See Figure 2-15. The Azure DevOps billing setting allows users to monitor current billings and set up new billings to the organization.

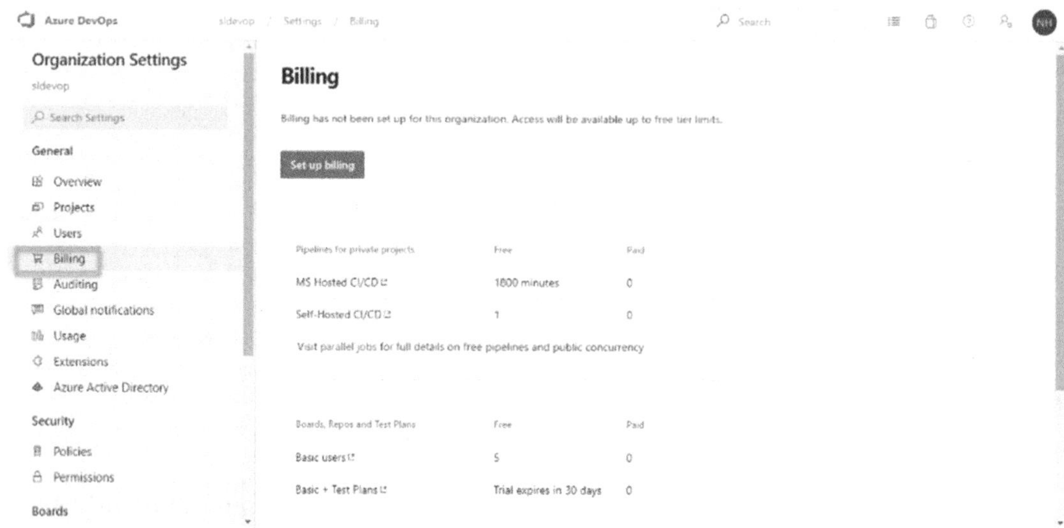

Figure 2-15. *Billing*

So far, we have discussed Azure DevOps billing and parallel pipeline execution capabilities. These types of information are very important for decision-making when working with Azure DevOps. You will learn more details on these billing and parallel jobs in future chapters.

Summary

In this chapter, we discussed several features related to Azure Pipelines. We identified build and deployment pipelines, Azure DevOps agents, and usage of agents. We then briefly discussed task groups and library options. Additionally, we were introduced to environments and billing on Azure DevOps.

In the next chapter, we will discuss setting up Agents Pools; Deployment Groups, and agents in them, which will continue to help us for the rest of the book.

CHAPTER 3

Setting Up Pools, Deployment Groups, and Agents

In the first two chapters, we discussed the concepts around Continuous Integration and Delivery and briefly explored concepts and features of Azure Pipelines. This has set the background for us to dive into each feature of Azure Pipelines, which will enable us to understand how to utilize Azure Pipelines to automate the software delivery process.

In this chapter, we are going to look at the agents in Azure Pipelines. As we already have discussed, we have two types of pipelines that can be used in Azure DevOps. One is Azure Pipelines, which is having Windows, Linux, and Mac agents hosted in Microsoft servers, facilitating and building many types of software projects. The next type is self-hosted agents, which can be used to add your own machine's virtual or physical components to agent pools that you can create in Azure DevOps.

The major advantage of having a self-hosted agent would be to facilitate a couple of needs that we would not be able to satisfy with Azure-hosted Pipelines. One such need is having custom versions of software requirements to build your software projects, such as if you need a particular SharePoint version and have a dependency on SharePoint libraries to your projects. Azure-hosted agents will not have this type of specific needs, and this is one of the situations where self-hosted agents come in handy as you can set up whichever software you want in your machines.

Another good use of self-hosted (on premises - could be even cloud VMs) agents would be when you try to deploy to on-premises environments where the machines sit behind cooperate firewalls. In this scenario the Azure-hosted agent does not have a line of sight to the machines behind cooperate firewalls. Another situation in which you will not have a line of sight from Azure-hosted Pipelines would be when you use Azure App

C. Chandrasekara and P. Herath, *Hands-on Azure Pipelines*, https://doi.org/10.1007/978-1-4842-5902-3_3

Service Environments (ASE) for total isolation and security. All these scenarios of self-hosted agents can help as they can reside within the cooperate network or inside ASE and perform the deployment jobs assigned by the Azure Pipelines, using local network accessibility to the required targets. See Figure 3-1.

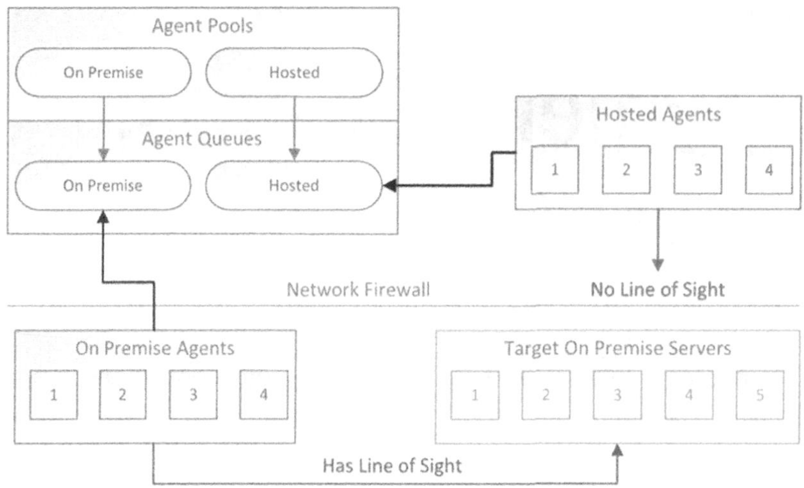

Figure 3-1. *Line of Sight*

First, let's look at how to create agent pools and set up the permissions in them. Then, using a couple of lessons, let's get agents added to the pools we create to understand how we can use them in this chapter.

Lesson 3.01: Setting Up Pools and Permissions

As already discussed, we can set up self-hosted, on-premises machines, virtual machines, or cloud virtual machines as agents. Before setting up an agent we need to define agent pools to keep agents as a group. One agent pool can have multiple agents with the same capabilities assigned to it to enable the consuming build or release pipeline to get facilitated with the service of an available agent at a given point in time.

Pools can be defined on two levels. First, you can define a pool at the Azure DevOps organization and have it added to all existing team projects. To do this, click on the organization setting in your Azure DevOps organization and click on Agent Pools ➤ Add Pool. You can see the default self-hosted pool named Default, if also available, for you to set up agents. See Figure 3-2.

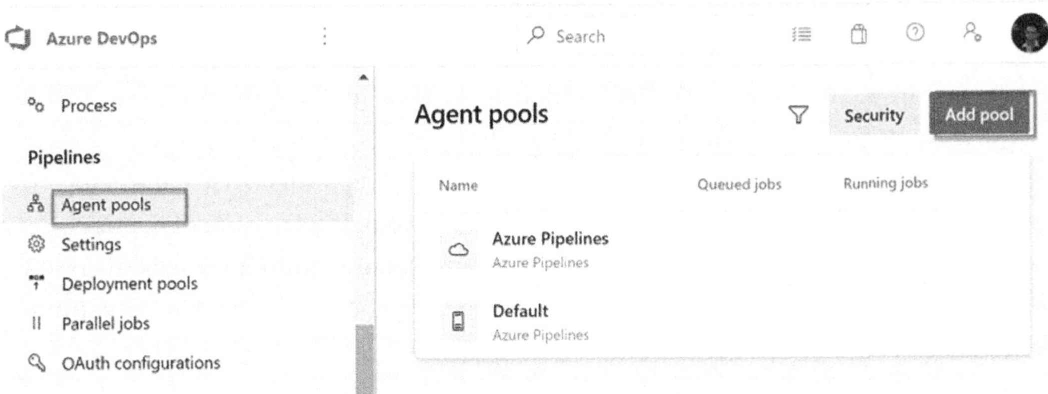

***Figure 3-2.** Add pool*

A pane will appear allowing you to provide a name for the new pool. You can allow all pipelines to use the agents in the new pool by granting permissions. The option to make the new pool available for all team projects is deselected if you want to add the new pool to only the required team project later on from the team project settings. See Figure 3-3.

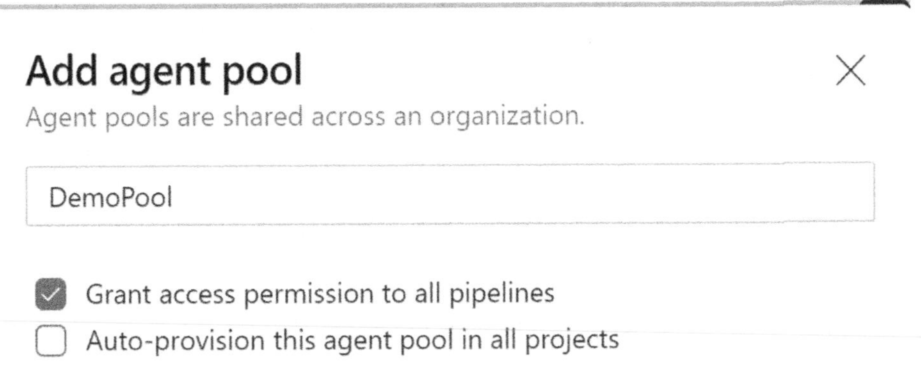

***Figure 3-3.** Add a pool*

Once the pool is added, you can click on the pool name to navigate to its jobs page, which shows running and queued jobs of the agent pool. You can click on the settings page and in the settings page, there are options to enable applying the pool as available to any new team project getting created in the organization. However, this setting will not provision the already created agent pool for any existing project. See Figure 3-4. You can only add the pool to existing projects at the time of the creation of the pool (see Figure 3-3) or by going to an individual team project and adding the existing pool. You can set up a maintenance schedule for the agents in the pool as well in the settings page. See Figure 3-4.

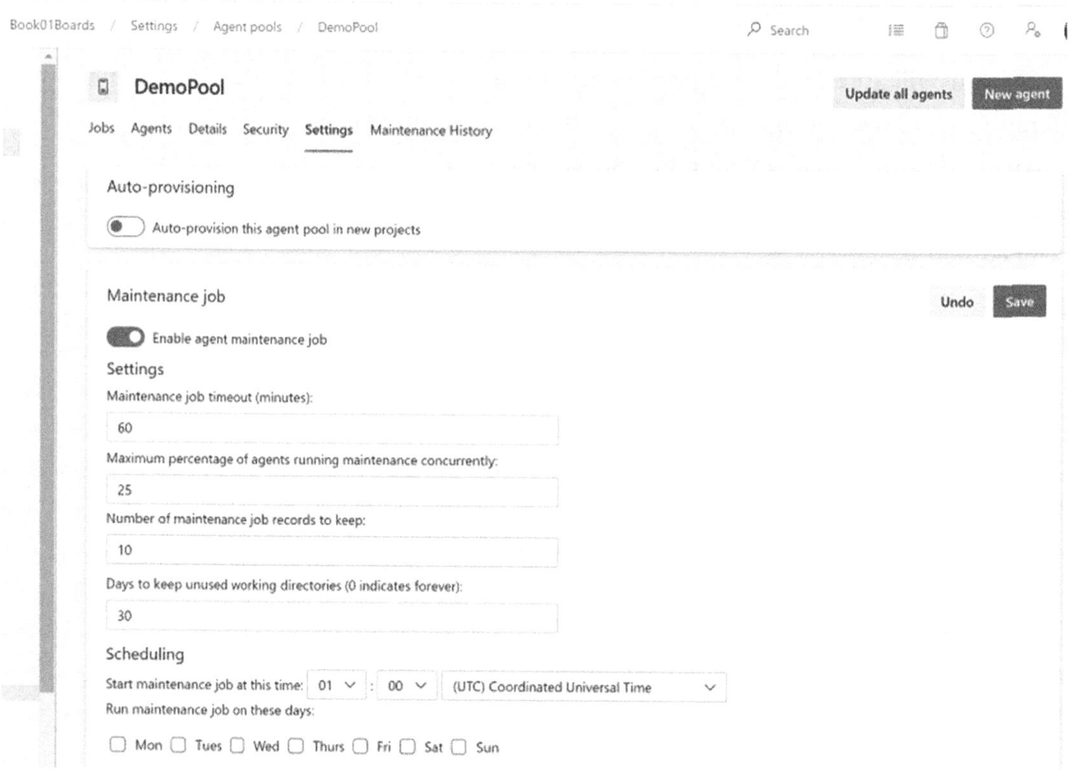

Figure 3-4. *Pool settings*

Maintenance history will show any maintenance activities performed for agents in the pool. The agent tab allows you to add the agents to the pool, and in the details tab, you can view details such as description and owner of the pool.

In the security tab, you can define the permissions for the created agent pool. As mentioned in Chapter 2, there are three types of permissions you can assign in the agent pool. The reader will be allowed to view the agent pools. The service account permissions will grant permissions to view agents, create sessions, and listen to jobs assigned by the pool. The administrator can administer and manage the pool and view and use it. See Figure 3-5.

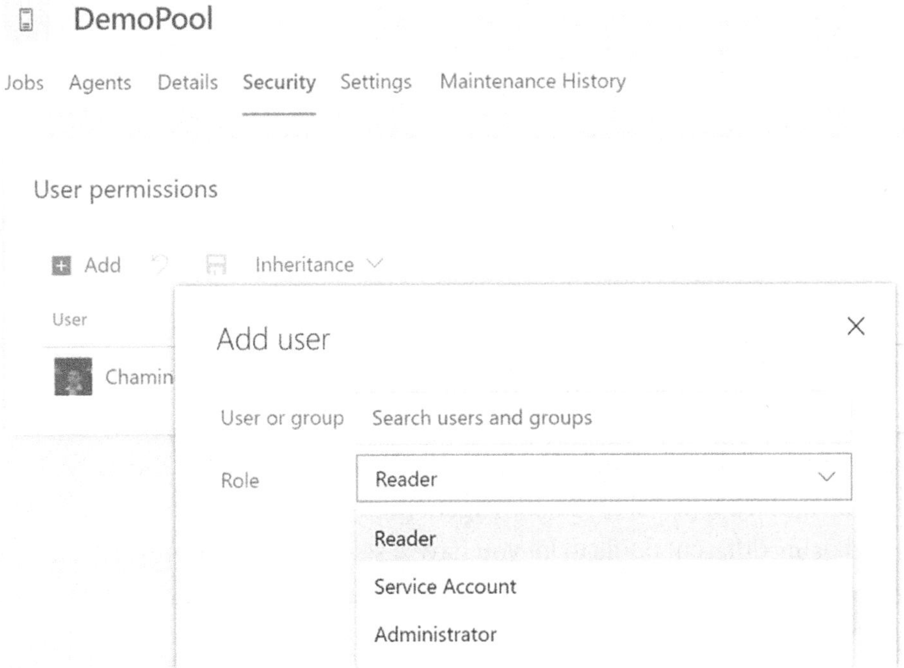

***Figure 3-5.** Agent pool permissions*

Go to a team project and click on project settings ➤ Agent Pools to navigate to the project settings agent pool page to add an agent pool to a team project. You can add an existing pool that is not provisioned for the team project or add a new pool from the team project settings page. When you add a pool from the team project, it only gets added to the current team project. If you want it to be added to another team project, you can do so by adding an existing pool to the other team projects. See Figure 3-6.

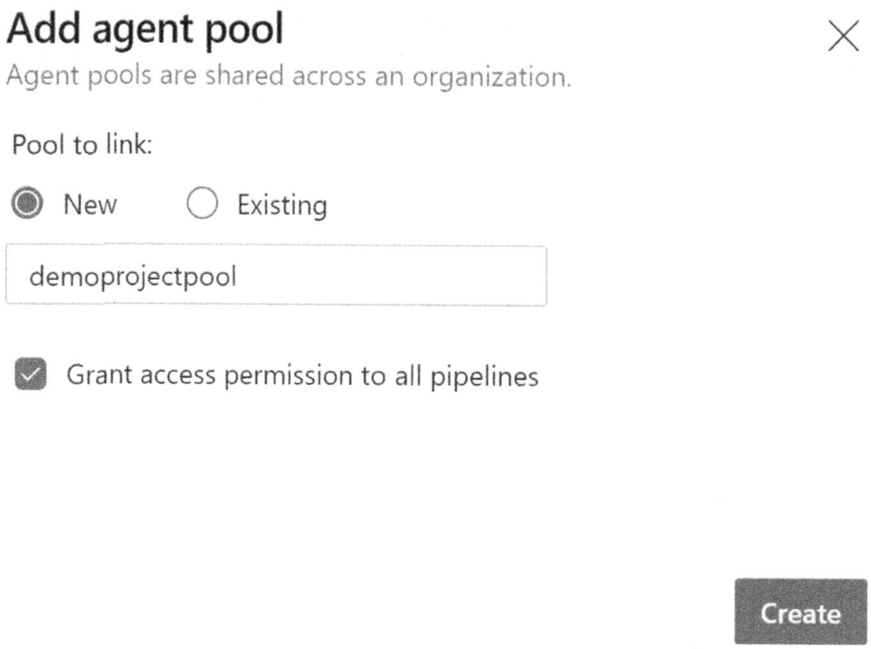

Add agent pool

Agent pools are shared across an organization.

Pool to link:

New Existing

demoprojectpool

Grant access permission to all pipelines

Create

Figure 3-6. *Add agent pool to a team project*

In this lesson we have explored options to add an agent pool to the Azure DevOps organization and team projects. Custom agent pools are useful for setting up self-hosted agents and using different pools to let you have a set of agents serving the same purpose to be grouped together as a pool. We discussed the usefulness of having agent pools in detail at the beginning of this lesson.

Lesson 3.02: Adding Agents to Pools

You can set up virtual machines or physical machines as self-hosted agents. These agents can be added to either a pool named Default, which is the default self-hosted agent pools; or as discussed in the previous lesson, you can add custom pools to team projects. We can use those pools to add agents. To add an agent to a pool, you need to have the Administrator role assigned in the pool where you are adding the agent. You can go to the pool in the project or organization's settings.

There are three types of machines - Windows, Linux, and Mac -that you can set up as agents in a self-hosted agent pool. The instructions for setting up each type of agent can be found in the panel loaded by clicking on the project/organization settings ➤ Agent pools, and clicking on a pool name ➤ New agent Button. See Figure 3-7.

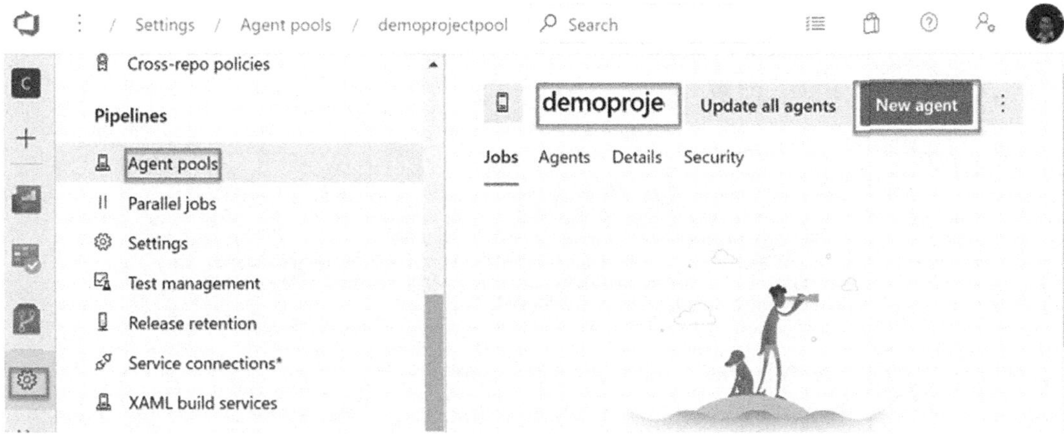

Figure 3-7. *New agent*

Let's start by adding a Windows machine as an agent to a pool. You can simply follow the instructions in the loaded panel Windows tab. See Figure 3-8.

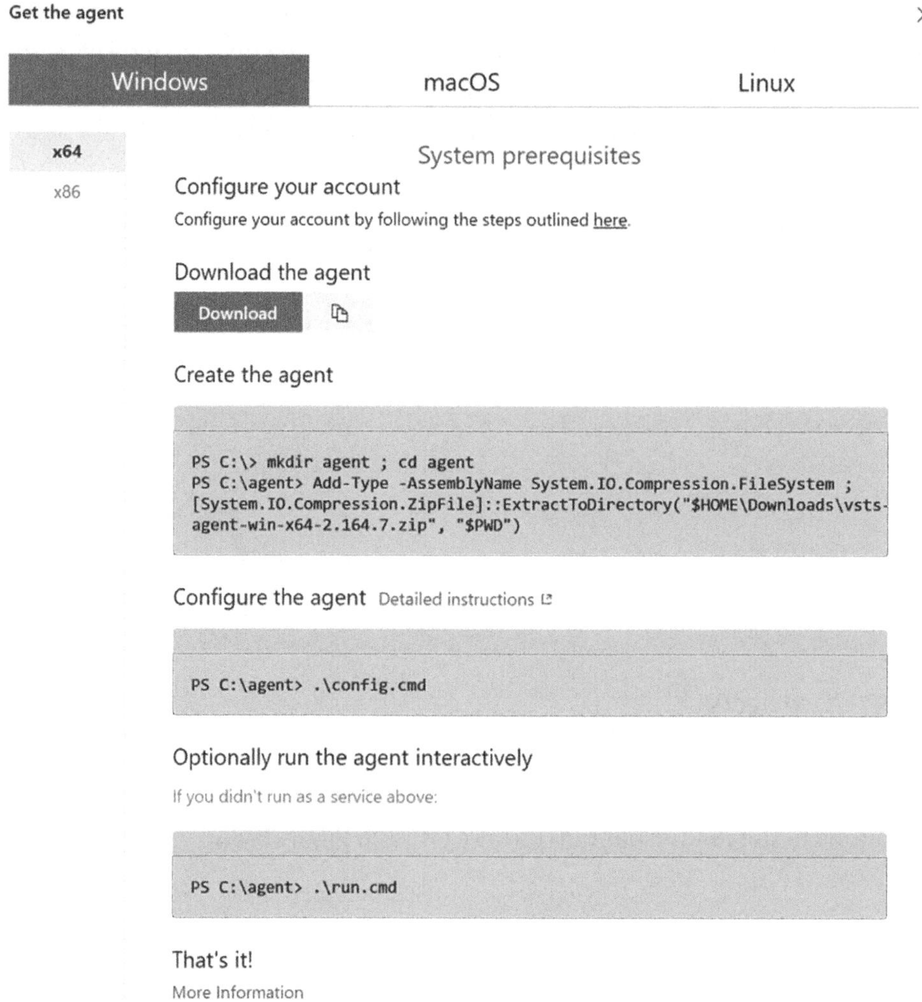

Figure 3-8. *Windows Agent setup instructions*

You can also manually download the agent zip file by clicking the download button shown in Figure 3-8. Then extract it to a folder. Use a command prompt or PowerShell window and run the config.cmd and follow the prompts. You have to provide the Azure DevOps organization url. Then you need to provide a Personal Access Token (PAT), and we have discussed how to create one in the Hands-On Azure Boards book of this book series. The PAT needs to have the Agent pool Manage and Read scope defined. Instead of a PAT, you can use negotiate or alt as an authentication option and provide the username and password to register the agent, or use an integrated authentication type to use logged-on windows credentials. The credential you use only needs to set up the agent and it would not be the credentials used to maintain the connectivity of the agent to Azure DevOps. Hence, it is not required for you to keep a PAT or other credentials active after setting up an agent as the agent and Azure DevOps communicate using a different secret token setup at the time of setting up the agent, which is not visible to you. You can get detailed information from the Detailed instructions link shown in Figure 3-8. You can provide a name of the agent pool that the agent needs to join. Running an agent as a service is advisable as long as it doesn't need to perform any interactive activity. In scenarios where you need to run a UI test that requires desktop interaction, you can configure it as interactive with auto login options. See Figure 3-9.

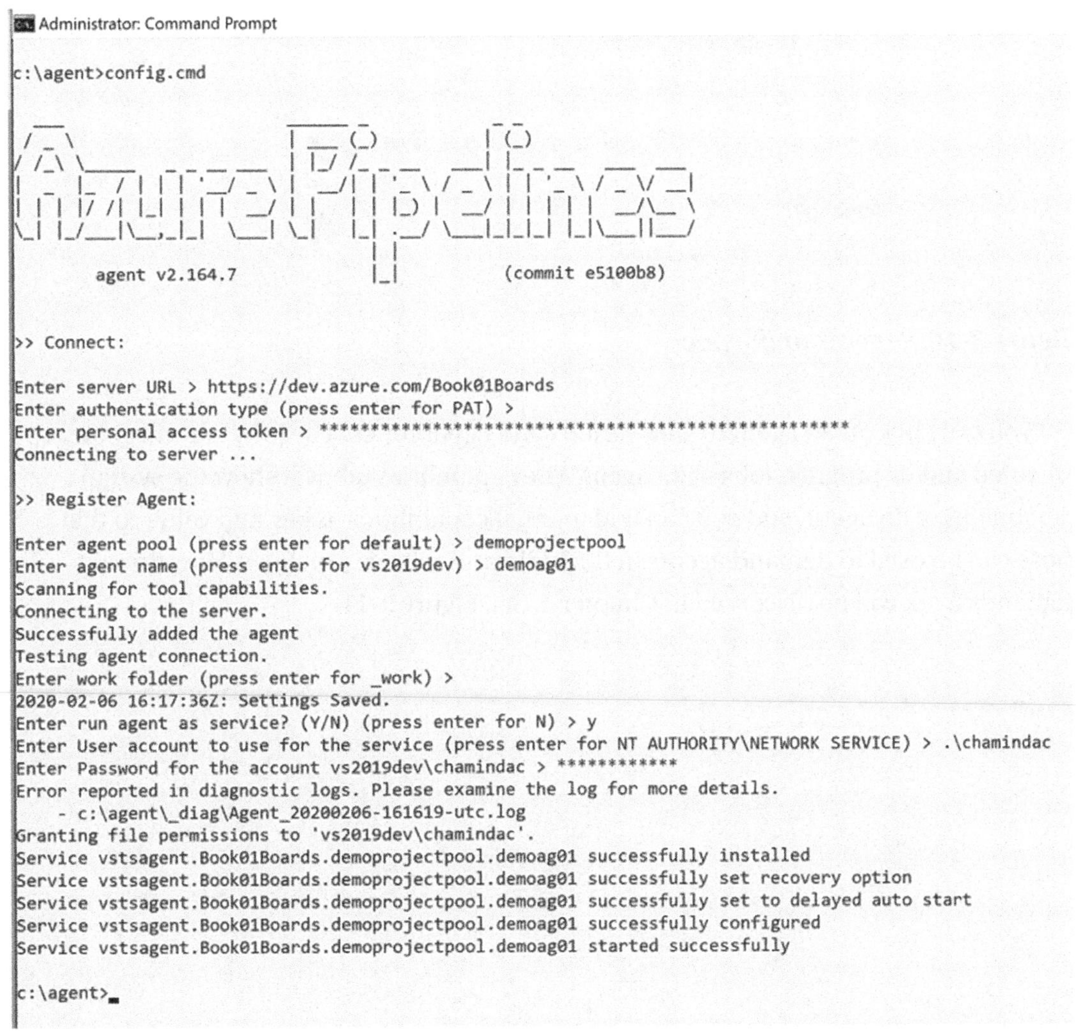

Figure 3-9. *Configure agent*

More or less, in a similar manner you can set up agents in Mac or Linux as per instructions available in the tabs in the panel shown in Figure 3-8. Once the agent is registered, it will become available in the agent pool, agents tab, and can execute jobs assigned by the pool. An agent can be enabled or disabled so that it allows the pool to assign jobs to it. See Figure 3-10. This would be useful if you are performing a maintenance task on a given agent in a pool, for example, applying security patches, installing software, or even applying Windows updates, etc.

Figure 3-10. *Agents in the pool*

You can click on an agent to view its jobs and capabilities. The jobs tab will show executed and in-progress jobs of an agent. The capabilities tab will show the system capabilities of an agent, and you can add manual capabilities as key and value so that these can be used to demand agents in the build and release pipelines. How these demands work will be discussed in Chapter 4. See Figure 3-11.

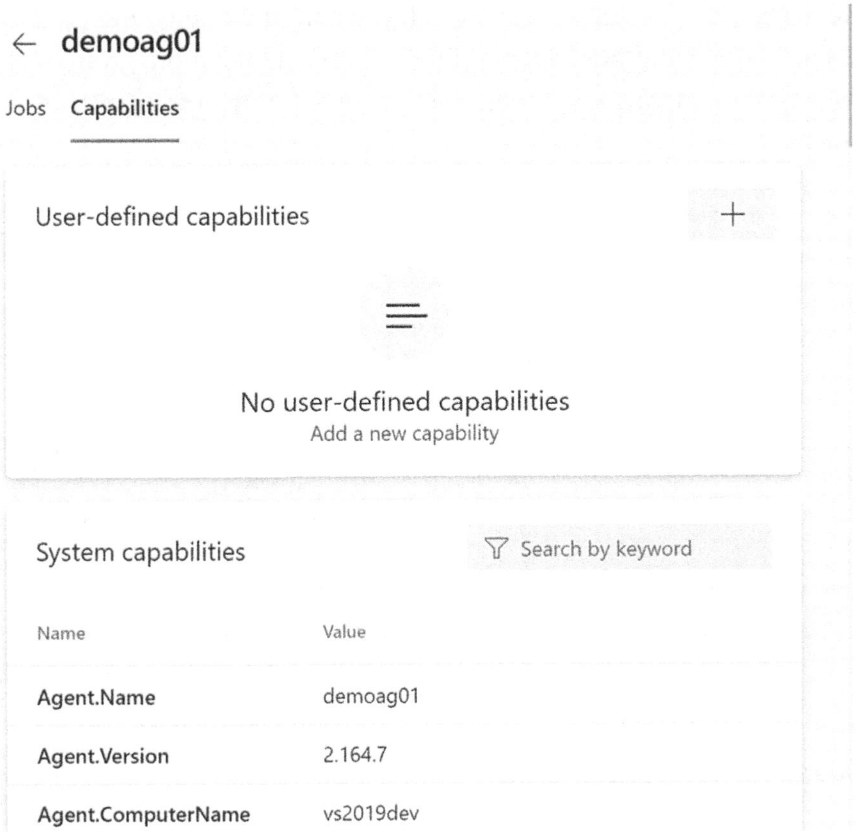

Figure 3-11. *User capabilities*

This concludes the lesson on adding agents to pools, where we explored the place where we can find the instructions to set up an agent in a pool for all platforms. Additionally, we discussed the important information of setting up an agent using a Windows-based agent as an example. Further, how to define user capabilities for a self-hosted agent and view the system capabilities were explained in this lesson.

Lesson 3.03: Setting Up Deployment Groups

Deployment groups can be used for the purpose of keeping deployment targets in machines. A deployment group can have multiple machines registered in it, and a deployment agent can be set up in these machines tagged with different roles such as webserver, dbserver, etc., denoting the purpose of the machine in the deployment group.

In the Azure DevOps organization level, you can find deployment pools in the settings. The deployment pool allows you to share a deployment group with multiple team projects. From organization settings, you can define new organization pools. See Figure 3-12.

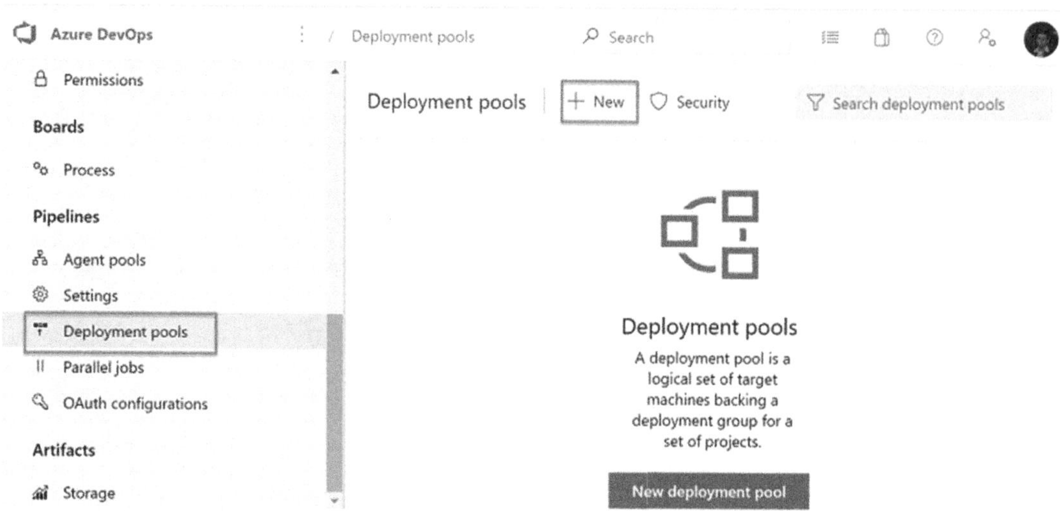

Figure 3-12. *Create new deployment pool*

The deployment pool can be provisioned as a deployment group in selected project(s) at the time of the creation of the deployment pool, if required. See Figure 3-13.

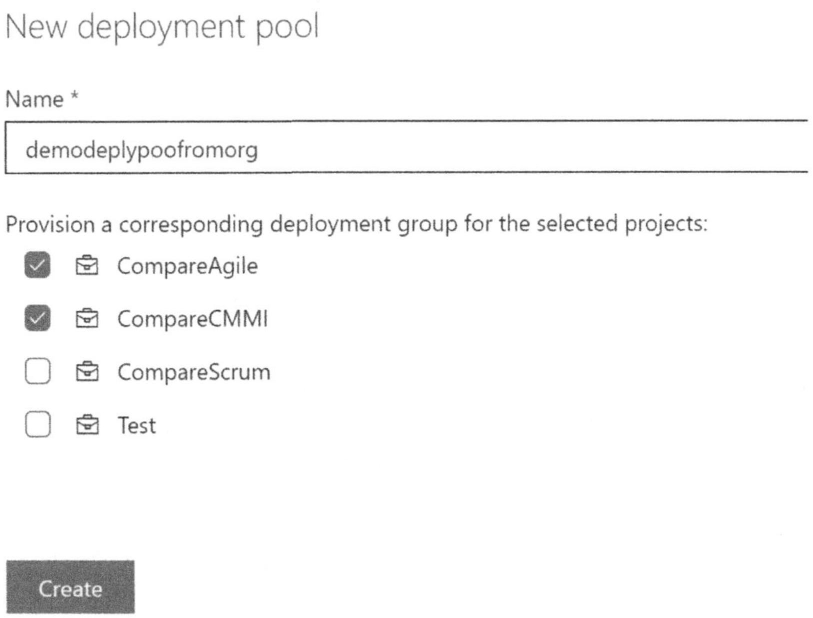

***Figure 3-13.** New deployment pool*

Once the deployment pool is created, you can click on the pool name and add the machines to the pool by executing the script available for Windows and Linux machines. The drop-down lets you select the operating system and available script changes depending on the machine type. You can click on Use a personal access token option to enable embedding a PAT to the script so that it can automatically execute, with minimal interaction, to set up a machine as a target in the deployment group. You can provision the deployment group/pool in the other existing team projects in the Azure DevOps organization, and even remove the deployment group from the current provisioned team projects. See Figure 3-14.

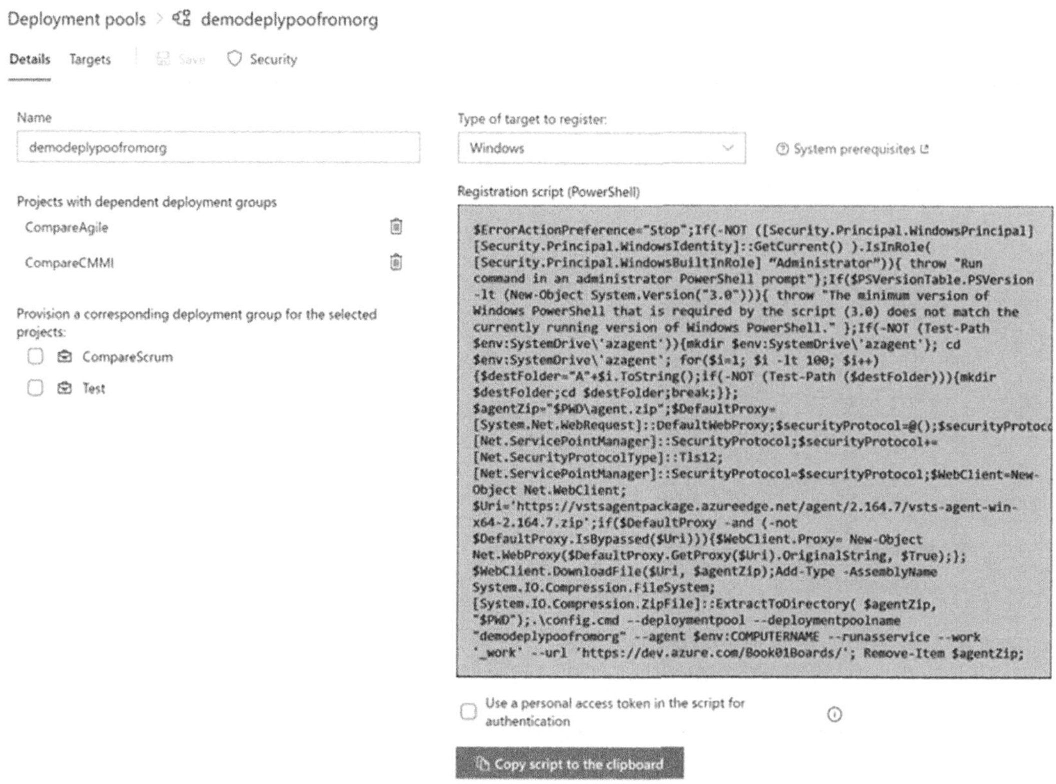

Deployment pools > demodeplypoofromorg

Details Targets Save Security

Name

demodeplypoofromorg

Type of target to register:

Windows

System prerequisites

Projects with dependent deployment groups

CompareAgile

CompareCMMI

Provision a corresponding deployment group for the selected projects:

CompareScrum

Test

Registration script (PowerShell)

```
$ErrorActionPreference="Stop";If(-NOT ([Security.Principal.WindowsPrincipal]
[Security.Principal.WindowsIdentity]::GetCurrent() ).IsInRole(
[Security.Principal.WindowsBuiltInRole] "Administrator")){ throw "Run
command in an administrator PowerShell prompt"};If($PSVersionTable.PSVersion
-lt (New-Object System.Version("3.0"))){ throw "The minimum version of
Windows PowerShell that is required by the script (3.0) does not match the
currently running version of Windows PowerShell." };If(-NOT (Test-Path
$env:SystemDrive\'azagent')){mkdir $env:SystemDrive\'azagent'}; cd
$env:SystemDrive\'azagent'; for($i=1; $i -lt 100; $i++)
{$destFolder="A"+$i.ToString();if(-NOT (Test-Path ($destFolder))){mkdir
$destFolder;cd $destFolder;break;}};
$agentZip="$PWD\agent.zip";$DefaultProxy=
[System.Net.WebRequest]::DefaultWebProxy;$securityProtocol=@();$securityProtoc
[Net.ServicePointManager]::SecurityProtocol;$securityProtocol+=
[Net.SecurityProtocolType]::Tls12;
[Net.ServicePointManager]::SecurityProtocol=$securityProtocol;$WebClient=New-
Object Net.WebClient;
$Uri='https://vstsagentpackage.azureedge.net/agent/2.164.7/vsts-agent-win-
x64-2.164.7.zip';if($DefaultProxy -and (-not
$DefaultProxy.IsBypassed($Uri))){$WebClient.Proxy= New-Object
Net.WebProxy($DefaultProxy.GetProxy($Uri).OriginalString, $True);};
$WebClient.DownloadFile($Uri, $agentZip);Add-Type -AssemblyName
System.IO.Compression.FileSystem;
[System.IO.Compression.ZipFile]::ExtractToDirectory( $agentZip,
"$PWD");.\config.cmd --deploymentpool --deploymentpoolname
"demodeplypoofromorg" --agent $env:COMPUTERNAME --runasservice --work
'_work' --url 'https://dev.azure.com/Book01Boards/'; Remove-Item $agentZip;
```

Use a personal access token in the script for authentication

Copy script to the clipboard

***Figure 3-14.** Deployment pool details*

In the security tab, you can define security for the deployment tool. You can define four types of roles and add users or groups to the pool permissions. Administrators can view, manage, administer, and use the deployment pools. The user role can use the pool to create a deployment group in team projects and view the pool. Service accounts can view agents/targets in a deployment pool and listen to the jobs from the pool. A reader can only view the pool. See Figure 3-15.

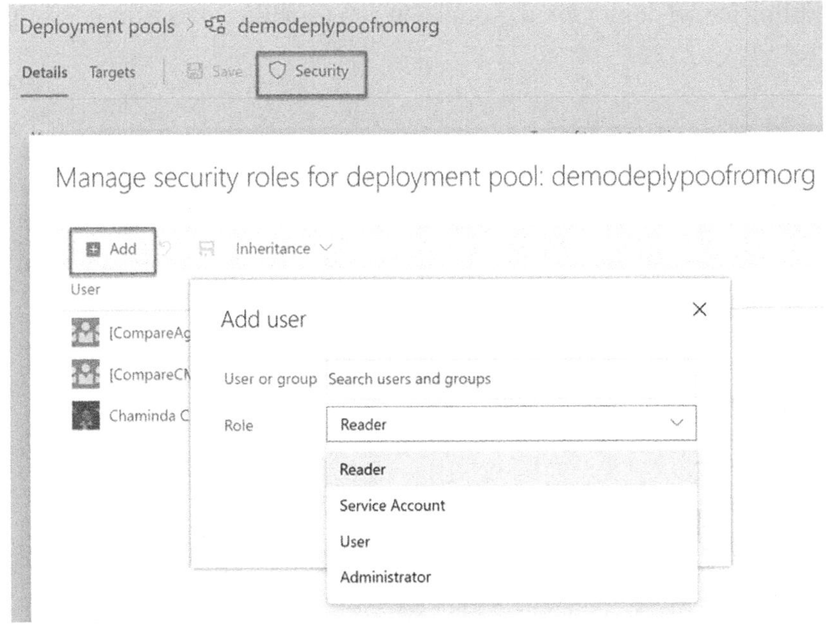

Figure 3-15. Deployment pool security

You can expand the Azure Pipelines left menu, and there you can find the deployment groups submenu, where you can create deployment groups or provisions already available in the deployment pool as a deployment group. See Figure 3-16.

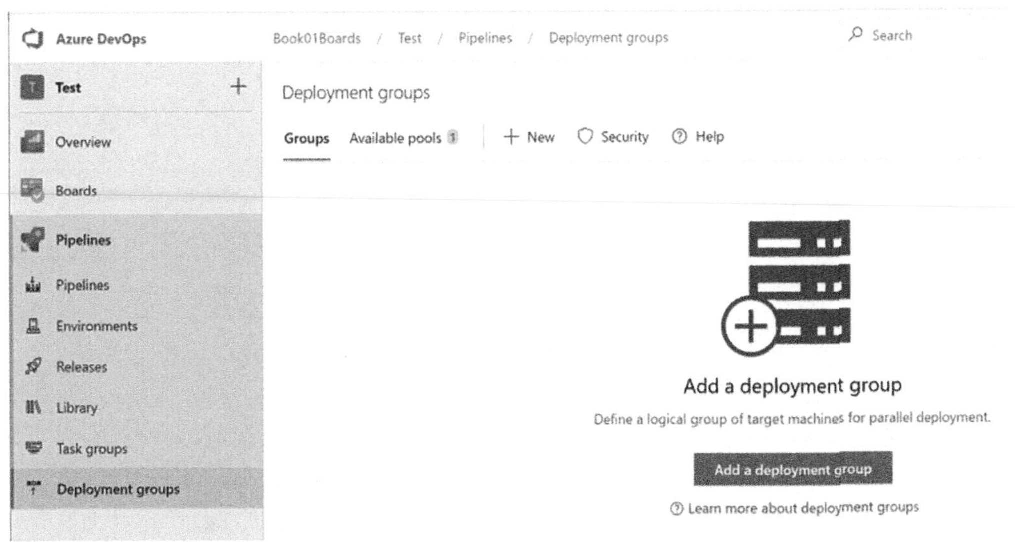

Figure 3-16. Deployment groups

When adding a new deployment group, you can provide a name and description to it. See Figure 3-17.

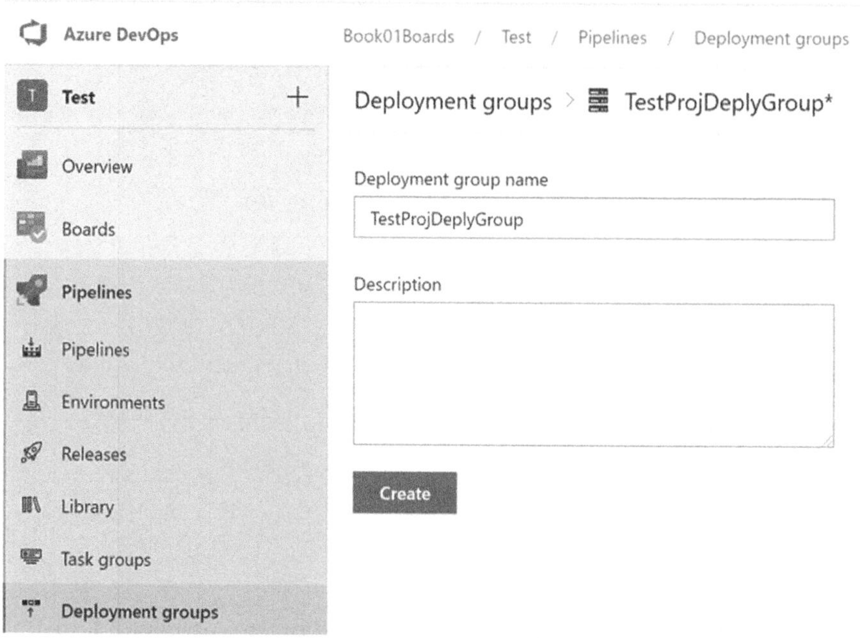

Figure 3-17. *Create deployment group from project*

Once a deployment group is created in the project, you have the capability to provision it in other team projects by sharing it with them. See Figure 3-18.

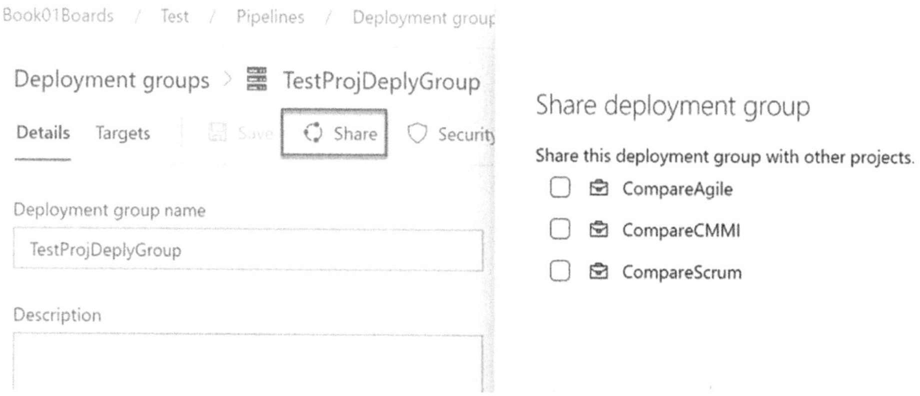

Figure 3-18. *Sharing deployment group*

In the deployment group, you can set up security for the roles reader, who can just view the group; the user who can use the group in pipelines; and for the administrator role who can manage and use the group. Similar to the deployment pool window, the deployment group inside the team project lets you copy and use the script to create targets in the desired operating system, Windows, or Linux. See Figure 3-19. In the targets tab, you will be able to see the targets of the deployment group.

Book01Boards / Test / Pipelines / Deployment groups
Search
Deployment groups > TestProjDeplyGroup
Details Targets Save Share Security Help
Deployment group name
TestProjDeplyGroup
Description
Deployment pool
Test-TestProjDeplyGroup Manage
Type of target to register:
Linux
System prerequisites
Registration script

```
mkdir azagent;cd azagent;curl -fkSL -o vstsagent.tar.gz
https://vstsagentpackage.azureedge.net/agent/2.164.7/vsts-agent-
linux-x64-2.164.7.tar.gz;tar -zxvf vstsagent.tar.gz; if [ -x
"$(command -v systemctl)" ]; then ./config.sh --deploymentgroup --
deploymentgroupname "TestProjDeplyGroup" --acceptteeeula --agent
$HOSTNAME --url https://dev.azure.com/Book01Boards/ --work _work -
-projectname 'Test' --runasservice; sudo ./svc.sh install; sudo
./svc.sh start; else ./config.sh --deploymentgroup --
deploymentgroupname "TestProjDeplyGroup" --acceptteeeula --agent
$HOSTNAME --url https://dev.azure.com/Book01Boards/ --work _work -
-projectname 'Test'; ./run.sh; fi
```

Use a personal access token in the script for authentication
Copy script to the clipboard
Run from an administrator command prompt

***Figure 3-19.** Deployment group details*

The deployment group created in the project is available in the organization settings as a deployment pool where you can provision it for projects, targets, or set up security. See Figure 3-20.

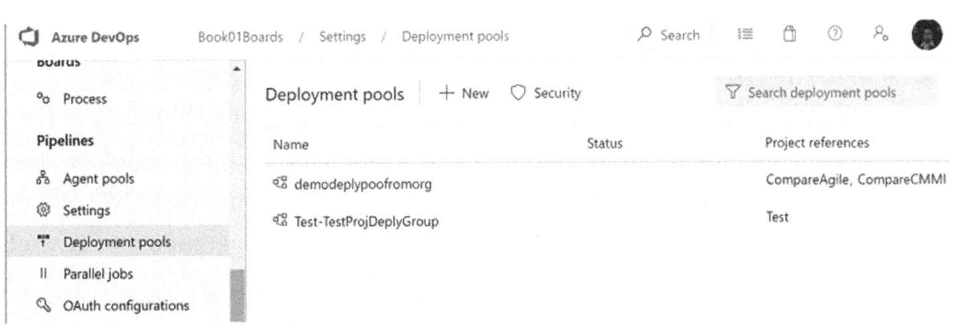

***Figure 3-20.** Deployment pools*

In a team project, you can use the existing deployment pool of the organization to provision a deployment group. See Figure 3-21.

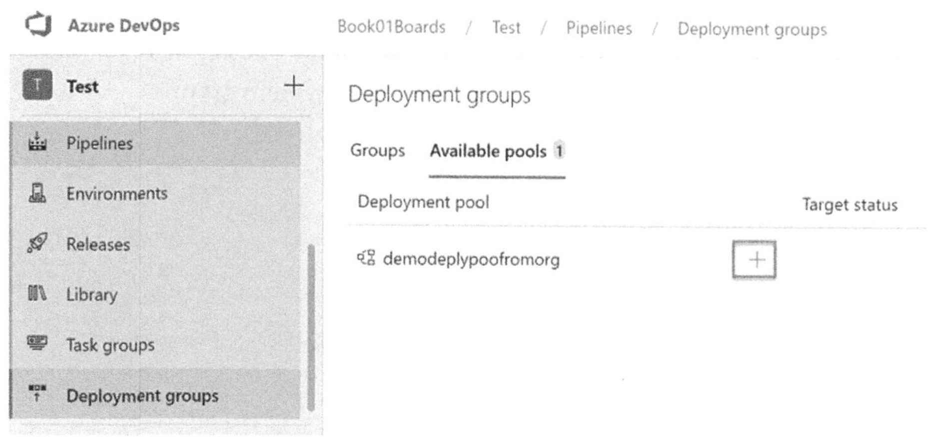

Figure 3-21. *Provision an available pool as a group*

In this lesson, we looked at how we can create deployment groups that can be used in Azure Pipelines to do the deployments.

Lesson 3.04: Adding Targets to Deployment Groups

Targets in deployment groups are targets machines that you can set up to participate as deployment, destinations, or targets that can be used in Azure Pipelines. You can set up Windows or Linux machines as deployment targets, which would be really useful when your software system is on premises or an infrastructure virtual machine set up on a cloud platform.

To add a deployment target, you can go to the deployment pool in organization settings or to a deployment group in the team projects. Once you open up the deployment details, you can find the script that can be copied for a Windows or Linux machine. Select a personal access token option to embed a PAT in the script so that it can authenticate with the Azure DevOps to set up the deployment target. By copying the script as shown in the previous lesson and executing it in the target machine PowerShell or Terminal windows with administration privileges, this will set up an agent and add the target machine as a deployment group. See Figure 3-22.

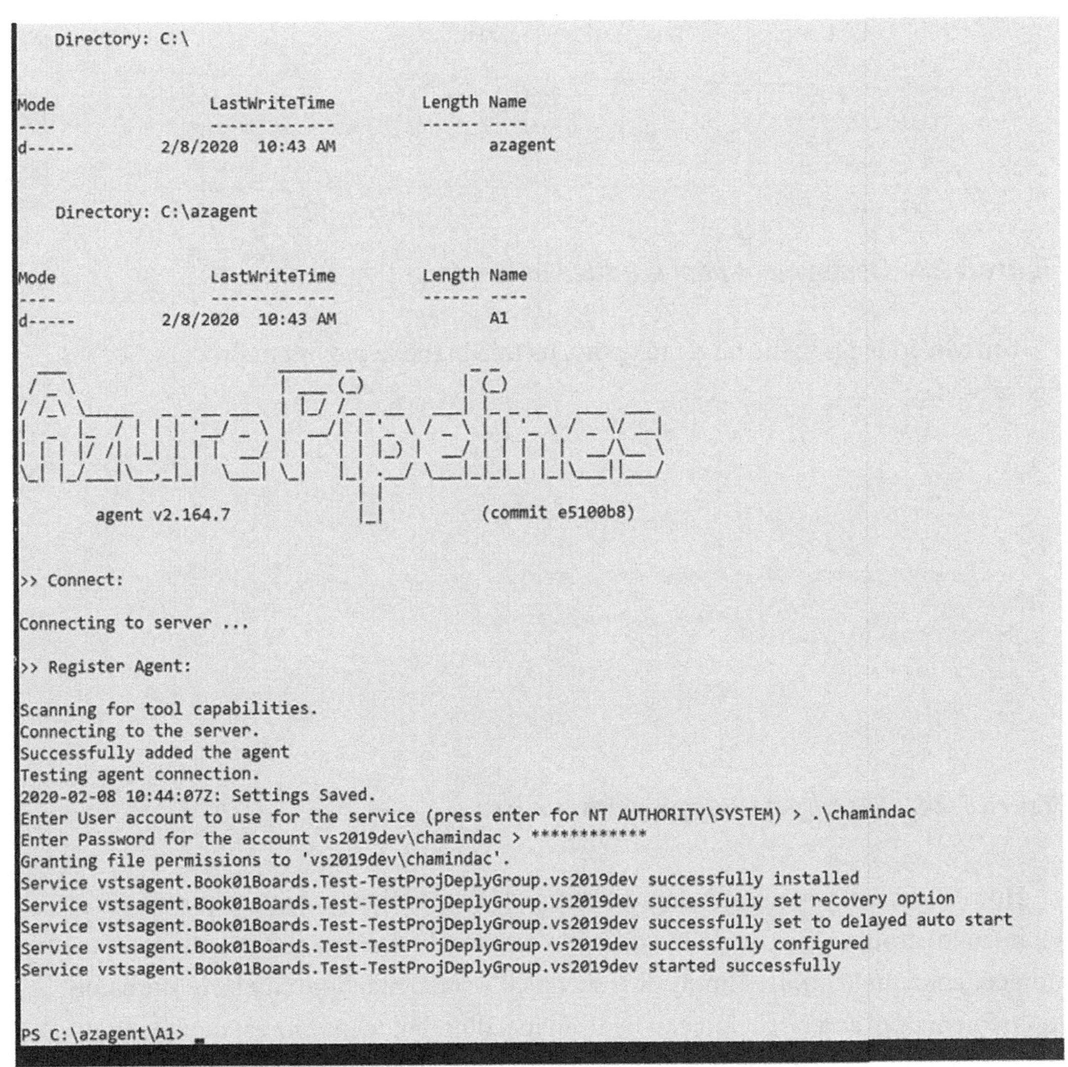

Directory: C:\
Mode LastWriteTime Length Name
d----- 2/8/2020 10:43 AM azagent
Directory: C:\azagent
Mode LastWriteTime Length Name
d----- 2/8/2020 10:43 AM A1
agent v2.164.7 (commit e5100b8)
>> Connect:
Connecting to server ...
>> Register Agent:
Scanning for tool capabilities.
Connecting to the server.
Successfully added the agent
Testing agent connection.
2020-02-08 10:44:07Z: Settings Saved.
Enter User account to use for the service (press enter for NT AUTHORITY\SYSTEM) > .\chamindac
Enter Password for the account vs2019dev\chamindac > ************
Granting file permissions to 'vs2019dev\chamindac'.
Service vstsagent.Book01Boards.Test-TestProjDeplyGroup.vs2019dev successfully installed
Service vstsagent.Book01Boards.Test-TestProjDeplyGroup.vs2019dev successfully set recovery option
Service vstsagent.Book01Boards.Test-TestProjDeplyGroup.vs2019dev successfully set to delayed auto start
Service vstsagent.Book01Boards.Test-TestProjDeplyGroup.vs2019dev successfully configured
Service vstsagent.Book01Boards.Test-TestProjDeplyGroup.vs2019dev started successfully
PS C:\azagent\A1>

Figure 3-22. *Register target machine to a deployment group/pool*

Similar to agent pool agents, communication between the target and the deployment group is maintained with a different token from the PAT that you use to set up, so there is no need for the PAT to be active to keep the targets available to the deployment group.

Once the target is added in the pool/group, it will be available to the projects provisioned with deployment groups using the same pool. See Figure 3-23.

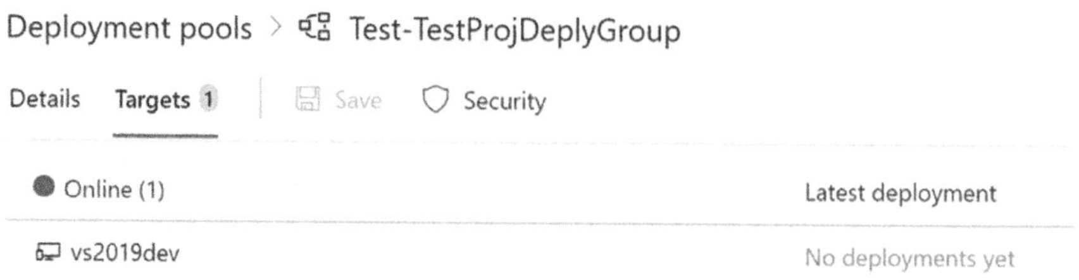

Deployment pools > Test-TestProjDeplyGroup

Details Targets 1 Save Security

Online (1) Latest deployment

vs2019dev No deployments yet

***Figure 3-23.** Deployment pool is added with a target*

You can add tags to the target to define its role in the deployment process. See Figure 3-24.

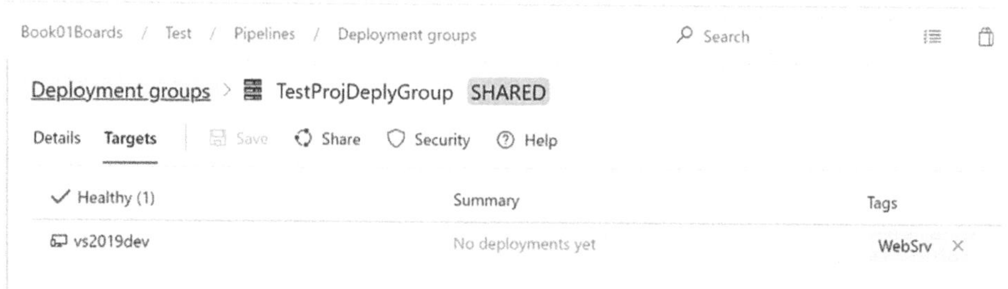

***Figure 3-24.** The target is tagged with WebSrv*

However, when you use the deployment pool in multiple projects to provision deployment groups, you can define different tags for the same target in a different team project deployment group. Simply, this means the same machine can be in the same deployment pool as a target but can be used in a different team project deployment group as a different deployment target role. See Figure 3-25.

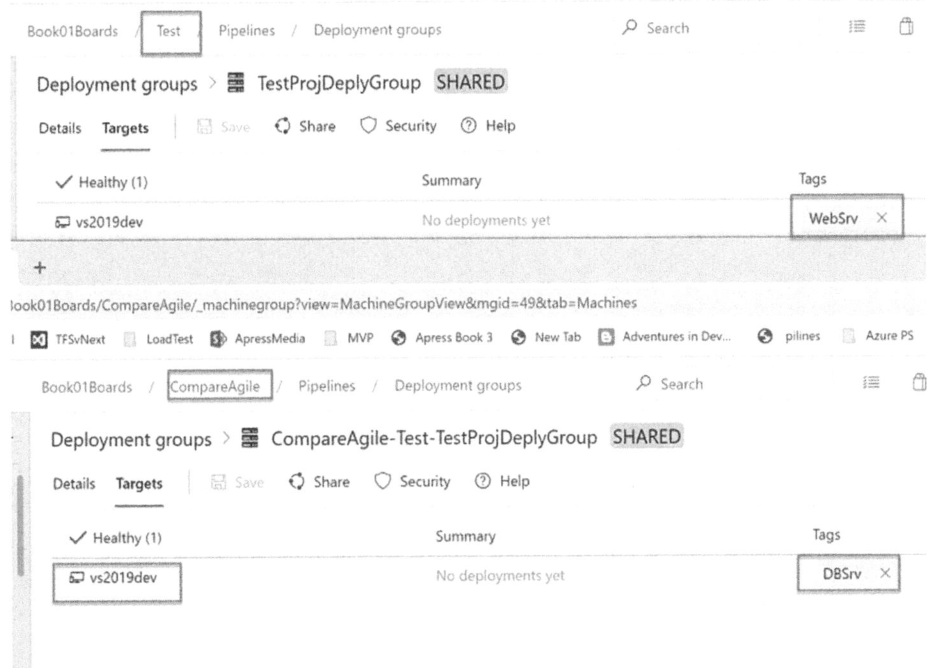

Figure 3-25. *Same deployment pool is used with a deployment target in different projects*

We have discussed the options to set up targets in deployment groups in this lesson, which will be useful in deploying to targets of your own infrastructure on premises or cloud.

Summary

In this chapter, we explored how we can create a self-hosted agent that can facilitate a custom-build pipeline execution with special software needs that can be satisfied with Azure Pipelines agents hosted by Microsoft. Further, if you have spare machines or your own datacenters with virtual machines, you might prefer to use them as build agents by registering them on your own agent pools. In addition, we discussed deployment groups and targets and how to set them up to facilitate software deployment on your own infrastructure.

In the next chapter, we will be exploring the options of creating Azure build Pipelines using the classic editor.

CHAPTER 4

Creating Build Pipelines-Classic-Source Control, Templates, Jobs, and Tasks

Build pipelines allow you to compile the source code, run unit tests, and publish your code as deployable artifacts. In classic build pipelines, you can easily drag and drop steps and set up the pipeline in a very visual way. You can use several settings available in the build pipeline to determine its behavior. Throughout the next three chapters, we will be exploring these features and their usage in detail.

In this chapter, we will discuss a few sections of the Azure DevOps build pipeline. You will be able to go through the build pipeline from selecting the source to building and packaging the built binaries for release.

Lesson 4.01: Using Source Control Providers

The main purposes of the build pipeline are building source code, executing unit tests, and publishing and packaging the built source code as deployable artifacts. We need to select the source code from a source control repository to build.

The first important feature of the build pipeline creation is selecting the source code repo. Azure DevOps provides two built-in source control providers. They are the centralized source control repo known as a team foundation version control (TFVC) and distributed source control repo Azure Git. So, the Project source can be managed as a Git source control or TFVC using the Azure DevOps. But when we create build pipelines

C. Chandrasekara and P. Herath, *Hands-on Azure Pipelines*, https://doi.org/10.1007/978-1-4842-5902-3_4

in Azure DevOps, it isn't limited to their own source control repos. You are allowed to connect external source control repos such as GitHub, Subversion, BitBucket, and other Git repos with Azure DevOps build pipelines and create the build packages.

Go to the Azure DevOps Pipelines section. Start creating the new build pipeline. Azure DevOps has two types of pipelines: YAML build pipelines (which we will discuss in Chapter 8) and classic build pipelines. Select the classic editor, and then it will direct you to the section where you can select the repository. See Figure 4-1.

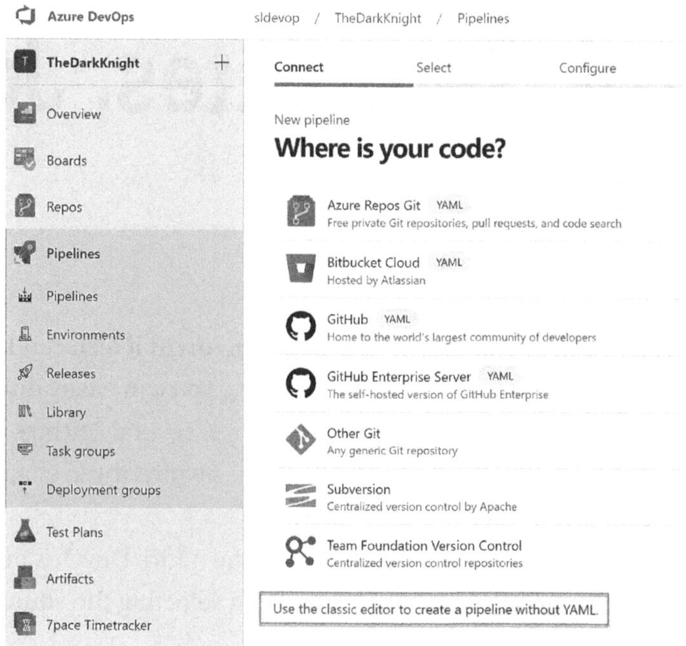

Figure 4-1. *Classic editor link*

Classic editor is a more visual version of a build pipeline creation. The Azure DevOps classic editor allows users who have less coding experience create the build pipelines easily. At the beginning of the build pipeline creation, you can select the repository where your source is located. See Figure 4-2.

4. Checkout submodules: If this option is selected, it allows the build pipeline to check out files from the submodule in the same repository or external repository.
5. Check out files from LFS: If selected, this option will check out large files such as audio and video files in the build agent during checkout for build.
6. Don't sync sources: This will not sync source code while the checkout process is going on.
7. Shallow fetch: It allows you to decide how many commits you need to fetch.

So far we have discussed what the features available in Azure DevOps are when we select Azure Repos Git as the source control.

Let's discuss the features available when we select TFVC as the source. See Figure 4-7.

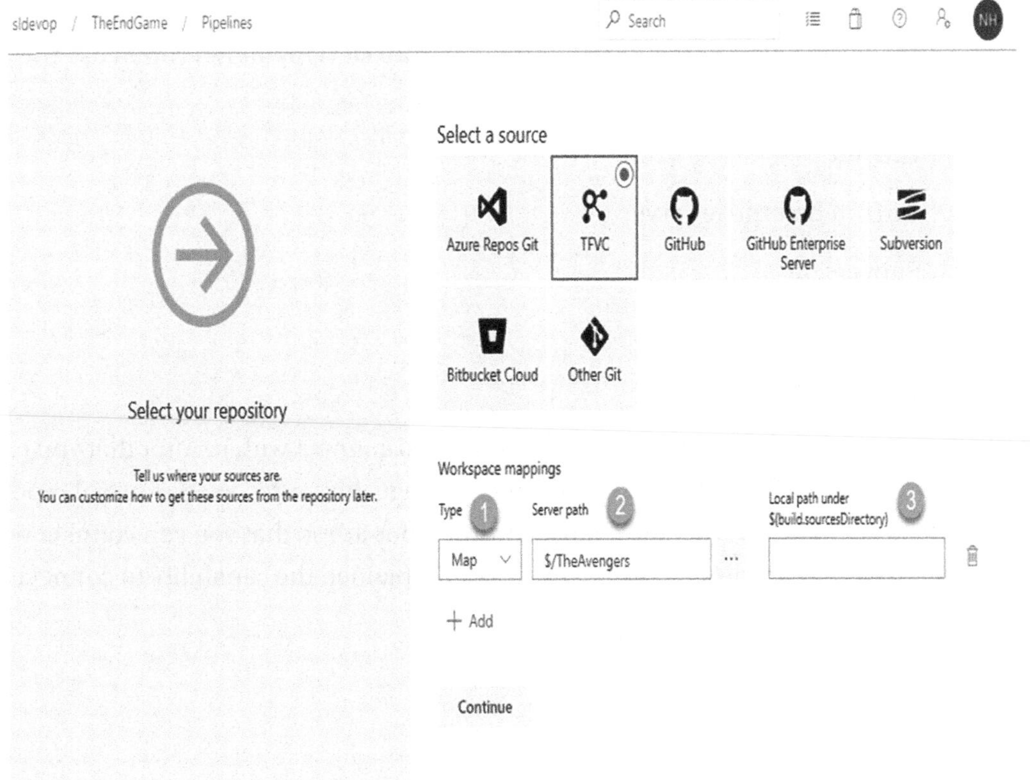

Figure 4-7. *TFVC as source*

Once you select TFVC as a source, it allows you to decide workspace mapping. You can decide which source codes are going to build using this build.

1. Type: There are two types: Map and Cloak. If you select Map, it will map the selected folders in the given server path to build using this build pipeline. If you select Cloak, it excludes the content of the selected folders.

2. Server path: Select the source code you want to include or exclude from this build.

3. Source path under $(build.sourcesDirectory): Decide the folders inside the source that need to be included or excluded from the build.

Once you create a build pipeline using TFVC as the source, it allows you to change the workspace mapping any time you want. Other than that, you can clean the working directory before build and label the builds upon successful build completion with the build number.

Other than using Azure Git and TFVC Repos, Azure DevOps allows you to use the following external Repos:

1. GitHub

2. GitHub Enterprise server

3. Subversion

4. Bitbucket cloud

5. Other Git repos

Select the required external repo and authorize to connect with it. After that you can use Azure DevOps build pipelines to build and package the source in an external repo.

This lesson discussed what the source control repos are so that you can connect with Azure DevOps build pipelines. Further, the lesson explained the capability to connect with internal repos and external repos.

Lesson 4.02: Using a Template

As new development tools and technologies are introduced to the industry more often, build and deployment tools also need to be improved consistently to work with those new development tools and technologies. Azure DevOps has various types of build templates supporting and setting up build pipelines with several technologies.

While you create an Azure DevOps build pipeline, you can create it using either an empty pipeline or using a template. This lesson will explain what templates are and how Azure Pipelines can be set up easily with them.

As we already know, the purpose of a build pipeline is to get the source code from the linked source repo, compile and build the source code, test the source code, publish the code, and finally package the published code as a deployable package. There are various build tasks available in Azure DevOps that we can use to configure the build pipeline steps. So, we have to add each relevant task one by one to set up a build pipeline. However, with Azure DevOps build templates, you can get multiple steps for a particular technology build setup added to a build pipeline, including generic configuration values required to successfully build the project, which makes setting up a pipeline straightforward and easy task.

Generally, an Azure DevOps build template is a set of build pipeline tasks created as a package. A template may contain all the tasks need to restore the required dependencies such as NuGet packages, build the source code, test the source code, publish the source code, and finally create a deployable package. It may also contain a generic configuration required for a particular technology-type project. After you add the relevant build template, you can complete your build pipeline with minor changes to the pipeline. So, it makes a build pipeline configuration process easier for a beginner. There are various build templates available in Azure DevOps supporting the setup of build pipelines, which are using different development tools and technologies. Let's identify a couple of available build templates.

ASP.NET core is a well-known technology. So, Azure DevOps has an ASP.NET core build template that we can use, as explained below.

While you create a new pipeline, it has a step where you can select the build template. See Figure 4-8.

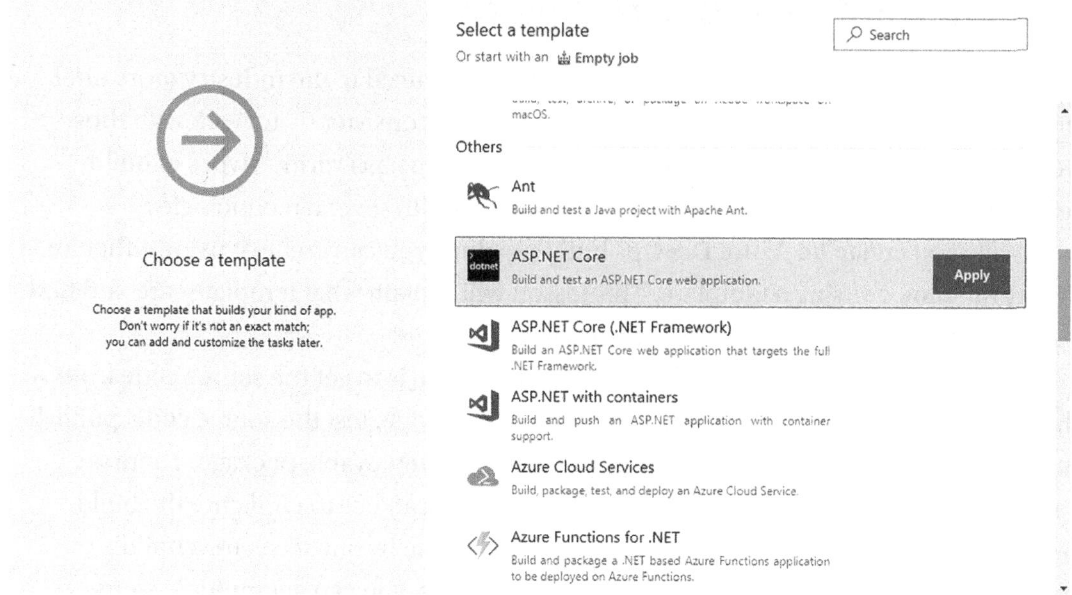

Figure 4-8. *Build templates*

Once you click on the apply button, it will be added to the build pipeline. See Figure 4-9.

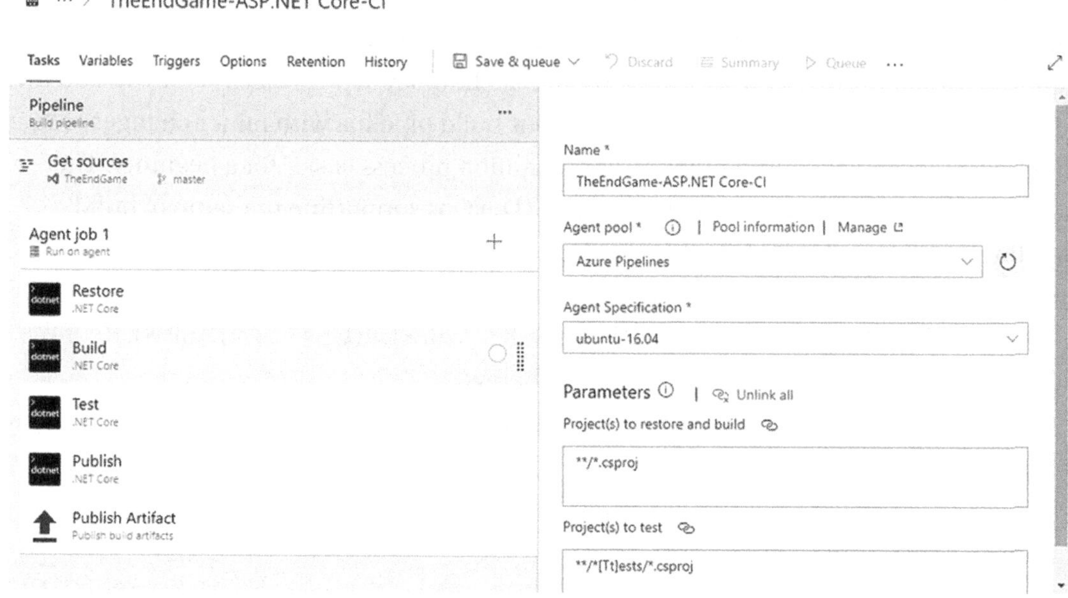

Figure 4-9. *ASP.NET core template*

Once you have added the build template to the build pipeline, it will add all necessary steps to the build. In the ASP.NET Core template, we can identify the following build tasks that are added.

Restore - If there are any NuGet packages or Azure DevOps artifacts feeds used in the project source, this will restore all the referencing packages.

Build - This step builds the selected project and verifies the compilation state of the source code.

Test - After building the project source, next we need to do unit testing on source code. This step can be configured to execute the unit tests.

Publish - This step will prepare the built binaries to publish as a website.

Publish Artifact - This will publish the deployable artifact.

As you have seen above with the ASP.NET core template, all the necessary steps are included in the template, and it makes the build pipeline configuration easy for anyone - even for a user who has no previous experience. After adding the template, you might need to make small changes if necessary. So, templates are very usable and it makes the build configuration process efficient.

If you go through a few other Azure DevOps templates, you will be able to get a good idea of how effective and helpful these templates are. If we consider a docker, it is a completely different deployment compared to directly deploying ASP.NET core. It needs to build a docker image out of the source code you have implemented. So, a docker build pipeline should be able to connect with the source and build the image using the build steps. A docker image build step needs to do more complex processes like downloading docker images available in the docker hub or other registries that are referred in the docker file contained in source code. After downloading the docker images, they need to be converted to docker containers. All the build process happens with these docker containers and finally it creates a docker container with your application and converts it to a docker image. Docker image is the deployable package created by the docker build. In docker, these images need to be stored in specific location call registries.

So, in the Azure DevOps docker template, it creates a docker image using the docker build step; after that, use another task to push the created image to the registry. See Figure 4-10.

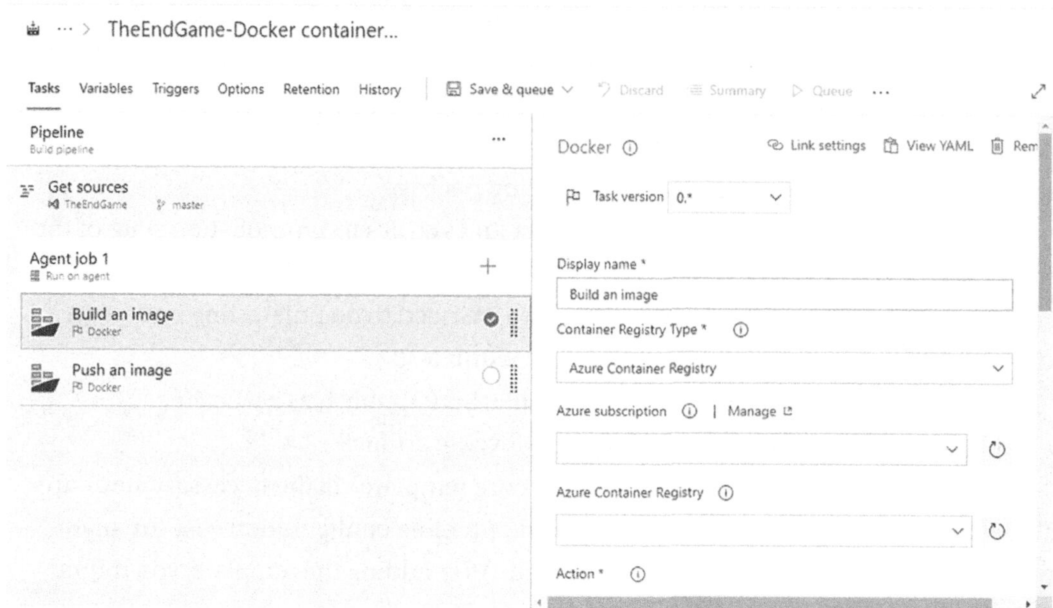

Figure 4-10. *Docker template*

You have seen how Azure DevOps templates support two completely different deployment technologies. Even if you are completely new to these technologies, you will be able to create a build pipeline easily using these templates. There are lot of templates available for the latest technologies like Machine Learning (ML). See Figure 4-11.

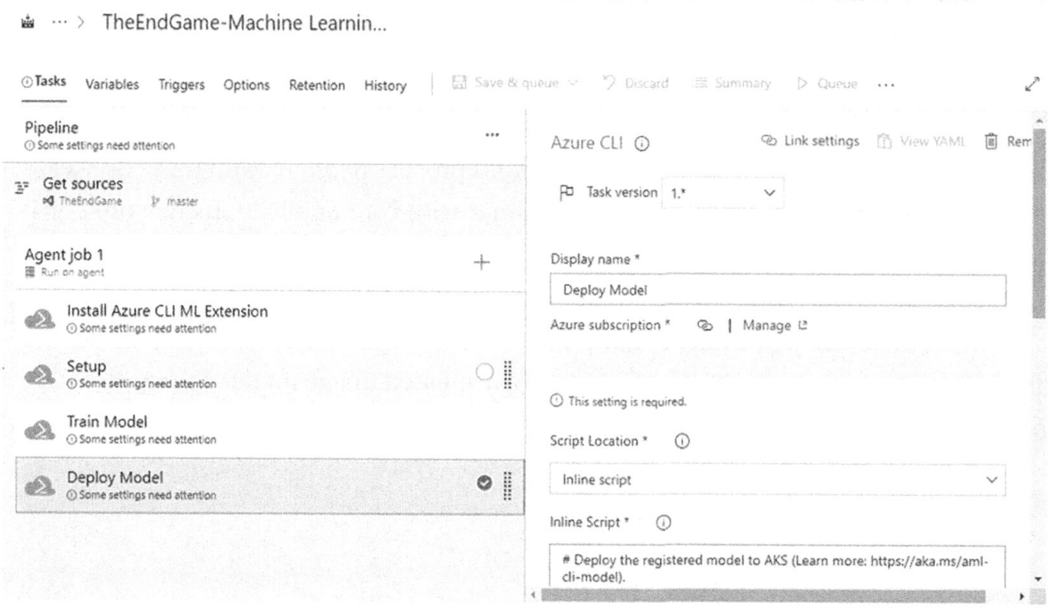

Figure 4-11. *Machine learning build template*

Machine learning is a latest technology and most of us don't have an idea of how to set up a build pipeline for machine learning. But Azure DevOps has introduced a machine learning template that can be used to train a model. When training a model, it is required to create an ML workspace in Azure. To create workspaces, normally we use Azure CLI (Command Line Interface) commands. To work with machine learning, it is required to install an Azure CLI ml extension. So, at the beginning of the pipeline, using the first step in the template, you can prepare the agent to work with Azure CLI ML commands. Basically, machine learning is developing an algorithm and training data to behave as the provided algorithm. Before training the model, it is required to create the workspace. After creating the workspace, you can train the model and deploy it using the next steps. All these steps can be done using an Azure DevOps machine learning template by providing relevant data to each step.

Azure DevOps build templates provide good support for users to create build pipelines that support various technologies. Also, it is a good option for any person even without having experience in each of these different technologies, to get started with the setting up of build pipelines.

Lesson 4.03: Using Multiple Jobs

As you already know, CI and CD is a very important part of the modern software development process. It will automate complex software build and test flows that can give you a lot of trouble if you do it manually. Sometimes we need to build the code with different versions of frameworks, and sometimes we need to build code with different platforms. There are so many scenarios that need to be followed to create a good deployable package. Azure DevOps multiple jobs provide good help when you need to create complex build pipelines that required the support of multiple frameworks or platforms.

Agent job a.k.a. agent phase is where you can define the build agent that is used to execute the tasks under a build pipeline. Also, the agent job/phase can be used to define some configuration that is relevant to all the tasks under that agent phase.

Agent phase allows you to select an agent pool and the relevant agent. As we already discussed in previous lessons, we know we can create hosted agents and private agents according to the project and billing requirements. In some scenarios you might need to build an ASP.NET application with some specific framework version that is available in the hosted agent. So, you can select a hosted agent pool for that agent phase. Also, there can be some scenarios like when you need to have specific framework version installed in your agent, and if there are other versions of the same framework available in the agent, the build gets failed. So, in that type of scenario, it is better to create a private agent with a specific framework version only. One such example would be the need to have SharePoint versions, which are not available in hosted agents. So, you can decide whether to go with private agents or hosted agents using an agent phase.

Also, there can be project requirements code that must be compiled using a specific version of the framework. As an example, you need an agent that has the .net framework 3.5 installed. So, you can add these types of demands using the demand section of the agent phase. You can set up a build agent with a specific framework version and set the agent name or a specific capability as a demand. When build is triggered, it searches for an agent that matches the defined demands in the agent phase.

As shown in Figure 4-12, you can add an agent name and agent version as the demand. Then when the build triggers, it will search the agent that meets all the requirements mentioned in the demands. Like the demands mentioned in Figure 4-12, it will search for the agent with the name "Agent01" and agent version "2.107.0" in the agent pool and run the pipeline tasks using that agent.

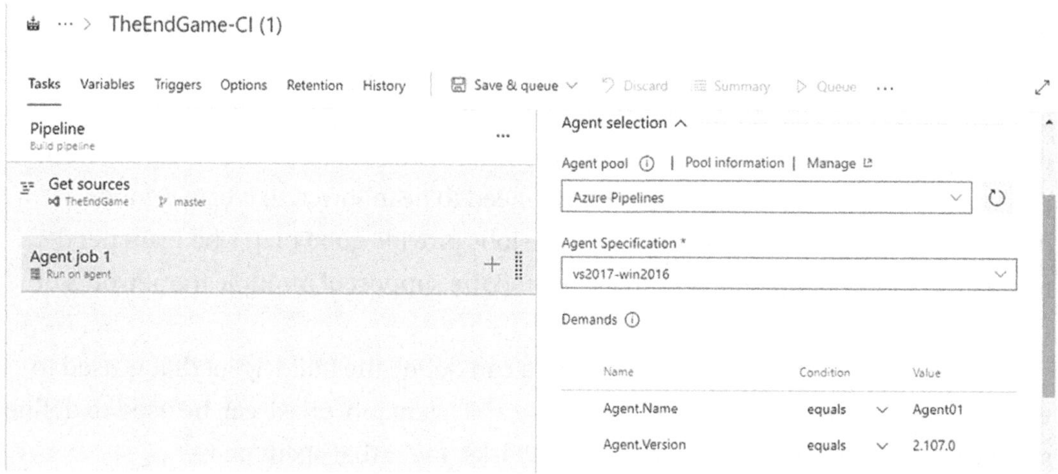

***Figure 4-12.** Agent phase demands*

So far, we have discussed a few of the capabilities of the agent phase. Now let's discuss the situations where we need to use more than one agent phase in the same build pipeline. In the mobile development business, developers mostly have to release a mobile application to both iOS and Android platforms. Further, it is necessary to release these versions under the same build number for both platforms. We can do this by using the same build pipeline to build both Android and iOS apps, by utilizing multiple agent phases in the same build, and setting one agent as MacOS for iOS app and the other as Windows or other platform as per the need of the Android application. See Figure 4-13.

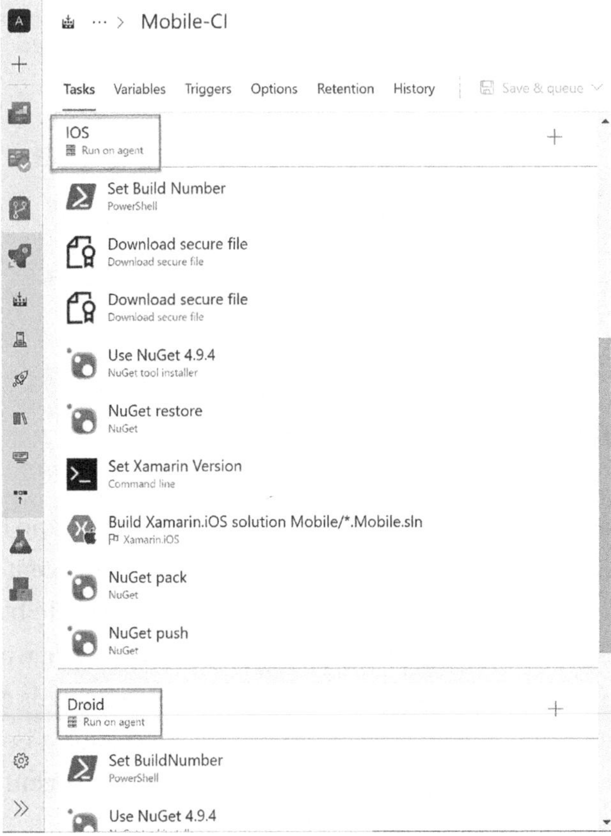

Figure 4-13. *Agent phase for iOS and Android*

As an example, we can create a build pipeline with three phases where one can be used to test the code by running the unit tests. For that agent phase, you can select an agent that can run the unit tests. The other two agent phases can build Android and iOS codes separately using two different agents. iOS uses the Mac OS agent and Android use suitable Windows agents from the pool. By using multiple agent phases, you can achieve two main build requirements here. One is that you can build a mobile app for different platforms with the same build number using the one build pipeline. Also, you can complete the build process quickly because agent phases can run in parallel without depending on each other. The parallel execution makes the build process more efficient and saves time. See Figure 4-14.

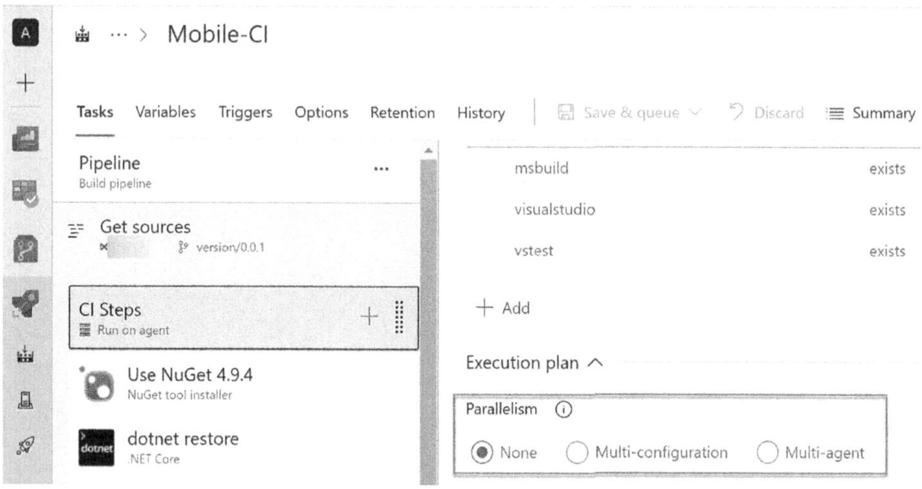

***Figure 4-14.** Agent phase parallel configurations*

We have discussed how agent phases can behave individually and build in parallel without depending on each other. There can be situations where agent phases need to be dependent on each other. Consider a situation where you need to build the source using an agent with specific software needs, and you need to decide whether to continue building the source using another agent with separate software needs and use the build output gain from the previous agent phase. You can easily develop a build pipeline that helps these types of situation run more easily with the use of agent phases and set dependencies. See Figure 4-15.

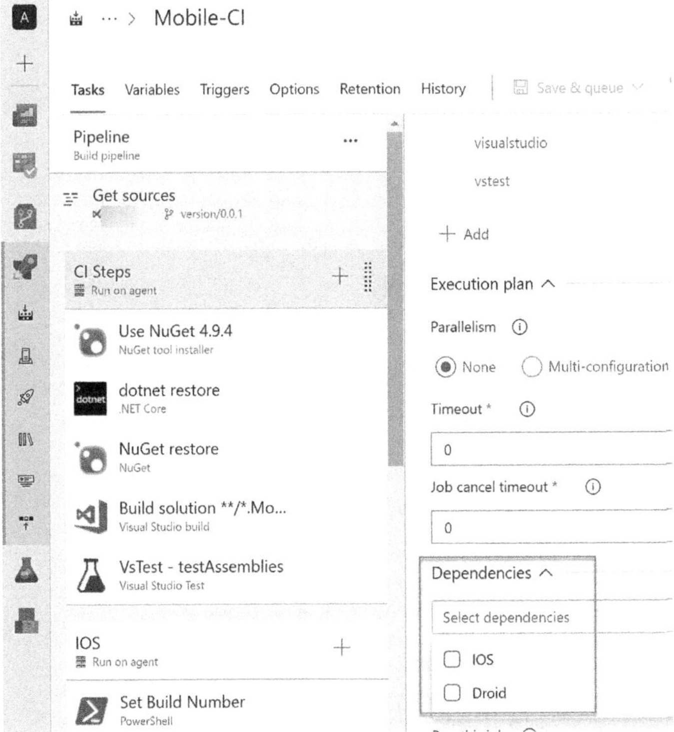

Figure 4-15. *Agent phase dependency*

Also, the Azure DevOps agent phase has the capability to parallelize job tasks. Sometimes there can be project requirements where the same code needs to be built using various configurations like debug and release. If you need to build using different configurations, the agent phase has that capability. Also, you can decide how many agents need to be used for the parallel execution, which allows us to use one agent for one configuration. If you have a limited number of agents in the organization, you might get into trouble when you do parallel executions using the multiple agents of all other build and releases that need to be in the queue until the agents become available. So, you can define a maximum number of agents to use by the agent phase at a given time occupied and keep the other agents in the pool available. See Figure 4-16.

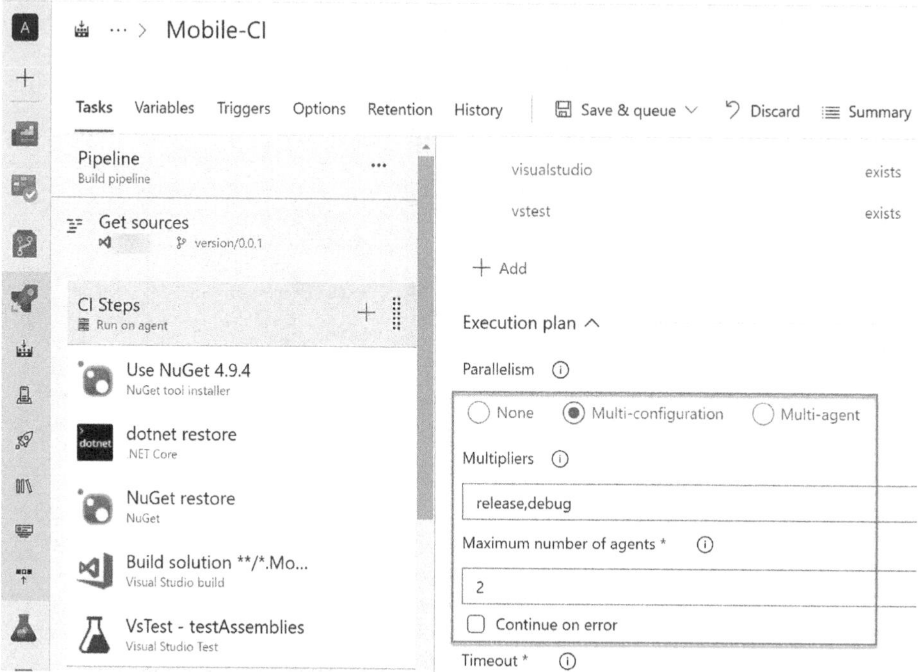

***Figure 4-16.** Multiple configuration build parallelly*

When building a source code, the build time varies due to different reasons. Anyway, it is good to have a timeout value defined for the agent phase. An example is that sometimes you might have experienced a situation where a build pipeline keeps running a greater normal execution time due to issues with the build tasks. In that type of a situation, it might affect the productivity of the builds and deployment process. This happens because there can be other builds waiting in the queue to use the agent, and a build running for a long time affects the queue waiting time for other builds. To control this type of issue, it is possible to add the agent phase timeout that would fail the build after a specified time duration. It can reduce the unnecessary waiting time of the other builds in queues. Other than this, there might be situations where more time is required to run the build pipeline tasks like test steps. As you know, some projects have automated test scripts runs at 4 to 5 hours or even longer, which require more of the time set as the timeout value of the agent phase. See Figure 4-17.

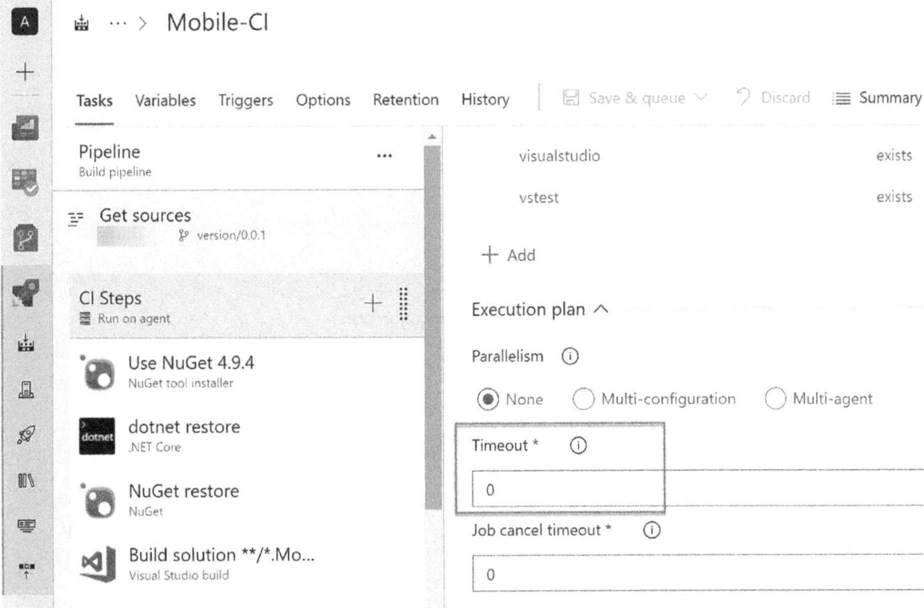

Figure 4-17. *Agent timeout*

There is another interesting feature in the agent phase that allows Azure DevOps users to use the OAuth token in the build pipeline. As an example, if there are PowerShell scripts used in the build pipeline that has the Azure DevOps Rest API calls to active its functionality, it is required to be authenticated to execute the calls to REST API. So, you can use a PAT (Personal Access Token) to authorize the access to API as one option and provide it as a parameter. Or if you enable "Allow scripts to access the OAuth token" in the pipeline, you can utilize the System.Accesstoken in the script for the same purpose. See Figure 4-18.

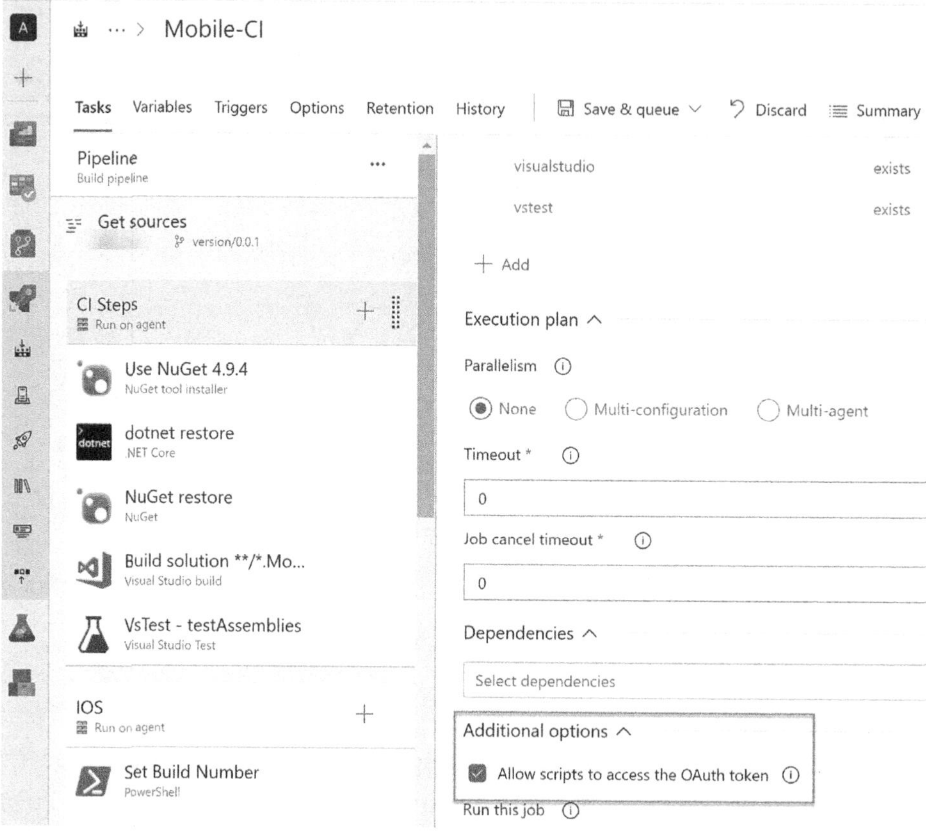

Figure 4-18. Auth token

In this lesson, we discussed a couple of features and usage scenarios of agent jobs/phases and parallel execution capabilities, and dependencies of phases as well as the usage of timeouts, which will be useful for you when you set up your build pipelines with Azure DevOps.

Lesson 4.04: Using Tasks

The Azure DevOps build pipeline can be used to make a business more productive and efficient due to its amazing capabilities. It has a lot of good templates as we discussed in the previous lessons. Also, it provides agent phases that allow the user to create more usable and complex pipelines. In these templates, we have steps we can use. Similarly, we can manually add steps/tasks to build pipelines to perform actions inside an agent job. Let's learn about pipeline tasks in this lesson.

Task is a package of the code segment that is created to do some specific work in the automated pipeline. There are several inputs required by each task to perform the actions with the source code you set up as linked in the build pipeline. Also, these tasks are available with several versions, which have minor changes as improvements in each.

As we already know, a build pipeline can be created using build templates or can be created by adding tasks one by one according to the requirements. There are various tasks available in Azure DevOps, which help to perform different actions like build, test, package, and so on. See Figure 4-19.

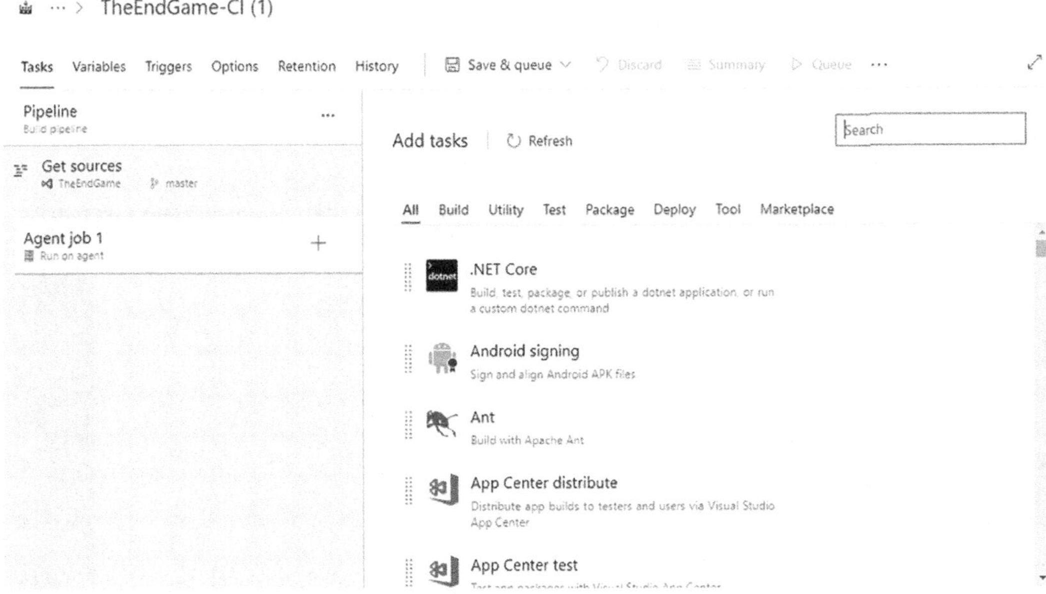

Figure 4-19. *Pipeline tasks*

While working with different technologies, it is required that you use different build tasks. As an example, we use ASP.NET Core build tasks with ASP .NET core source code. While we work with Android development, we need to use Android signing tasks. Likewise, Azure DevOps provides several build tasks for different technology needs and purposes.

In some situations we need to execute commands to do several things. As an example, in the machine learning build pipeline, we use a PowerShell task to execute Azure CLI commands to create an ML workspace. We have PowerShell, bash, and other utilities available as an Azure DevOps task.

We have discussed the built-in tasks available in Azure DevOps. If the available tasks don't suit your needs, you can install tasks from the marketplace. The marketplace has various free tasks available that you can install to the Azure DevOps organization and use in pipelines. However, the marketplace is an open platform and you may find some extension tasks from the marketplace are not reliable or effective at times. So, it is recommended to use tasks from trusted providers with good reviews or have good documentation and availability of the task implementation source code, which allows you to create your own version - maybe with a bug fix. It is better to install these tasks from the marketplace to your Azure DevOps instance in a controlled manner. For this control purpose, only admin users are allowed to install the marketplace tools. If a user or users do not have admin rights needs to install a marketplace extension, they are required to make a request so that an admin can evaluate and approve such a request and install the required extension. See Figure 4-20.

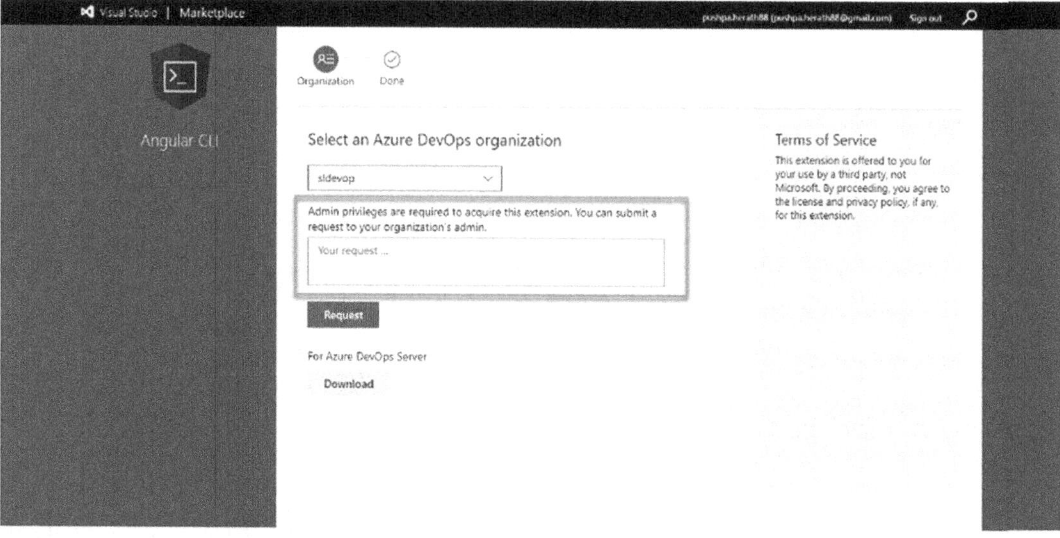

***Figure 4-20.** Admin permission request*

After sending the request admin, get the request mail with all the necessary information. See Figure 4-21.

Angular CLI has been requested

pushpa.herath88 is requesting Angular CLI by Raul A. Ruiz be installed to sldevop.

pushpa.herath88:

Need this for test

View requests

About this extension

Angular CLI by Raul A. Ruiz

Build, tests, lint, e2e an Angular project, or run a custom Angular CLI command.

Learn more

We sent you this notification due to a default subscription. View | Unsubscribe

Microsoft respects your privacy. Review our Online Services Privacy Statement.

One Microsoft Way, Redmond, WA, USA 98052.

Sent from Azure DevOps

Figure 4-21. *Marketplace extension installation request*

After getting this request, the admin can decide whether to install the extension or not. Also, if there are no tasks that suit your requirements, you can create your own custom tasks and publish them in the marketplace or share them only to the Azure DevOps organizations where you want the extension to be shared.

Tasks in Azure DevOps build pipelines have common configuration values available with almost all the tasks, which allow you to decide some control options for the task. As an example, when we run the test using the pipeline task, all the tests don't get passed all the time. So, if you want to continue the build pipeline, run it even if a test step failed, and you can do that using the task configurations. Another common experience while you work with pipelines is if the task is going to fail, it takes too much time to complete. In that type of situation, we can give a task timeout in which the server stops the task after a specified timeout period. See Figure 4-22.

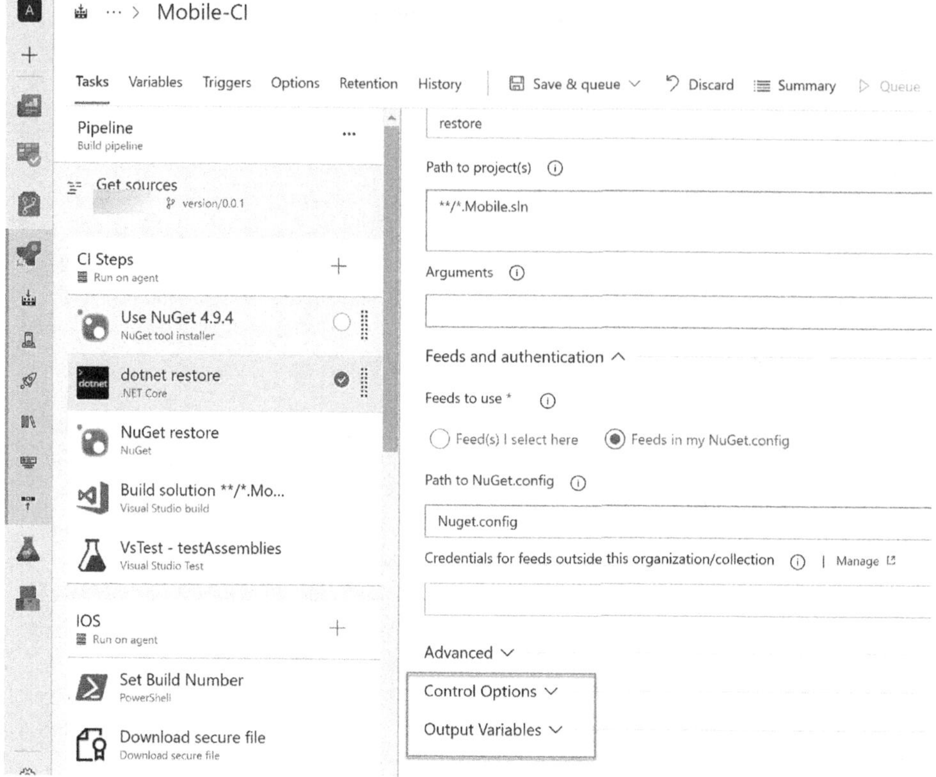

Figure 4-22. *Common configurations of tasks*

While working with multiple tasks, it may be necessary to keep some dependency between each task. Sometimes you can decide to execute the build pipeline step depending on a situation, such as if the pipeline is not triggered based on a pull request (PR). In situations like when you create a build pipeline to build the PR requests, it is not necessary to package the published code as it is a dummy work that is done before merging the source to the master branch to verify how the code changes affect the source after merging the code to the target branch. For this purpose, you can set custom control conditions to make the step/task executed if it is not a pull request triggered build and all previous steps succeeded. See Figure 4-23.

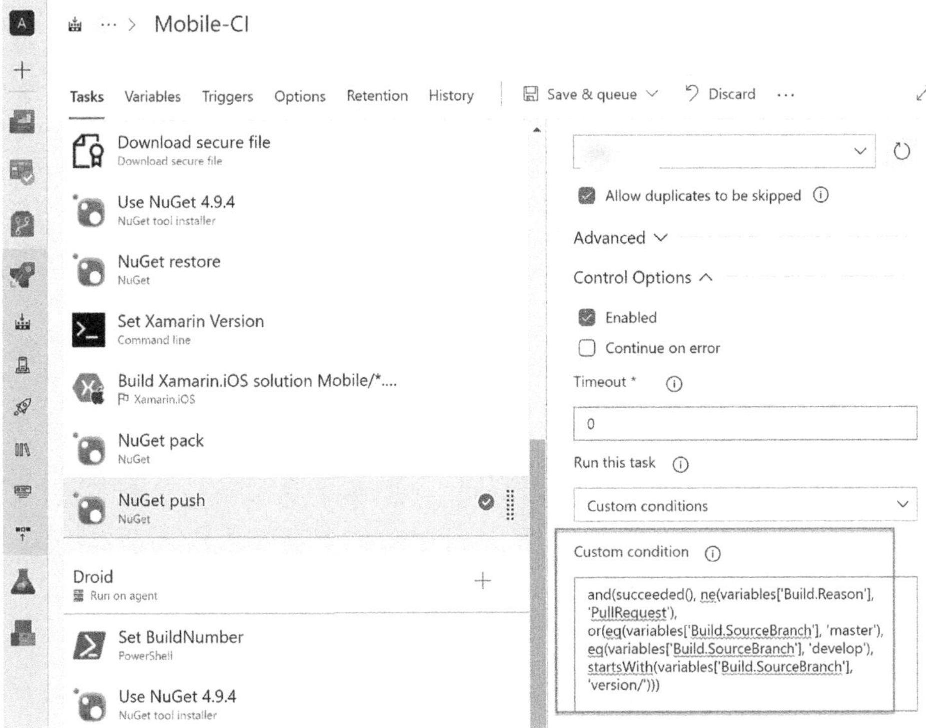

***Figure 4-23.** Custom condition of NuGet push*

We have explored the Azure DevOps task usage and common control options in this lesson. Further, we have discussed the usage of marketplace extensions and considerations you should have while using such extensions.

Summary

We have started discovering the classic build pipelines in this chapter, with a detailed look at the ways to connect various source control repos and the usage of templates to get the build pipeline setup done easily. Additionally, we discussed the purpose of agent jobs and several settings in agent jobs, which help to optimize the build execution needs of a project. Then we had a look at build tasks and their common control options and usage of extensions.

In the next chapter, we will further explore the classic build pipelines to understand how to use variables, how to set up triggers and path filters, format build numbers to support versioning of software and packages, and several other useful build pipeline features and properties.

CHAPTER 5

Creating Build Pipelines – Classic – Variables, Triggers, Filters, Options, and Retaining

In the previous chapter, we looked at a couple of features that you can use while setting up Azure build pipelines with the classic editor. Those included the capability to use different source control systems, applying common step templates to set up a build, usage of multiple jobs inside a build, and parallelism including multi-configuration builds. Further, you explored the capability to add tasks or build steps to a build pipeline and even getting additional tasks by installing marketplace extensions. Then you had a good look at the task control conditions and usage of custom conditions to satisfy for various scenarios.

With that knowledge, we will be stepping into more features of classic build pipeline setup in this chapter, exploring how we can define and use variables, setting up build triggers including applying branch protection policies builds with path filters. Additionally, we will be discussing formatting build numbers; enable, disable, and pause builds linking your work items to builds; applying demands, timeouts, and editing the history of classic builds; as well as retention options.

C. Chandrasekara and P. Herath, *Hands-on Azure Pipelines*, https://doi.org/10.1007/978-1-4842-5902-3_5

Lesson 5.01: Using Variables

Variables are useful to keep settings in a common location for multiple steps used in a build. They can be paths, common values such as names and passwords, or even configuration values used in your apps. There are two types of variables you can use in a build pipeline. Predefined variables available with Azure DevOps can be found at `https://docs.microsoft.com/en-us/azure/devops/pipelines/build/variables?view=azure-devops&tabs=classic` and you can define the variables in the Azure Pipelines as custom variables. Let's try to understand each type of variable and usage in this lesson.

You can use system variables as well as custom variables in any pipeline task by using the syntax of $(variableName). To define a custom variable, you can use the variables tab in the classic build pipeline. Clicking on Add+ will allow you to add new variables to the pipeline. A predefined variable link will take you to the Microsoft documentation page on predefined variables.

If your variable contains a sensitive value such as a password, you can hide it by entering the value and clicking on the padlock icon to lock it in each variable. Once a variable value is locked and saved, it cannot be seen again. If you unlock it, the value will be empty and you have to provide the value again and lock it.

The option to enable setting at the queue time will let you change the value of the variable at the time of queueing a new build. System.debug is a variable that is useful to set at the queue time, as it allows you to decide to run the current build you are queueing in the debug mode emitting more diagnostic log details, at the time of queueing the build. It will be useful you to identify issues in a broken build pipeline to get them fixed. See Figure 5-1.

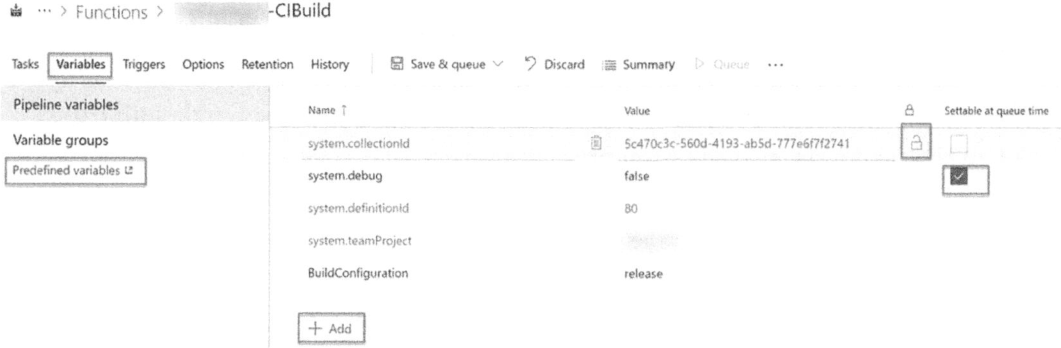

***Figure 5-1.** Variables in a build*

At the time of queueing the build, you can click on variables to view the settable variables at queueing. See Figure 5-2.

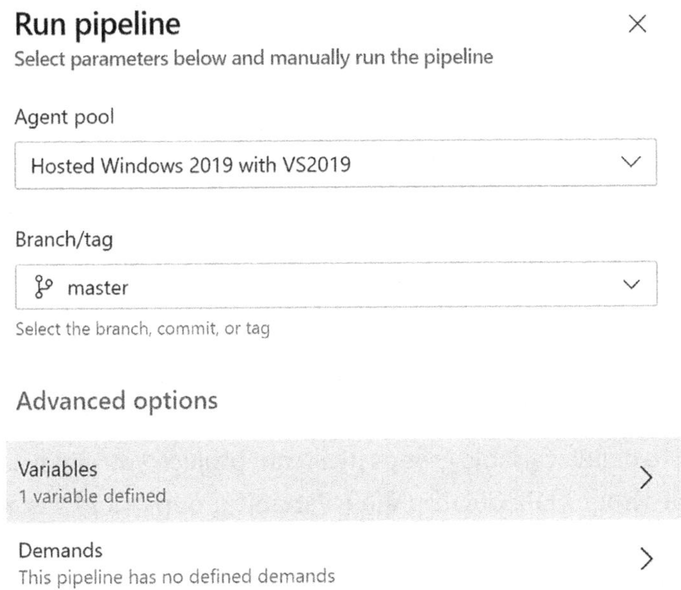

Figure 5-2. *Variables settable at queue time*

Then you can click on the required variable to update it. See Figure 5-3.

Figure 5-3. *Variable to update before running the pipeline*

Updating the value of the variable is possible when clicking on the variable. See Figure 5-4.

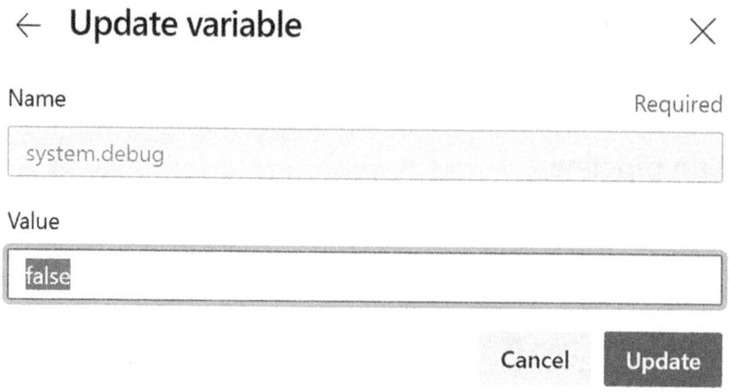

Figure 5-4. *Update variable at the time of queueing*

The variables can be defined as variable groups so that you can share them across multiple build pipelines in the team project or even share variables between build and release pipelines. To define variable groups in a team project, you can use the Pipelines ➤ Library, Variable Groups tab. Click on the + Variable group to add a new variable group. See Figure 5-5.

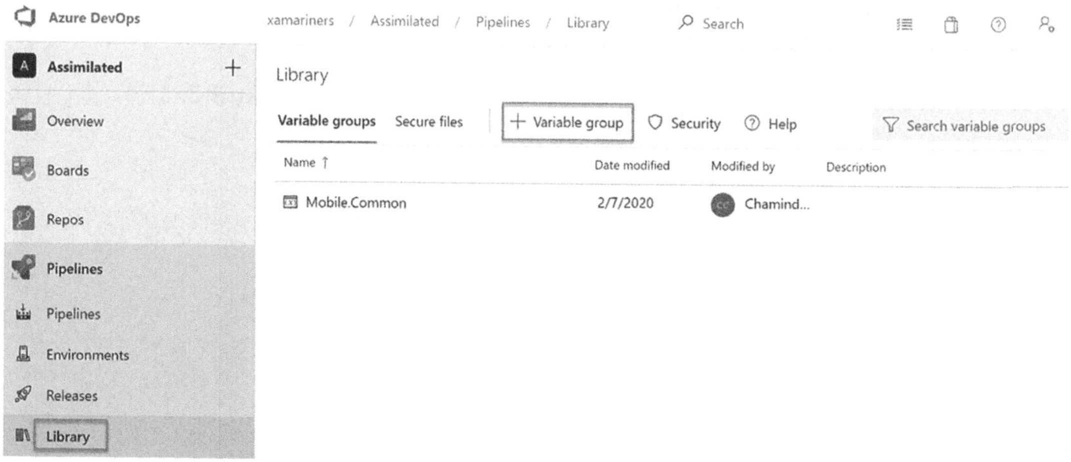

Figure 5-5. *Add new variable group*

A variable contains a name to identify it and you can add a description to it. For a variable group, you can enable access for pipelines making it available to use in Azure Pipelines. You are able to clone variable groups, which is useful for creating the same set of variables for multiple scopes such as deployment target environments. See Figure 5-6.

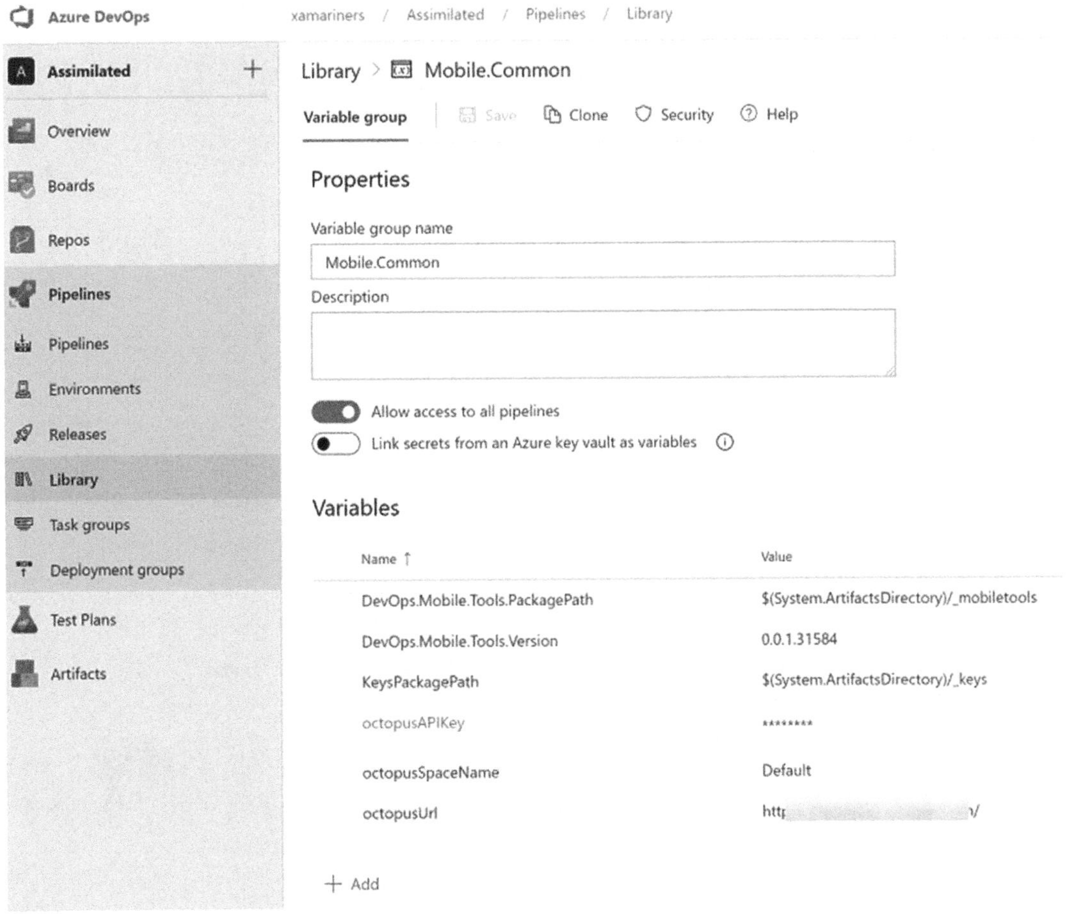

Figure 5-6. *Variable group*

Linking secrets from the Azure Key Vault allows you to set up a variable group based on selected variables from a given Azure Key Vault. You will be able to store all your secret variables in a common secure vault in the Azure Key Vault and use them in required pipelines because of this capability. See Figure 5-7.

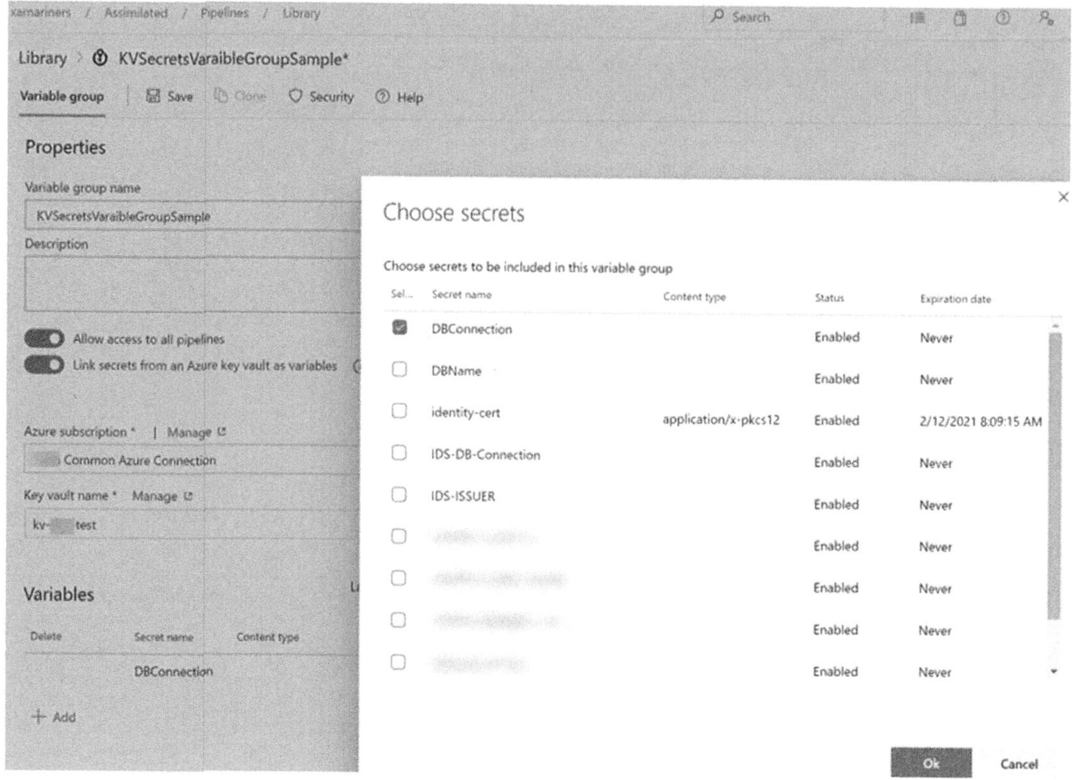

***Figure 5-7.** Azure Key Vault secrets in a variable group*

Usage of variable groups in Azure build pipelines helps you to share common variables across multiple build pipelines. In a classic build definition, you can select the variable group in the Variables tab and add it to the build pipeline so that you can use the variables in the group in the pipeline. Similar to the build pipelines, you can use variable groups in Azure release pipelines. It is possible for you to scope the variable groups to a given stage or to release them in Azure release pipelines. You can use clone the capability of variable groups and create the same set of variables into another group with different values, which helps you to keep values for each stage in a variable group scoped to that stage. See Figure 5-8.

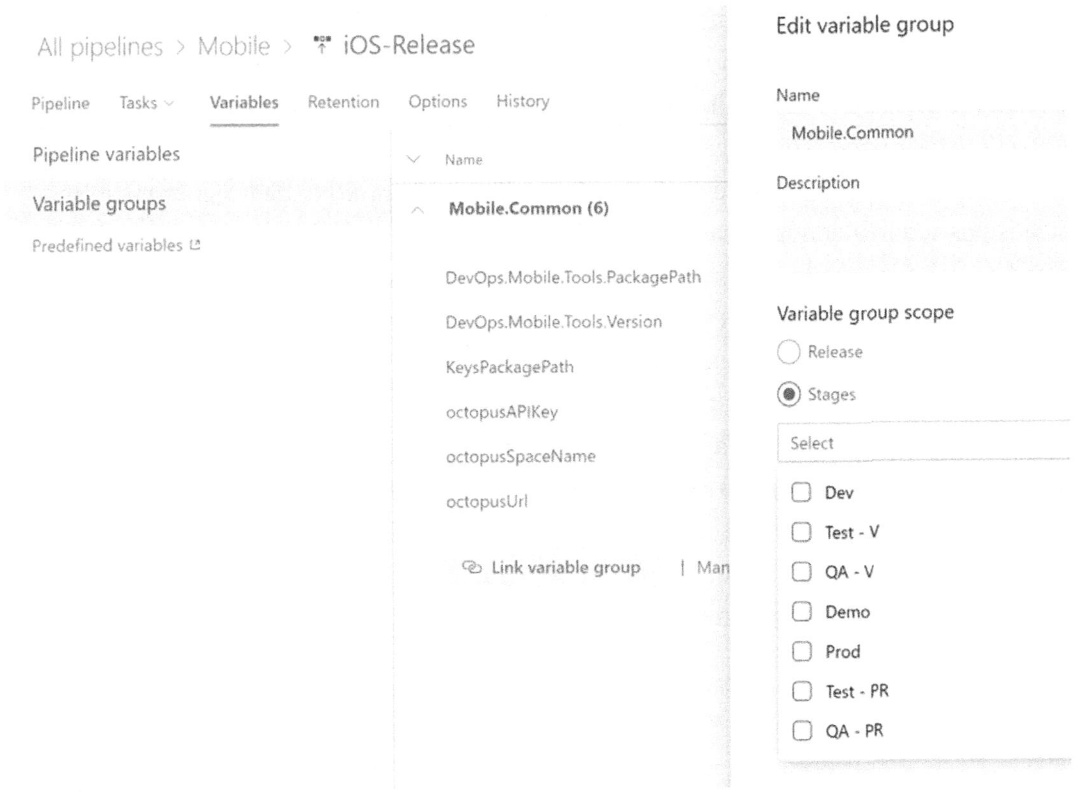

Figure 5-8. *Using variable groups in release pipelines*

We have discussed the usage of variables, how we can define them as pipeline variables, and share variables across pipelines using variable groups. Further, we looked at the capability of using Azure Key Vault secrets as variables.

Lesson 5.02: Setting Up Triggers and Path Filters

Build pipelines can be triggered manually. However, it is important to have different trigger options for builds. For example, once code is pushed to a repository to validate the code compilation state and evaluate the unit test state, you may want to run the builds. Or it could be your nightly schedule of regression test validation.

You may have a large code base that contains several projects. Imagine a situation such as an implementation of a large system with microservices-based implementation. In this kind of a scenario of microservices, you may only want to build a relevant microservice when the code pushed with changes for that microservice, but may not want to build other parts of the applications with builds related to them. Hence, with triggers it should have a filtering mechanism to determine which code paths should trigger a build.

Let's explore different trigger options for builds.

Enabling a continuous integration trigger will make a build to be triggered when a code is pushed to a defined branch or a branch meets the defined branch patterns. Each commit pushed to the branch will be built, and you can even execute unit tests in such a build to ensure the code that is committed is compiling without any issues as well as the tests are not broken, proving the validity of the code. The path filter option lets you filter a path as included, so that you can make sure if some code changes happen in that given path and in the given branch, that meets the pattern, gets build on code push. The exclude allows the path to be ignored so that a push to that path alone would not trigger the build pipeline. The batch changes option lets the multiple pushes to a branch be batched together and execute in one build instead of executing a build per push, if a build is already in a running state. See Figure 5-9.

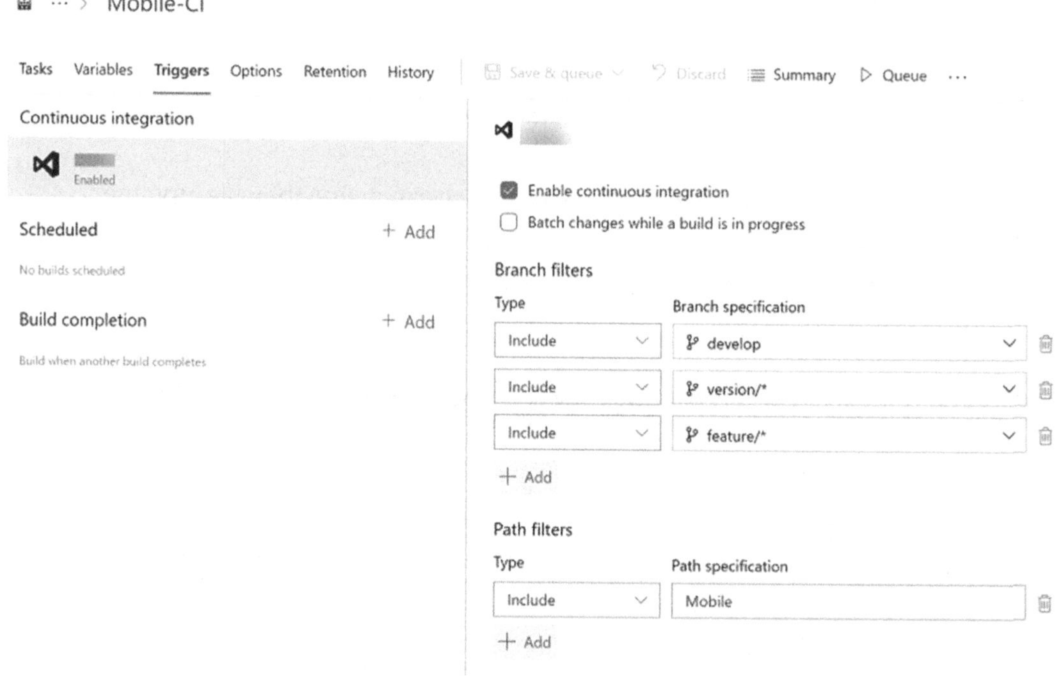

***Figure 5-9.** Continuous integration trigger*

A scheduled trigger can be used to set up a trigger that executes the build pipeline on a given scheduled time on selected days of the week, and using a selected branch or branches by a defined branch pattern. For scheduled triggers, also, you can set to exclude branch patterns. Further, the option is there for you to set the build to trigger only if a change in source or pipeline, after the last schedule build is executed. You can add multiple such schedules to a build as triggers. This scheduling of builds allows you to run your builds, say nightly, or a couple of times of a day, to evaluate your code base against vulnerability scans and to execute long-running unit tests. See Figure 5-10.

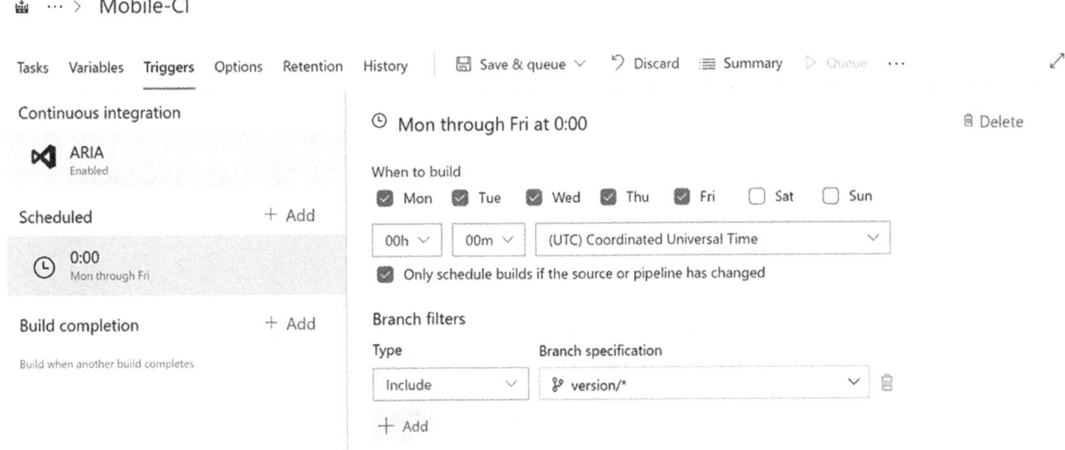

Figure 5-10. *Scheduled triggers*

There is another type of build trigger that allows you to create chains of builds. This option allows you to trigger a given build pipeline based on a completion of executions of another build pipeline. Maybe you can use one build in a schedule and run another upon completion of that build, which may let you execute some dependent steps or test runs. Or you may even split multiple tests into different builds and get them triggered after a given prerequisite build is completed. You can even add exclude include branch filter patterns to consider triggering builds if a given build is executed for the branches meeting the branch pattern defined. See Figure 5-11.

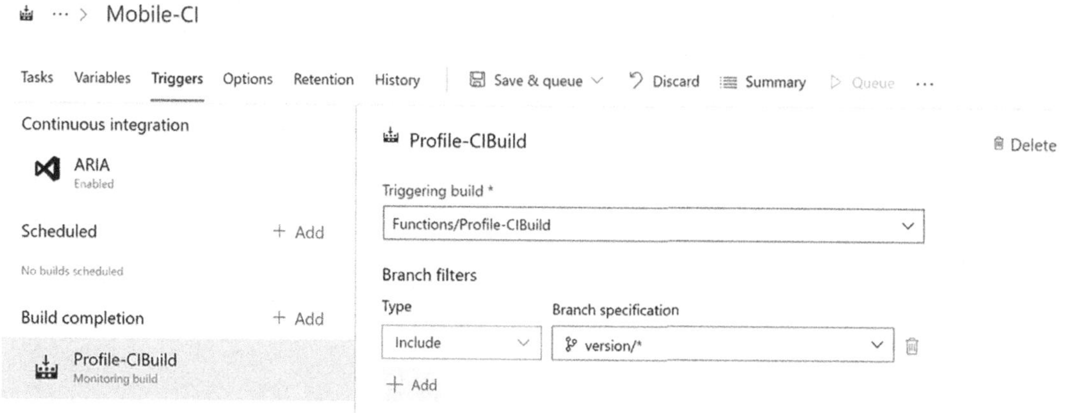

Figure 5-11. *Build completes trigger*

In this lesson, we have looked at different triggers you can set for build pipelines, which helps you to execute based on different contexts.

Lesson 5.03: Formatting the Build Number

The build number can be used to apply a version to a package/artifact generated as output from a build pipeline. Further, it allows you to properly version your software releases. You can follow and implement different build number patterns with Azure build pipelines, which we are going to have a quick look at in this lesson.

The simplest way to format a build number is by setting the build number format in the options tab in a given build pipeline definition. You can use predefined variables in the Build number format to create builds with the number format of your preference. See Figure 5-12.

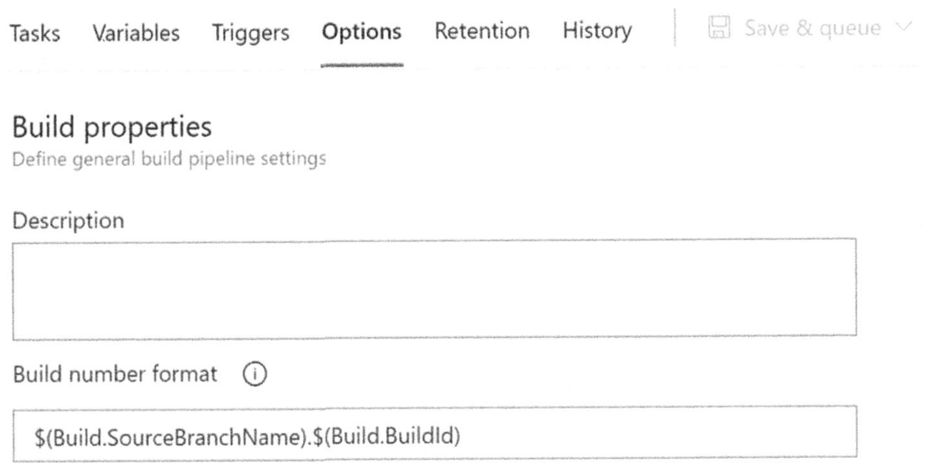

Tasks Variables Triggers **Options** Retention History | Save & queue

Build properties
Define general build pipeline settings

Description

Build number format

$(Build.SourceBranchName).$(Build.BuildId)

***Figure 5-12.** Build number format*

The $(Rev:r) or revision can be used to add a revision format to the build number, making each build number unique. It will start from 1 for any build number format and continue to increment the number until the base format changes. For example, if you define your build to use a branch name and revision, $(Build.SourceBranchName)$(Rev:r) as the build number format, for a branch named master, the build number will be master.1, master.2, and will continue. If the branch you build changes to develop, it will be starting as develop.1. The $(Rev:rr) can be used to add a two-digit revision number as with a preceding zero when the revision is a single digit. For example, the first build will have the revision as 01.

The build number can be manipulated using scripts such as PowerShell, which can run as a build pipeline step. In PowerShell, you can use the syntax below to update a build number of the current build.

```
##vso[build.updatebuildnumber]buildnumber
```

For example, the following PowerShell statement will apply the content of PowerShell variable $ BuildNumberToSet to the current build, as the build number.

```
Write-Output "##vso[build.updatebuildnumber]$BuildNumberToSet"
```

It is possible to use bash scripts to do the same as well.

```
echo "##vso[build.updatebuildnumber]$BuildNumberToSet"
```

You may use the scripting capabilities of yours to manipulate your source code packages version numbers with the build number of your build to apply proper versioning to the packages you create. For example, in a C# project, you could manipulate the AssmplyInfo.cs file, version information to update the assembly version and the assembly file version of a dll or exe that is getting built in the build. Or in build tasks such as creating NuGet packages, you are allowed to use a current build number to apply the version of the NuGet package. See Figure 5-13.

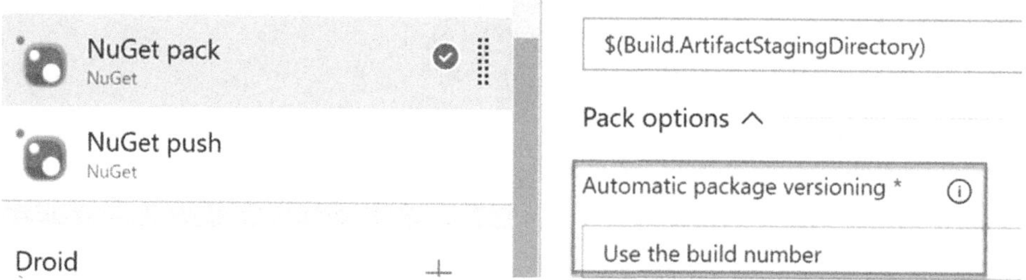

Figure 5-13. *Using build number in NuGet packages*

The build number can be referred in any script or task in the Azure Pipeline with a predefined variable $(Build.BuildNumber).

In this lesson, we have discussed the usage of a build number and setting it with build options or with scripts.

Lesson 5.04: Enable, Disable, and Pause Builds

The build pipelines in Azure DevOps allow you to keep them enabled, disabled, or paused. Let's look at what the behavior of each setting is and discuss a bit about the usage.

You can set the enable, disable, or pause option in the options tab of a build pipeline. See Figure 5-14.

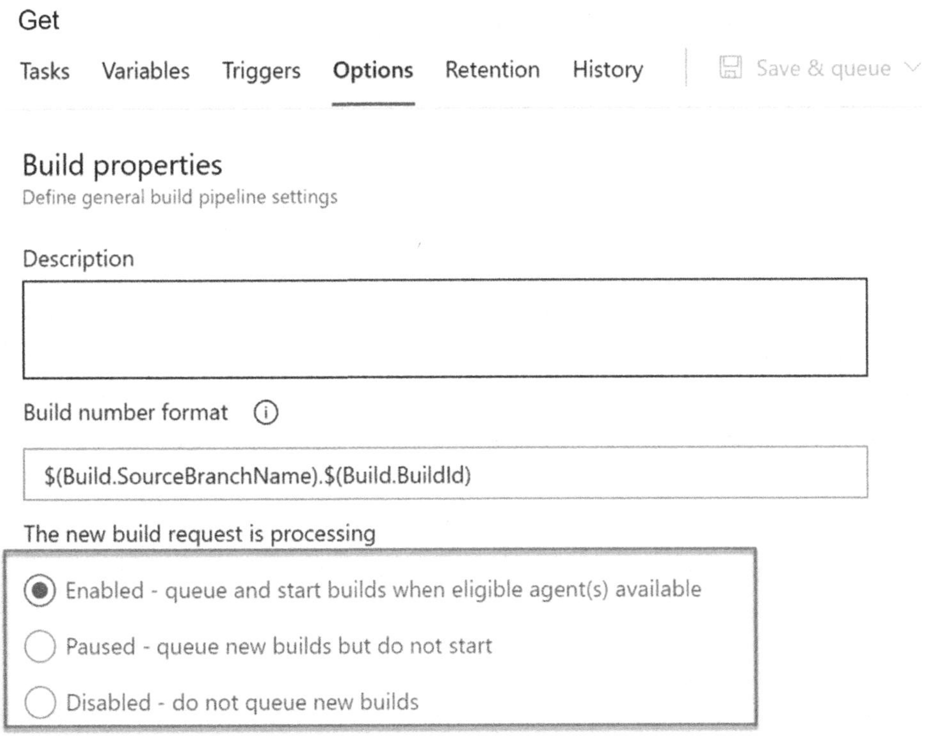

***Figure 5-14.** Enable, disable, or pause build pipeline*

The Enabled option allows the builds to get queued and get started with the execution of the build steps when an agent with the required capabilities is available. This is the normal expected case of a build pipeline, as it should get triggered and executed based on the triggers set in it.

The Paused option of a build pipeline allows the builds to be queued, but the build execution will not start until the build is enabled again. This option Paused is useful when you want to commit/push changes to a source code repo that could trigger multiple builds, but you want to get another build executed as priority before the build you are setting is Paused.

The Disabled option will not get the builds to be queued for the triggers until it is set to Paused or Enabled. This is useful at the time of performing a maintenance or improvement to the pipeline while making intermediate changes saved in the pipeline definition, as it would prevent the execution of work in progress build pipeline steps.

In this lesson, we have discussed the three options available in build pipelines defining the build pipeline getting queued and executed behavior, which allow you to effectively use them for the intended scenarios described.

Lesson 5.05: Build and Work Items

Work items are used to track the work you do in a project, and we have discussed them in detail in the first book of this book series on Hands-On Azure Boards. These work items can be integrated into the build pipelines so that they can be later used to generate automated release notes at the time of deployments. Further, to notify build failures and to make sure someone takes responsibility over the failure build, we can create a work item on failure builds. Let's look at how we can use builds with work items in this lesson.

You can define in the build options to automatically link the work items based on the associated work items to commits in branches that match the specified branch pattern. Once the build succeeds, links will be created to all the work items associated with commits, which were newly built in the given build. Later these work items can be used to generate a release note, while deploying to a given target based on the previous build deployed and the current one getting deployed. See Figure 5-15.

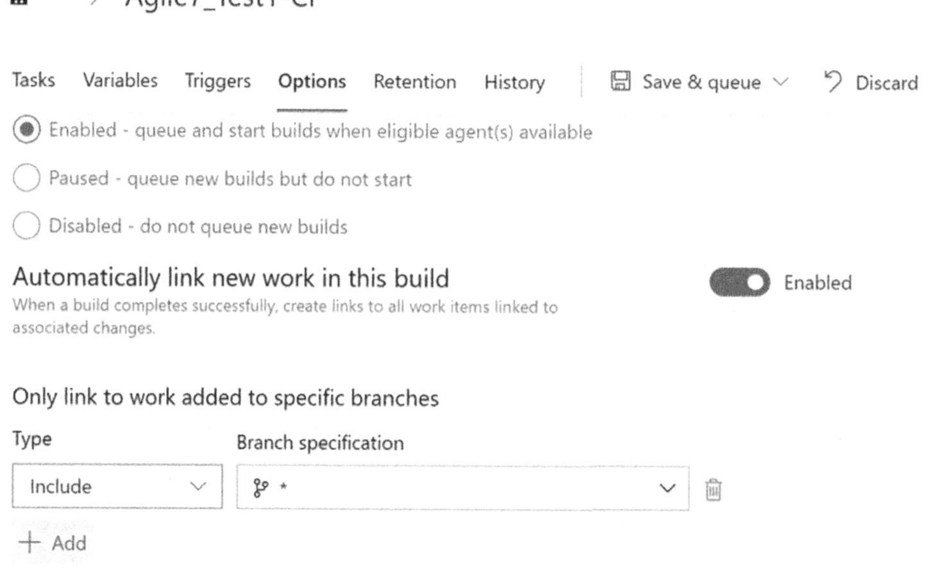

***Figure 5-15.** Link work items with builds*

Creating work items for failure builds allow you to select a work item type and set field values of the work item being created with preferred values. The values can be variables from the build or any other value you define. The work item can be assigned to the requester, so that in a situation of a commit, that would treat the commit user as the build requester, who would be assigned the work item. The responsibility of the failed build can be assigned to the developer who commits the code that is making the failure. This capability makes the failure builds to be attended on time without getting ignored. See Figure 5-16.

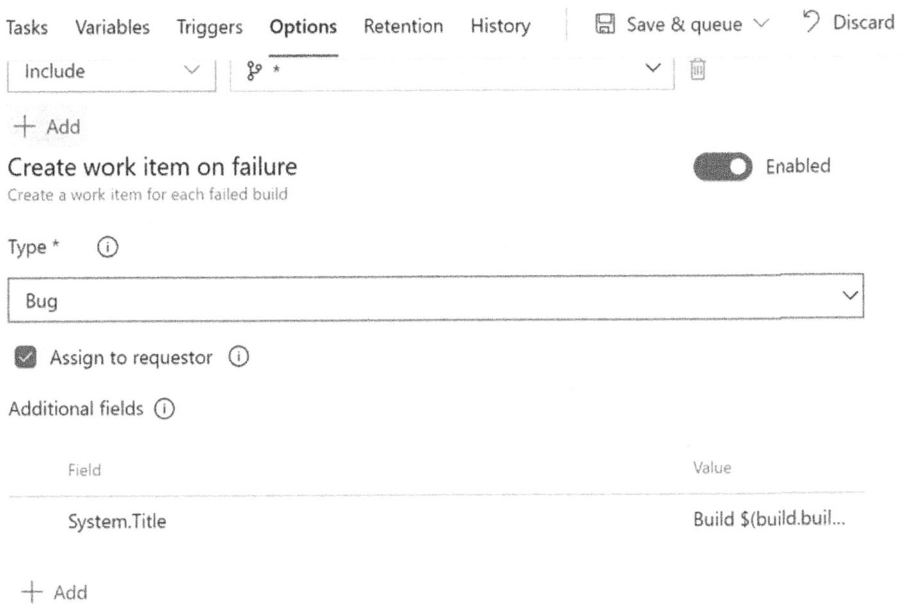

Figure 5-16. *Create work item on failure build*

We explored the work item and build association as well as creating a work item to assign build failure responsibility in this lesson.

Lesson 5.06: Build Status Badge

A build a status badge is a useful way to identify the current build state of a given build. It can be used in documentations such as wikis, or any other web page, etc., where you want to report the status of your builds.

The status badge is available in the option page of the build pipeline. It can be used as three formats. An Image URL will provide a build status image that can be used in a web page or a wiki page, etc. You can use an Image URL for a specific branch, reporting the status of the build considering a given branch. A markdown link is available as a markdown syntax so that you can use the build badge in any markdown documentation such as a wiki. See Figure 5-17.

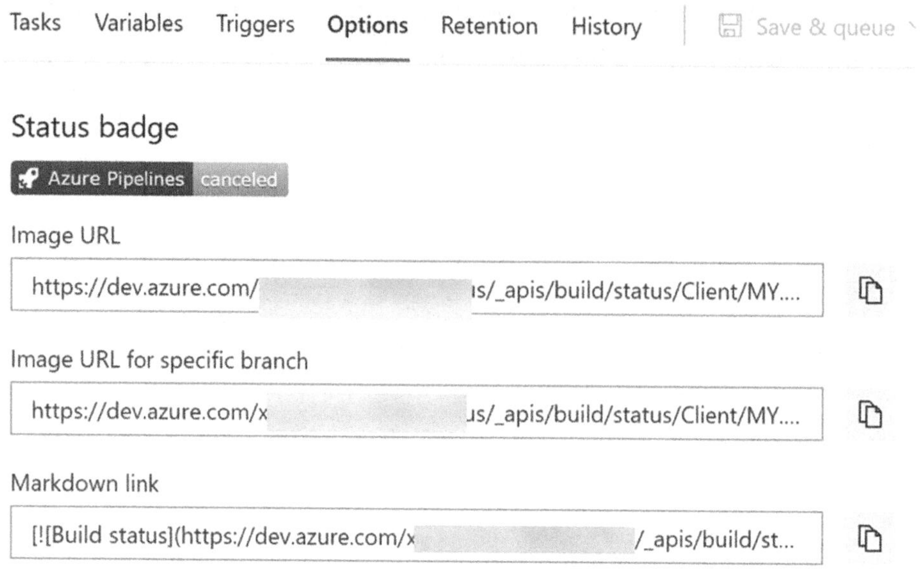

Figure 5-17. *Build status badge*

In this lesson we discussed the build status badge, which can be used to show the build status in documentations.

Lesson 5.07: Other Build Options

There are a couple of more build options worth looking at such as scope, timeouts, and demands.

The scope of authorization for the build can be set to either the project collection or current project. The project collection scope allows build jobs to access information for the level of project collection (Azure DevOps organization scope). A current project limits the access to the current project. An example scenario would be a PowerShell step using a system access token and the REST API of Azure DevOps to access information, which would be scopes based on the setting of the authorization scope to the Azure DevOps organization/project collection or to the current project scope. A build job timeout specifies the maximum number of minutes that build steps can be executed in a given agent before cancelling it. If you make a cancel request on a build job, the time in minutes that the job will wait before the server terminates the job if the cancel has not occurred, is determined by the build job cancellation timeout.

The demands let you define how to look for an agent based on its capabilities in a given agent pool. You can set it to check for capability existence or check for the capability value as a demand. It is possible to set multiple demands for a build job. See Figure 5-18 for the options discussed in this lesson.

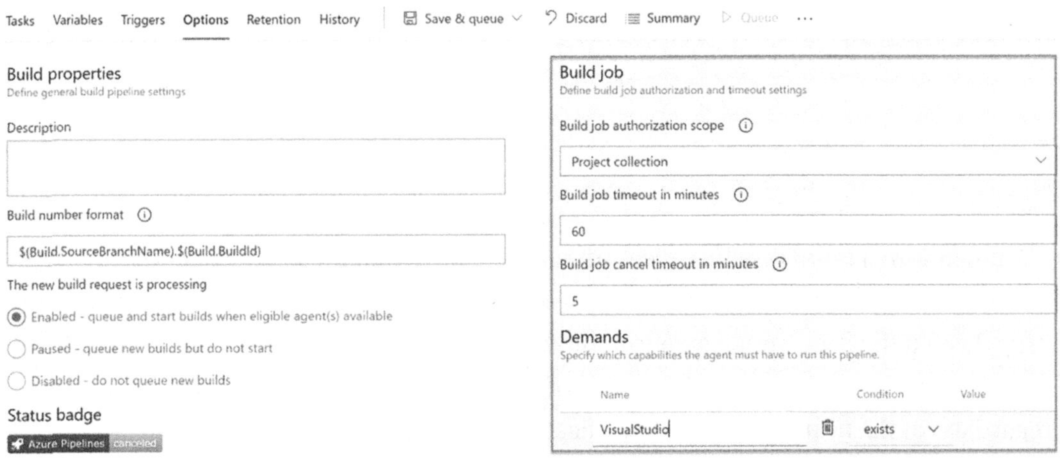

Figure 5-18. *Scope, timeouts, and demands*

We have explored a few other options such as authorization scope, timeouts, and demands for build jobs in this lesson.

Lesson 5.08: Build History and Retention

Build history and retention are two other useful features available in Azure Pipelines, which are worth having a look at so as to understand the purpose and usage of them.

The changes you make to an Azure build pipeline are recorded as history. While making changes to pipelines, it is possible to add comments to ensure changes made can be identified easily. The history can be used to compare the changes made to a pipeline between two history records. It is possible to revert back a pipeline to a given history point, which would be really useful while doing maintenance or upgrade work on a build pipeline. See Figure 5-19.

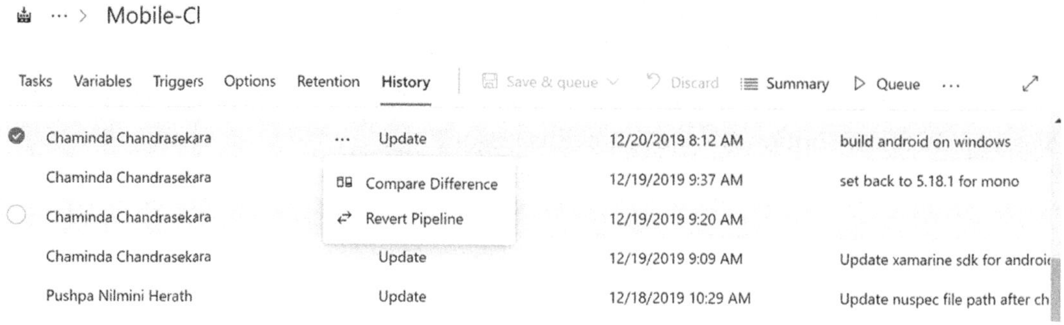

Figure 5-19. *Pipeline history*

Retention of build pipelines are streamlined and available as a project setting. We can set days to keep runs of builds, pull request builds, and attach artifacts in a pipeline drop. Even if the time limit exceeds to retain builds, the "number of recent runs to keep" value will decide, how many of last runs of builds will be kept available or retained, regardless of the number of days specification. See Figure 5-20.

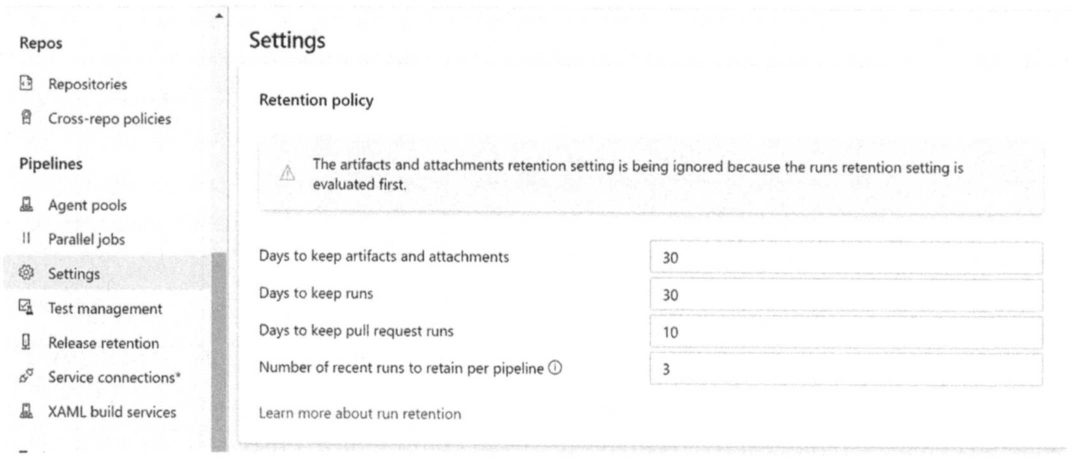

Figure 5-20. *Build retention*

In this lesson, we discussed the build pipeline history, capability to revert to a previous version of the pipeline, and retention options for the build runs.

Summary

We have explored the variables and their usage in detail in this chapter. Various triggers for builds and formatting build numbers for proper versioning purposes were discussed in detail. Additionally, we looked at several other options and features in build pipelines such as enable, disable and pause build pipelines; creating work items on failure and enabling linking of work items; usage of a build status badge; job scopes and timeouts; history; reverting build pipelines; and retention options.

In the next chapter, we take a closer look at features of classic build pipelines, such as queueing, usage of PowerShell scripts to set variables in builds, accessing secret variable values in scripts, usage of system access tokens, task groups, agentless phases, publishing artifacts, exporting and importing build pipelines, and organizing builds to folders.

CHAPTER 6

Creating Build Pipelines –Classic-Queuing, Debugging, Task Groups, Artifacts, and Import/ Export Options

We have discussed many useful features of Azure build pipelines in the previous two chapters. In them we talked about how we can set up a build pipeline using build tasks, variables, build job options, usage of different source control systems with builds, using builds to protect branches, and several other options and features.

In this chapter, we explore a few more features such as queueing builds and enabling diagnostic info with the debug build mode using variables in PowerShell scripts, usage of OAuth tokens, grouping tasks for reusability, usage of an agentless phase, importing and exporting builds, and organizing the builds into folder structures for maintainability.

C. Chandrasekara and P. Herath, *Hands-on Azure Pipelines*, https://doi.org/10.1007/978-1-4842-5902-3_6

Lesson 6.01: Queuing Builds and Enabling Debugging Mode for More Diagnostic Information

While working with build pipelines, we need to learn how to fix build failures quickly. Consider a situation where you are in the middle of a critical client release and it needs to be pushed quickly to production, but what if your build gets failed. You all may have experienced the pressure you get from the team when these types of failures happen. To solve the build failure quickly, it is necessary to identify the issue quickly. After the build fails, we need to read the build logs to understand the reason for failure. But sometimes log data provided are not enough to identify the real reason for the failure. Let's see the same build task logs with the debug state as false and the debug state as true to see the benefit we get when we diagnose issues with the debug mode on.

The following NuGet restore task has executed with the debug mode set to false. It has 178 log lines available. See Figure 6-1.

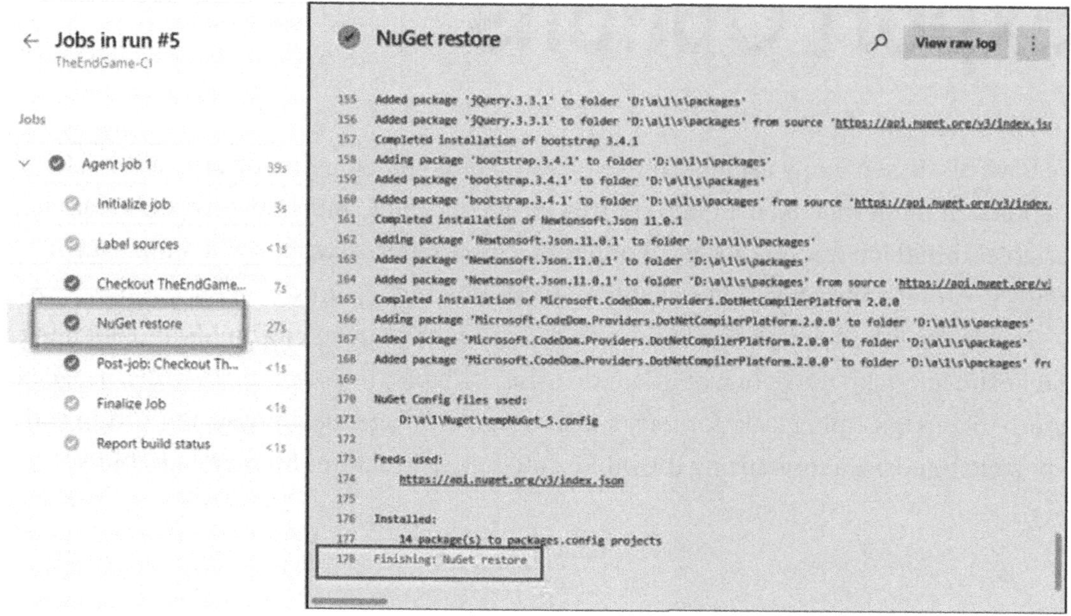

***Figure 6-1.** Build log with debug false state*

If we run the same build with the debug set as true in the variables (system.debug variable), you are able to see the difference between the two logs. It provides more details than the previous one. As shown in the following image, the same NuGet Restore step has 785 log lines, which means it provides more information than the debug false. See Figure 6-2.

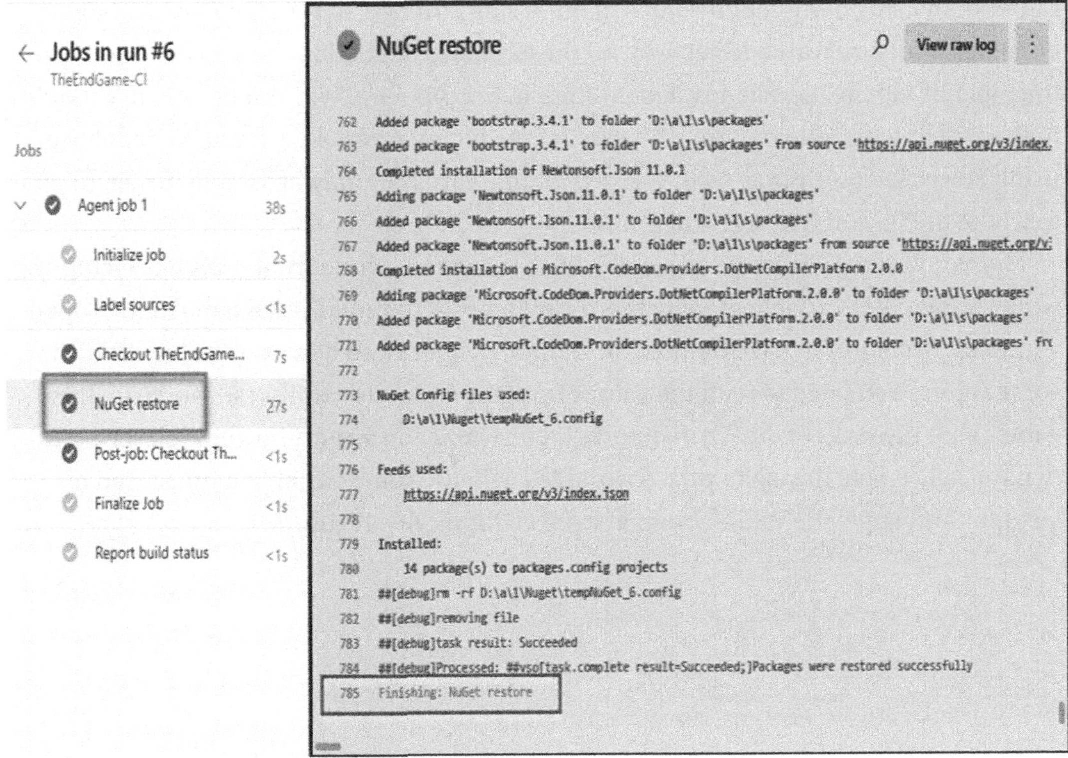

Figure 6-2. *Build log with debug true*

So, after the build failure, execute the build with the debug value set as true, which provides more details that you can use to identify the build failure reasons easily.

This lesson discussed that we can set the debug variable value to true and get more information on the failures with which we can easily identify the issues with the build.

Lesson 6.02: Setting Variable Values in PowerShell Scripts

While configuring build pipelines, pipeline tasks need various input values. Sometimes it can be a project name or a folder path, or a different set of values based on the type of project you are building. We all know it is good practice to have parameterized values rather than using hard-coded values in build steps. Hence, in pipelines we declare variables under the variable section. All the variables defined in the variable section of the pipeline can be used in any agent phase in the pipeline. Without declaring variables in the pipeline variable section, you can define dynamic variables for an agent phase using PowerShell scripts as well. These dynamic variables only belong to the agent phase to where the PowerShell script belongs.

Dynamic variables are very useful when you work with external tools like Octopus, which has greater variable management capability with multidimensional and scoped variables. Assume you have defined an Octopus project and it has a variable set with some values. You need to read the values from the Octopus variable set and use those values with the tasks of the Azure build pipeline. You can write a PowerShell script to dynamically create the agent phase variables with the same variable names used in Octopus and apply the value obtained from Octopus. See Figure 6-3.

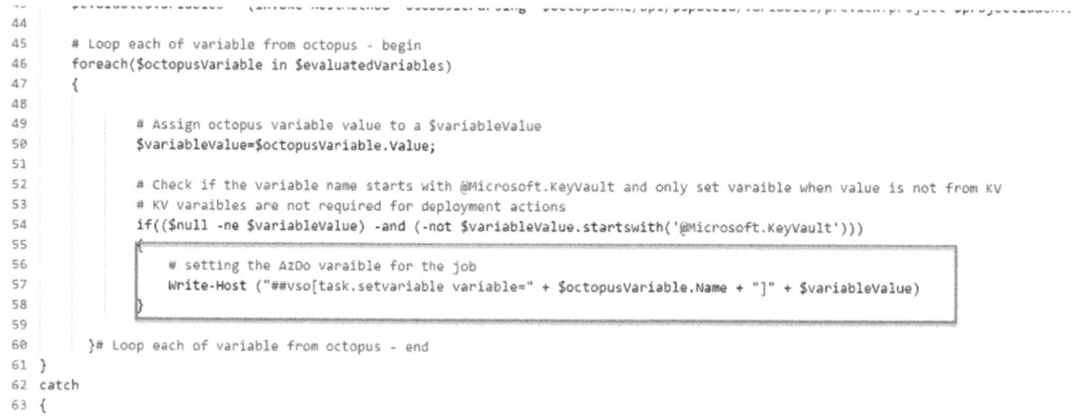

```
    # Loop each of variable from octopus - begin
    foreach($octopusVariable in $evaluatedVariables)
    {

            # Assign octopus variable value to a $variableValue
            $variableValue=$octopusVariable.Value;

            # Check if the variable name starts with @Microsoft.KeyVault and only set varaible when value is not from KV
            # KV varaibles are not required for deployment actions
            if(($null -ne $variableValue) -and (-not $variableValue.startswith('@Microsoft.KeyVault')))
            {
                # setting the AzDo varaible for the job
                Write-Host ("##vso[task.setvariable variable=" + $octopusVariable.Name + "]" + $variableValue)
            }

     }# Loop each of variable from octopus - end
}
catch
{
```

Figure 6-3. *Using Octopus variables in Azure DevOps pipelines*

All magic is done using this code line.

```
"##vso[task.setvariable variable=" + $octopusVariable.Name + "]" +
$variableValue
```

It creates a variable with the given variable name and assigns the given variable value. For example, a variable could be specified in Octopus as environment and it could have value develop or prod, etc., which is getting applied as a new variable in the Azure Pipeline. These variable values can be used by any task inside the agent phase.

This lesson discussed the very useful feature that allows you to create the build pipeline variables by dynamically using a PowerShell script.

Lesson 6.03: Accessing Secret Variable Values in PowerShell

As discussed in previous lessons, there are various types of build tasks that can be used to configure build pipelines for various requirements. In most situations, we need to use PowerShell scripts to automate some pipeline tasks. So, it is good to have an idea about how PowerShell scripts can use variables in a pipeline. See Figure 6-4.

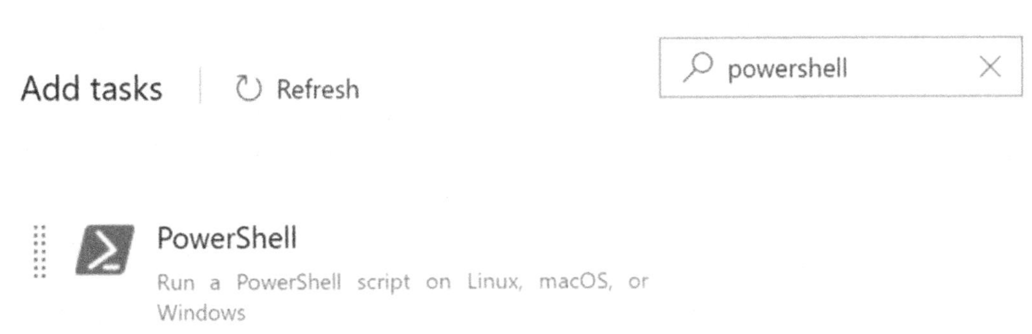

Figure 6-4. *PowerShell task*

While working with projects, we need to work with different types of values. Some can be shared publicly and some need to be secret. So, these secret values need to be treated differently due to the protection level required by them.

The variable values defined in the build pipelines are used by the agent by creating environment variables inside the agent. But for the secret values, it doesn't add any values in the agent environment variables. So, in the PowerShell scripts, we can only access the variables by using a $env:variablename or $(variablename) for the non-secret variables. But for secret variables, as the agent does not create environment variables in it, we cannot access the secret variables with the $env:variable format. The only possible way to access secret variables in PowerShell would be with a $(variablename) format.

We were able to learn how the secret variables get handled in the PowerShell scripts and how those secret variables behave in the pipeline. Also, we discussed the reasons for behavior of the secret variables in build pipelines in this lesson.

Lesson 6.04: Using Auth Tokens in the Builds

As we already discussed in previous lessons of this book, there are so many configuration options available in the Azure DevOps build pipeline agent phase. Those configurations values can be used to make the build process efficient and effective. In this lesson, we will talk about the OAuth configuration in the agent phase.

While working with Azure DevOps, sometimes it is required to use the Azure REST API endpoint to create, delete, update, and retrieve the Azure DevOps service resources. So, mostly PowerShell tasks are used to execute REST API calls in the build pipelines. As we are already aware, before executing any REST API call, it is necessary to use authentication mechanisms to allow the API to perform authorized operations. In Azure DevOps, the Personal Access Token (PAT) is the most common way of providing authentication. But a OAuth configuration in the agent phase allows us to execute API calls without using a PAT as a parameter for authentication.

The enable OAuth token configuration in the Azure DevOps build pipeline enables the scripts and other process launched by tasks to access the OAuth token through the SYSTEM.ACCESS.TOKEN variable. When access to the system access token is enabled, it is possible to use a $env:SYSTEM_ACCESSTOKEN environment variable in the task scripts that you are executing in a build pipeline job. See Figure 6-5.

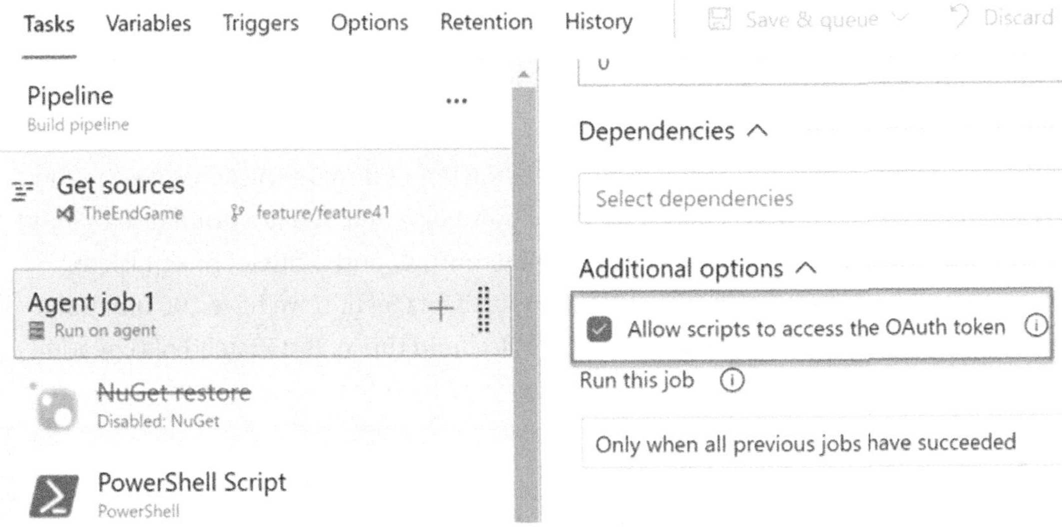

Figure 6-5. *Enable OAuth token*

The following code sample shows how to list the builds using an API script. It uses a $env:SYSTEM_ACCESSTOKEN variable in a task script for authentication. If the Build pipeline OAuth configuration is not enabled, the script will not work because the $env:SYSTEM_ACCESSTOKEN cannot get a value as it is only allowed when a build pipeline OAuth configuration is enabled.

```
$url = $env:SYSTEM_TEAMFOUNDATIONCOLLECTIONURI + $env:SYSTEM_TEAMPROJECTID
+  "/_apis/build/builds?api-version=5.1"
Write-Host "URL: $url"
$pipeline = Invoke-RestMethod -Uri $url -Headers @{
    Authorization = "Bearer $env:SYSTEM_ACCESSTOKEN"
}
Write-Host "Pipeline = $($pipeline | ConvertTo-Json -Depth 100)"
```

In this lesson, we have discussed how to use the OAuth configuration in build pipelines and the importance of this configuration.

Lesson 6.05: Creating and Using Task Groups

One of the important features of the pipeline is a pipeline task. While we configure build pipelines, sometimes we need to use the same set of tasks in multiple build pipelines. Assume a project developed with the microservices architecture. Let's say that Azure functions have been used to develop the microservices architecture and we need to configure a separate build pipeline for each function. In this type of situation, we use the same set of steps in each function build pipeline. It has a build task to build the code, a NuGet pack task to package the built output, and a NuGet push task to push the packed content to the Azure DevOps artifacts feed. If we have 100 functions in the project, we need to create 100 pipelines to build those. But instead of repeating the same work 100 times, we can create task groups to reduce the effort we put in to configure the pipelines.

A task group is grouping a set of repetitive tasks and maintaining it as the shared component for multiple pipelines. If we consider the situation where the project has more build pipelines that use the same set of tasks, we can create a task group using the repetitive tasks and pass parameters to it, using each build pipeline so that it builds and packages different projects.

Let's see how we can create a task group easily with an existing set of build steps. Create one complete pipeline with the all necessary tasks included in it. After that, if there are any input values to each task, parameterize those values. Now select the tasks that you want to add to the task group and create a task group. See Figure 6-6.

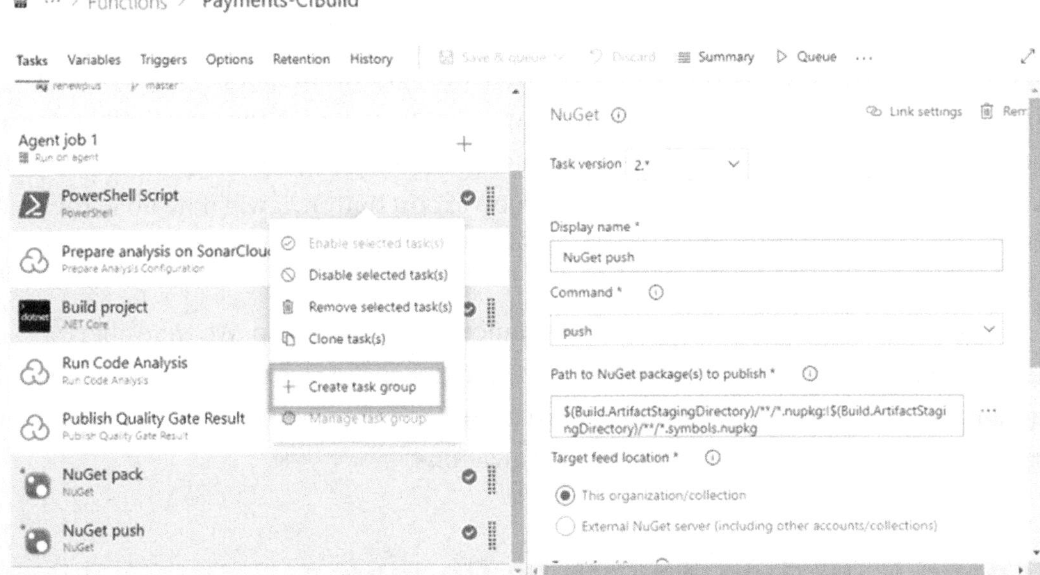

Figure 6-6. *Creating task group*

After adding the task group, it will be available under the Azure DevOps task group section. Now we can use the task group to create the build pipelines. See Figure 6-7.

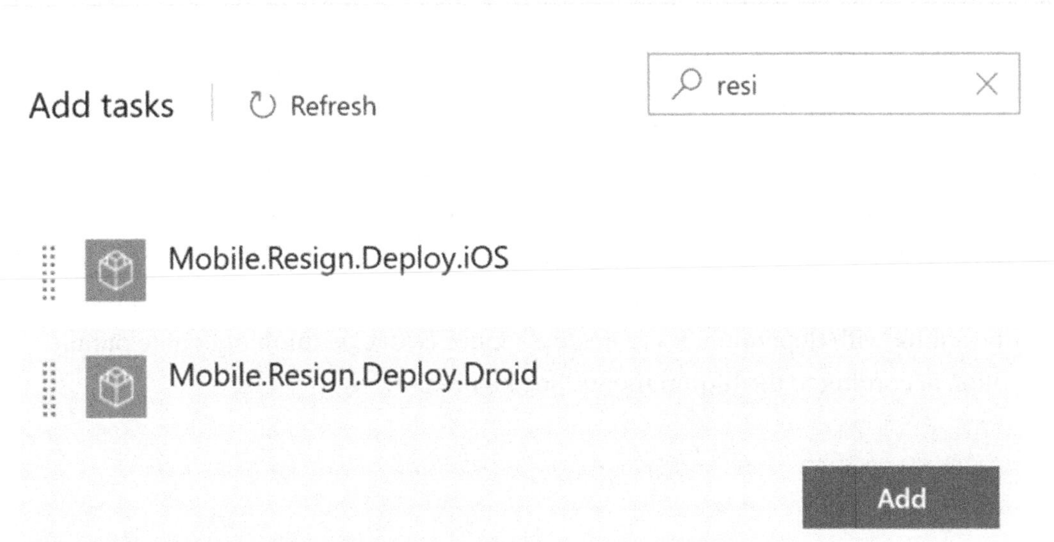

Figure 6-7. *Adding a task group to build*

If we create a task group, we can share this with other projects too. You can export the task group from one project to another project either in the same organization or an external one. Task groups are very usable and productive components that we can configure in Azure DevOps. For example, if you want to configure the same build tasks in the build pipeline in another project or a project in another organization, you can export the task group. When you click on the task group export button, it will download the json file. You can import this file in another team project, and it will automatically create a task group for you.

This lesson explained the use and importance of the task group. We were able to get an idea how to create a task group and the purpose of it. Further, we discussed its capabilities and reusability by allowing us to export and import to projects in the same organization and to projects in external organizations.

Lesson 6.06: Use Agentless Phases

Automated build uses a machine or more machines to do some work for us without any human interaction. We call the machines Agents, and they play a very important role of a task executor when it comes to automated pipelines. However, there are situations where you need to do some activities that do not require a machine to perform tasks such as waiting for an approval. For these waiting type of purposes, you can use agentless phases in build pipelines. Let's discuss agentless phase capabilities in this lesson.

An agentless phase has the tasks that can perform without help from the agent machine. Most of the tasks are manual intervention tasks or actions that depend on the data retrieved from the external query or API. As you already know, one build pipeline can have more than one agent phase. Similarly, you can add more than one agentless phase to the build pipeline if required. See Figure 6-7. You can order the agent phase or agentless jobs, with dependencies to make a sequence of execution or enable parallel execution according to the requirements. See Figure 6-8.

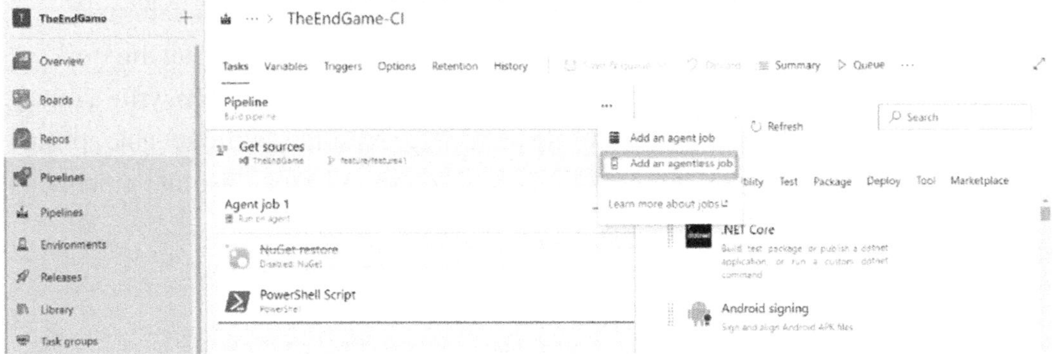

Figure 6-8. *Add agentless phase*

When it comes to an agentless phase, it has tasks available with it that do not require the agent machine involvement to perform the task. As an example, in some situations we might need to make a time gap between two tasks available in the build pipeline. Assume we execute a script to apply changes to an existing resource in Azure or want to provision a new resource. It takes some time to apply those changes to the resources in Azure. It might be required to wait until the change is fully applied before continuing the build pipeline execution in the next task as it depends on the availability of the change you made to the Azure resource. Hence, we can use agentless tasks to wait for the required time period to get the changes to be applied to the Azure resource and continue with another agent phase for the next task, which depends on the Azure resource change. See Figure 6-9.

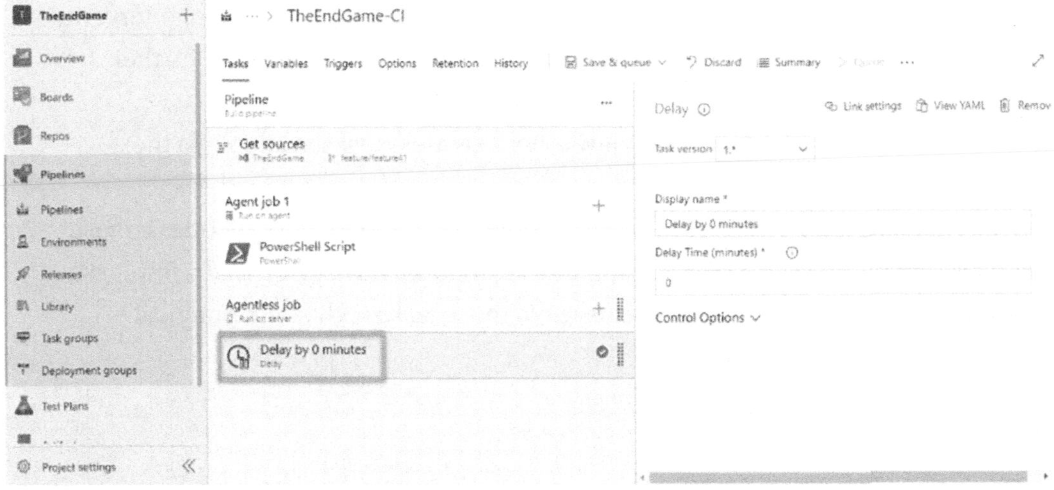

Figure 6-9. *Delay task of agentless phase*

Another useful task available in the agentless phase is the Query work items task. Consider a situation where you need to package the artifacts if and only if all the work items are marked as completed in the sprint. Hence, what you need to do is write a query to get the count of the work items in the to-do or in-progress status in the specific sprint. If there are any incomplete work items in the sprint, you should stop the build pipeline without creating the artifacts. See Figure 6-10.

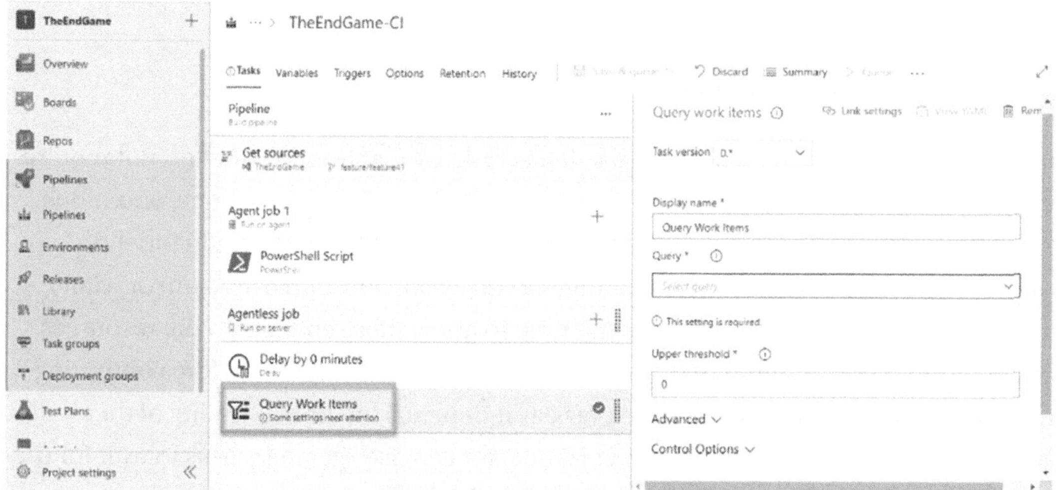

Figure 6-10. *Query work items task of agentless phase*

Another useful task is a manual intervention task that can wait for the user to approve or reject the further execution of the pipeline. This type of manual intervention helps to do any required manual verification of the executed steps before further executing the pipeline.

Other than these tasks, there are a few other agentless tasks available in the marketplace.

After going through this lesson, you were able to learn about the agentless phase available in the Azure DevOps build pipeline. Further, we have discussed a few tasks specific to the agentless phase and the usage of those tasks with some practical scenarios.

Lesson 6.07: Publishing Artifacts

Azure DevOps build pipelines are used to get the source from the repo, build the code, test the code, publish built binaries, and package it as deployable artifacts. Published artifacts are the outcome of most of the build pipelines. Azure DevOps uses different ways to save the build artifacts. One method is keeping the published artifacts in the same build pipeline. Further, you can publish the artifacts as NuGet packages to the Azure DevOps NuGet feed or an external NuGet feed. Their way of saving artifacts is keeping those in a shared file location.

The most well-known, simple way of keeping artifacts is to save the published artifacts to the pipeline itself using the publish artifacts task. After completing the build, you will be able to find the artifacts attached to the build pipeline if you utilize the artifacts drop as the same build. See Figure 6-11.

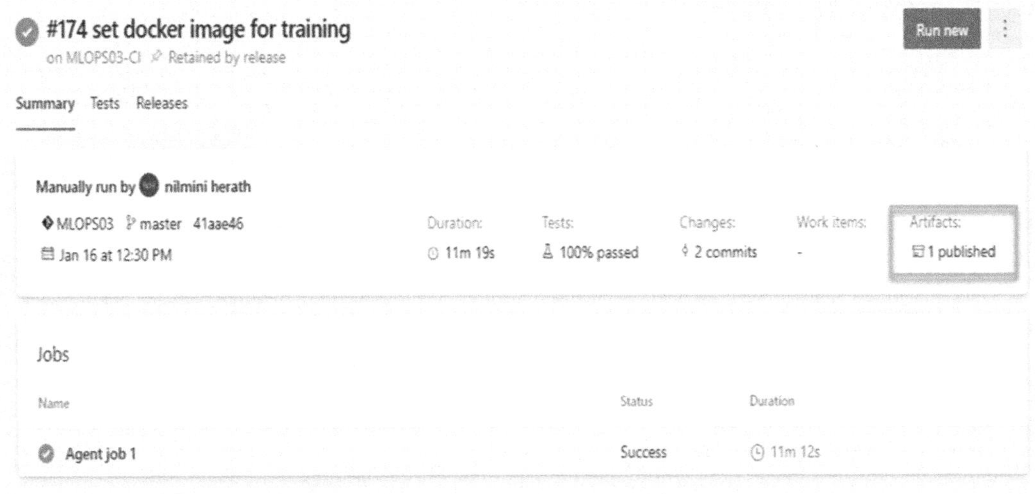

Figure 6-11. *Published artifacts attached to pipeline*

Artifacts attached to the build pipelines have a shorter lifetime as they will be dependent on the build retention time.

Using the same publish build output task, it is possible to publish the artifacts into a given file's share path. It is worth it to keep a file share when your concern is security and you want to use it as an on-prem agent to publish your build artifacts to a shared folder with your network, which is not accessible by those outside of your corporate network.

In this lesson we briefly discussed build artifacts. In Chapter 7, we discuss these different artifact publishing options, discussed in more detail, and with usage scenarios.

Lesson 6.08: Exporting and Importing Build Definition

As we know, sometimes we get requirements to set up build pipelines for multiple projects, mostly for a similar type of build needs. In that type of situation, it would not be worth it to spend more time to set up each build pipeline manually from scratch. Azure DevOps has the capability to export and import the build pipelines that allow us to set up build pipelines easily when we need similar builds in multiple projects.

In a situation where you have to set up multiple, similar build pipelines in a single project, you can easily clone the build pipeline and update according to the requirements. Or you can export the existing build and import to create a new build pipeline in the same team project. Go to the build pipeline, which you need, to export and click on export options. See Figure 6-12.

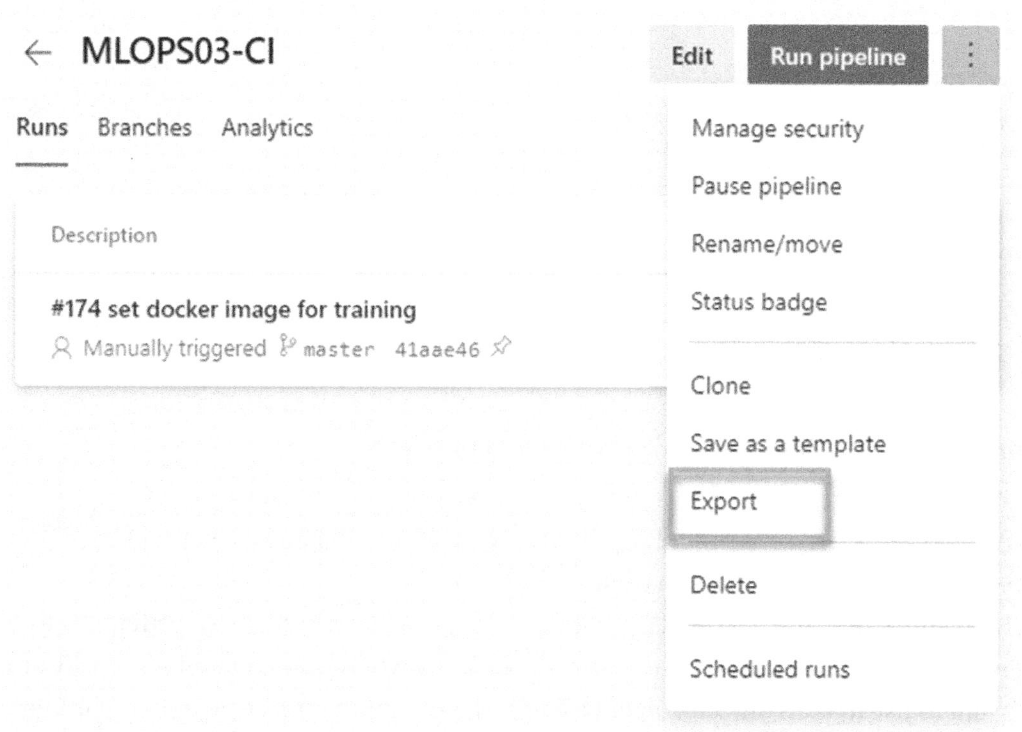

Figure 6-12. *Export build pipeline*

It will download the json file. For importing the pipeline, you can import the json file to the Azure DevOps project and it will create a build pipeline. See Figure 6-13.

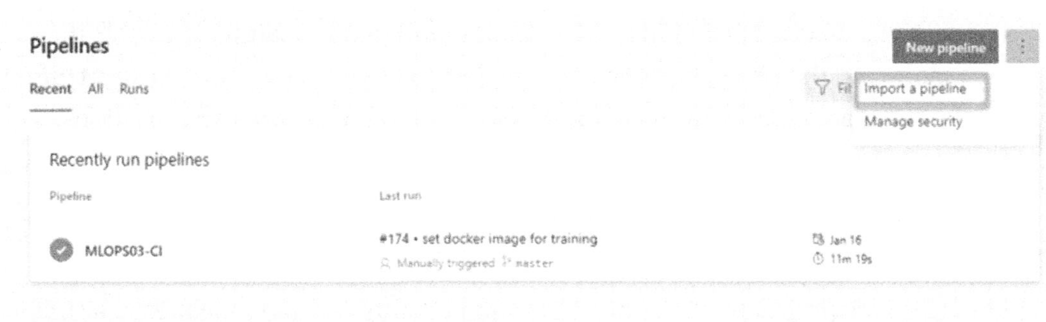
Pipelines
New pipeline
Recent All Runs
Import a pipeline
Manage security
Recently run pipelines
Pipeline
Last run
MLOPS03-CI
#174 • set docker image for training
Manually triggered master
Jan 16
11m 19s

Figure 6-13. *Import json of build pipeline*

But if you want to export a pipeline and import it to a different team project in the same or in a different Azure DevOps organization, it is not as straightforward as explained above for importing to the same team project.

Before we import the build pipeline json to another project, it is required to make a small change to the exported json file. Azure DevOps projects have unique ids for each team project. When you export the build pipeline, it contains the project id of the source team project in the json file. This project id is required to be replaced with the project id of the destination team project id. Otherwise, it gives an error when trying to import the build for a target team project and saving it, due to the differences of the project id in the json. So, first you must find the destination and source project ids using the following REST API call. You can run the following REST API call by changing the relevant organization name and project name to find the project id. See Figure 6-14.

```
https://dev.azure.com/yourorgname/_apis/projects/teamprojectname?api-version=5.0
```

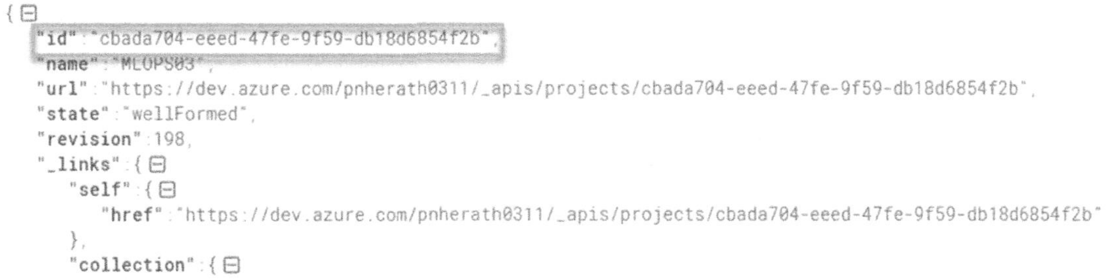
{
"id": "cbada704-eeed-47fe-9f59-db18d6854f2b",
"name": "MLOPS03",
"url": "https://dev.azure.com/pnherath0311/_apis/projects/cbada704-eeed-47fe-9f59-db18d6854f2b",
"state": "wellFormed",
"revision": 198,
"_links": {
"self": {
"href": "https://dev.azure.com/pnherath0311/_apis/projects/cbada704-eeed-47fe-9f59-db18d6854f2b"
},
"collection": {

Figure 6-14. *Project id*

After finding the destination project id and source project id, replace the exported json file and source project id with the destination project id. Then you can import it to the destination team project and save it to create a build pipeline.

This lesson discussed the build pipeline export and import features available in Azure DevOps and their uses. Further, we were able to learn a technique to export and import the build pipelines between team projects and Azure DevOps organizations.

Lesson 6.09: Organizing Build into Folder

Depending on the project architecture, there can be multiple build pipelines in a single team project. As an example, if the team is developing the system using microservices architecture, it is required to set up separate build pipelines for each microservices component. It would be good to organize the build pipelines in a more manageable way to increase its maintainability.

This lesson discusses how to create a folder structure and organize the build pipelines in a more manageable way within the team project. See Figure 6-15.

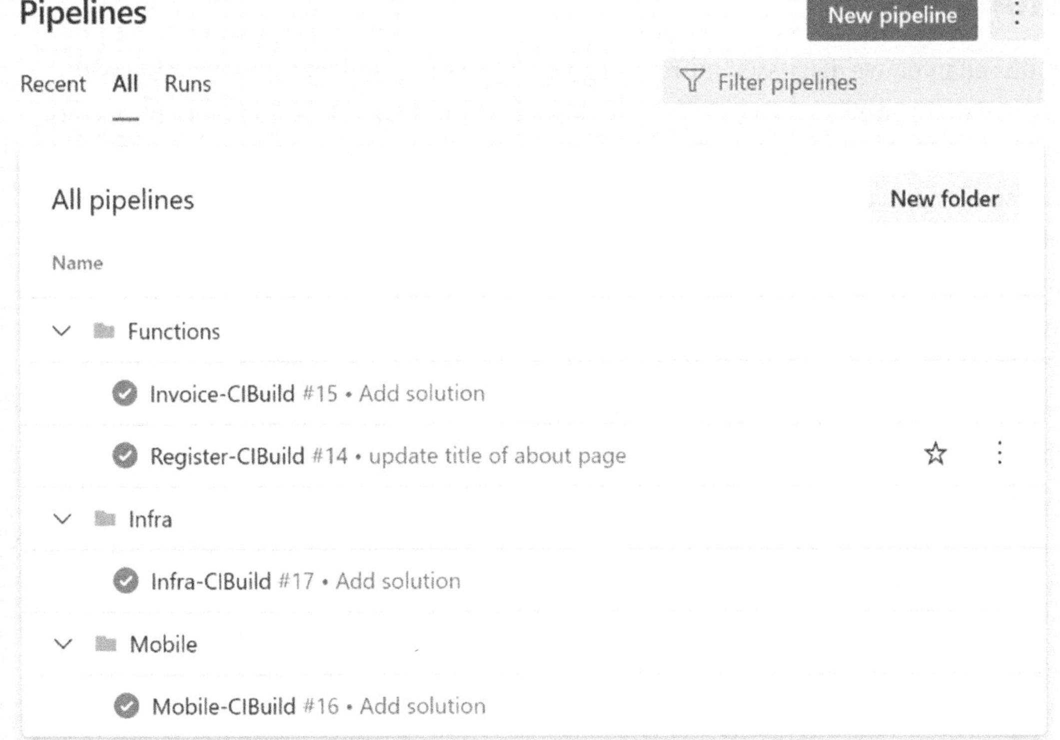

***Figure 6-15.** Build folder structure*

Let's consider a mobile development project that uses Azure functions as back-end microservices components. The function builds can be put under a folder named Functions. The mobile build can be organized under a folder named Mobile. Also, if the Infrastructure provisioned using the scripts, those Infra builds can be put to an Infra folder. Likewise, all the build pipelines should be categorized using meaningful folder structure. It will help users to easily access the relevant build pipelines without scrolling through all of the build definitions.

This lesson discussed the importance of having a good, organized folder structure to keep build definitions, which helps users to easily identify and maintain build pipelines.

Summary

In this chapter, we discussed more useful configurations and features available with Azure DevOps builds. As we explained, the debug mode of the build is very important to go through the build failure logs and identify the failure reasons. Also, we were able to discuss some useful features available in the Azure DevOps Pipelines while working with PowerShell scripts. Further, we talked about the use of the task groups and build artifacts, which are a very important part of Azure DevOps build pipelines. Additionally, we were able to get an idea of how to import and export build pipelines between team projects in the same organization or external organization, which is very useful when there is a requirement to copy similar build pipelines between projects. Finally, we discussed the importance of having a well-organized folder structure to keep build pipelines.

In the next chapter, we discuss build artifacts in detail to identify different options we can use to publish artifacts with usage scenarios.

CHAPTER 7

Using Artifacts

Artifacts or output from the build contain the binary files and required supportive files to deploy software to a target environment. Depending on the type of project that is being built, and depending on the deployment and testing requirements, the content of artifacts may vary. They may contain deployment specifications such as scripts or templates such as YAML files, test data, test execution scripts, etc.

There are a couple of ways to publish artifacts in a build, such as making it available with the build, putting the artifacts to a shared path, or creating it as a package and uploading it to a feed. Let's explore each of these options in this chapter in detail. Additionally, let's look at how to consume packages uploaded to a feed from another build as well as in development tools.

Lesson 7.01: Publishing Build Artifacts

As we briefly mentioned before, there are a couple of ways that we can publish artifacts generated by a build. You can use artifacts made available in each published method in release pipelines to deploy the software to the intended targets. Let's discuss each type of publish mechanism.

The first way is to publish an output of a build as an artifact inside the same build. This allows simplicity in implementation of the build pipeline. The steps in the build will generate the required content for deployment. The generated content is normally staged into a build artifact staging directory. Then the artifact staging directory will be published to the build, as a drop. See Figure 7-1.

C. Chandrasekara and P. Herath, *Hands-on Azure Pipelines*, https://doi.org/10.1007/978-1-4842-5902-3_7

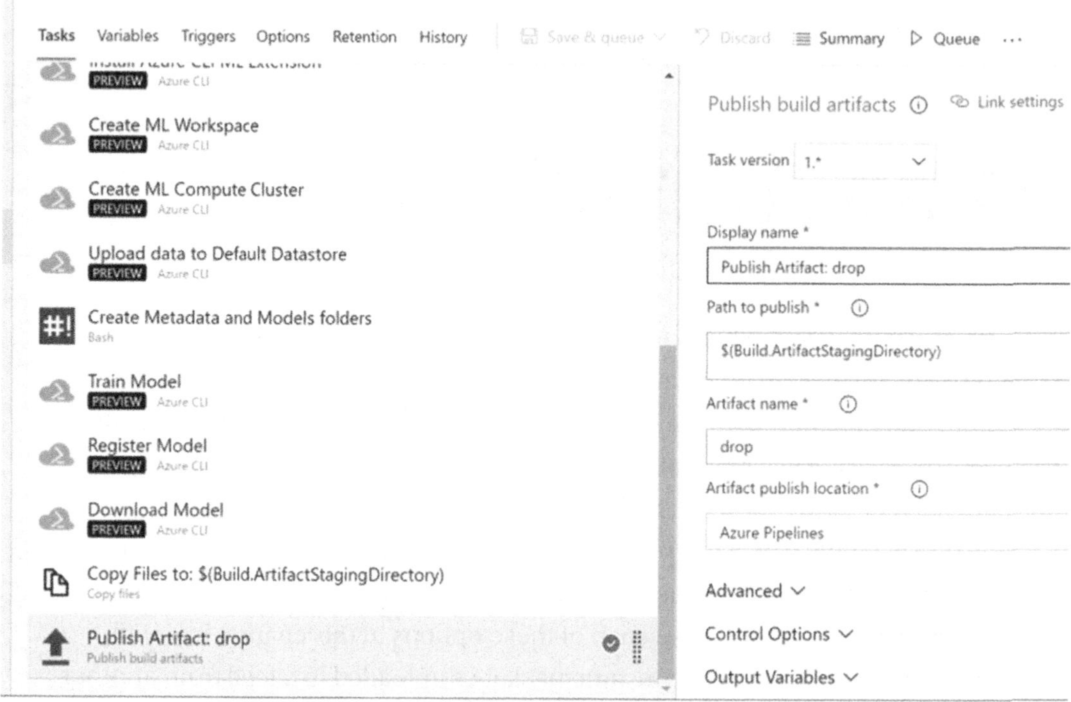

Figure 7-1. *Create a drop and publish artifacts in a build*

The second option is to use a shared path. This option is useful mainly when you are using a file server. You can make the file server path available to an on-premise agent scenario, where the agent can be allowed to have access to the shared path in your network.

The third option is to use an FTP upload task where you can set up a service endpoint in your team project to the FTP server. For this purpose, you can use a generic service connection type where you provide the FTP server URL and the credentials to the FTP server. See Figure 7-2.

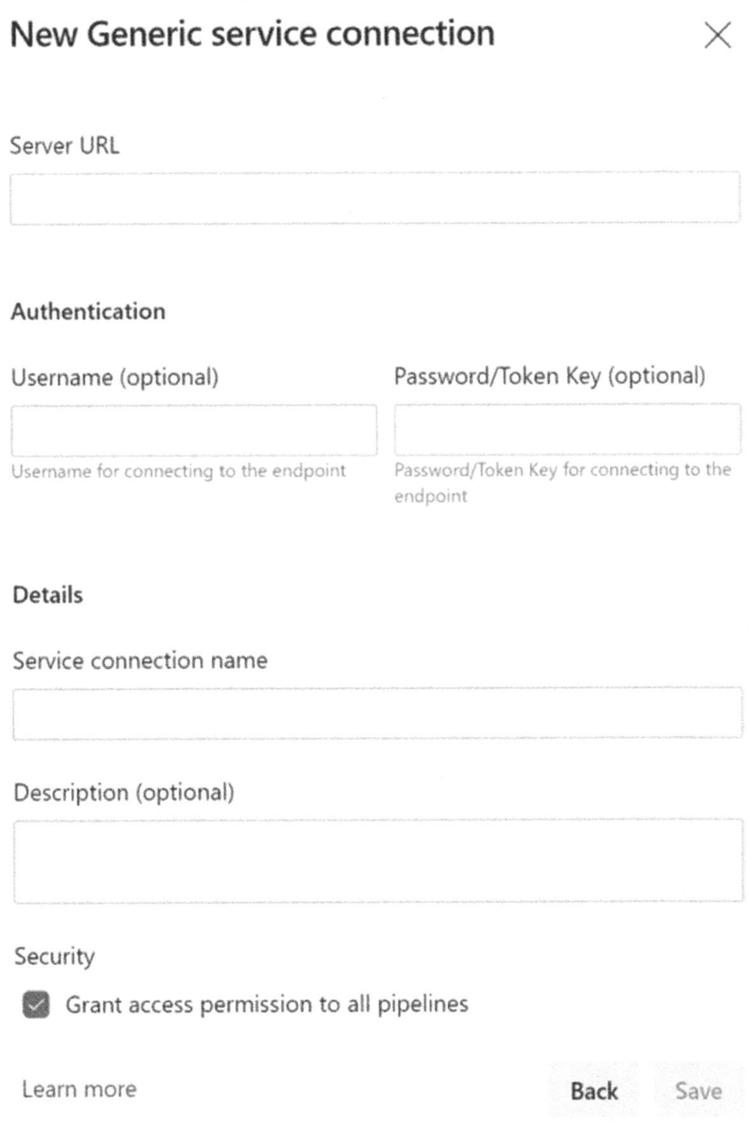

Figure 7-2. *Generic service connection*

The next option would be to package your build artifacts as a NuGet package and upload it to a NuGet feed. For this purpose, you can use the artifact feeds available in the team project, which we will discuss in detail in the next few lessons of this chapter.

In this lesson, we discussed different options the we can use to publish artifacts from a build.

Lesson 7.02: Packaging and Publishing Artifacts as NuGet

One of the options to publish build artifacts is to use NuGet packages. There is a great benefit over other methods in using a feed to keep the build packages. Primarily it allows you to keep the packages released regardless of whether the build is removed from Azure DevOps due to retention limits set for builds.

You have the capability to apply the build number as versioning to packages when you are using the NuGet package task, or you can use another preferred version mechanism. NuGet packages support semantic versioning, which is a preferred and reliable way of versioning software releases. Further, it allows you to use external deployment pipelines such as Octopus, deployed using the NuGet packages. Additionally, you can share common code components for your solutions by building and packaging them as NuGet packages.

To package contents of a build output as a NuGet package, you can use a file that is called a nuspec. A nuspec file contains specifications to create a NuGet package such as the name of package, version (version can be overridden in the NuGet pack task), author details, and even the specifications to include files or files in specified path patterns. You can refer to the nuspec reference here at `https://docs.microsoft.com/en-us/nuget/reference/nuspec` to learn more about nuspec files. If you are copying all your build content to build an artifact staging directory in the build tasks, you can package them as a NuGet package, using a basic nuspec file that is not having specifications of the files to include in the package. It will add all contents from the specified folder in the Base path. See Figure 7-3.

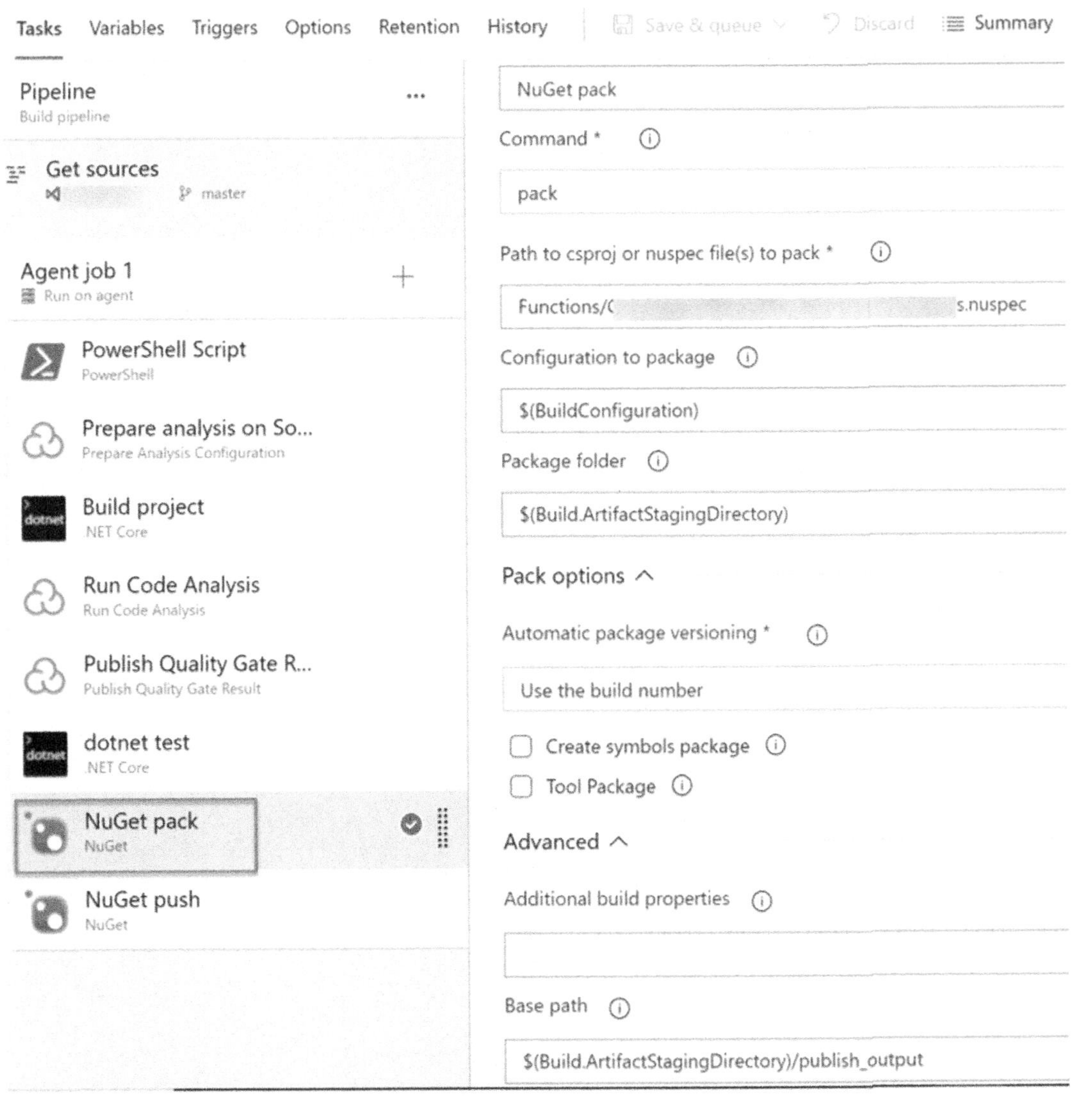

Figure 7-3. *NuGet pack*

You can use a NuGet push task to push the packaged NuGet package to a NuGet feed. It can be an artifact feed created in the team project. Or you can use a public or private NuGet feed of your own, or third-party package feed such as an Octopus server/cloud NuGet feed allowing Octopus deployments to be used as the deployment pipeline. If you are using external NuGet feeds, you have to set up a service connection to the external feed with a URL of the feed and access keys such as the API key. See Figure 7-4.

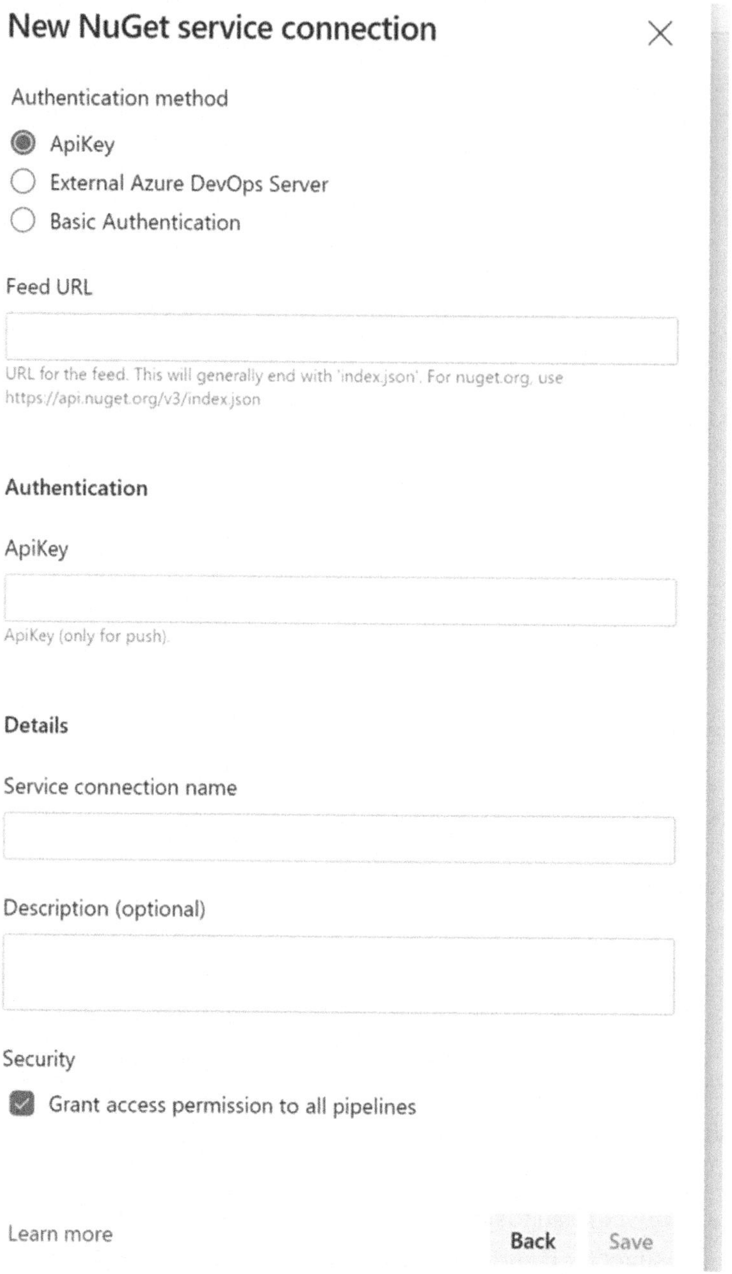

Figure 7-4. *NuGet service connection*

The artifact feeds can be created in a team project. These feeds can now be created publicly, by making the team project of the feed as public. Such feeds allow you to share your packages publicly. See Figure 7-5.

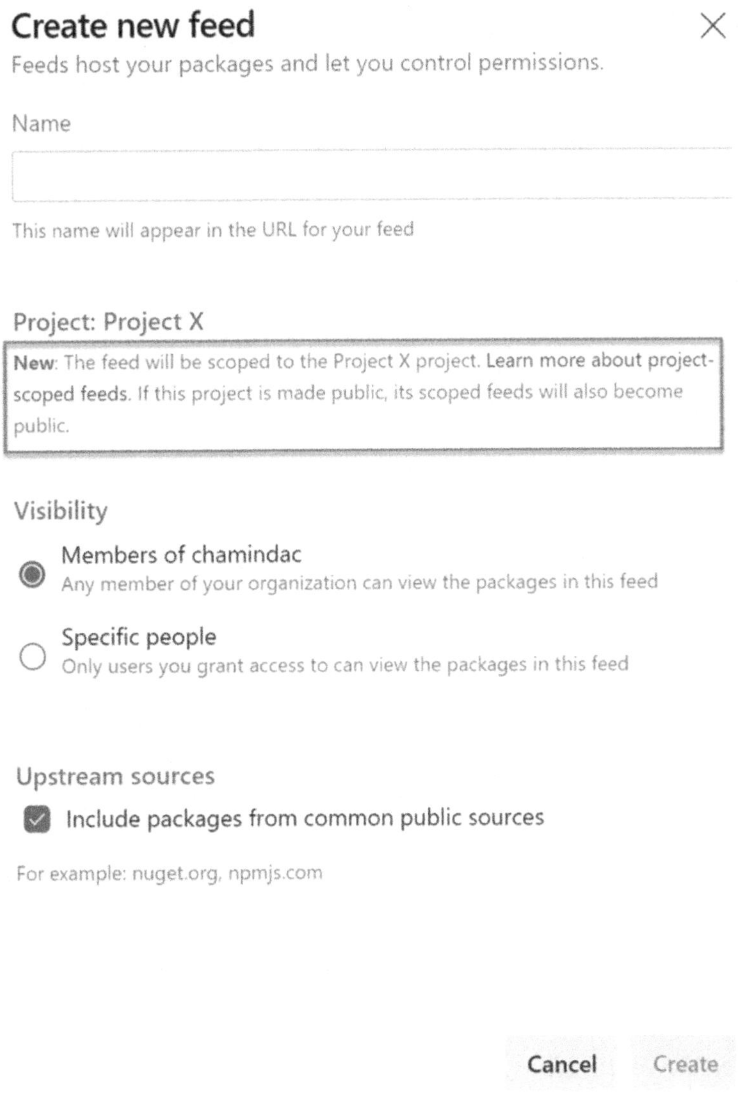

Create new feed

Feeds host your packages and let you control permissions.

Name

This name will appear in the URL for your feed

Project: Project X

New: The feed will be scoped to the Project X project. Learn more about project-scoped feeds. If this project is made public, its scoped feeds will also become public.

Visibility

Members of chamindac
Any member of your organization can view the packages in this feed

Specific people
Only users you grant access to can view the packages in this feed

Upstream sources

Include packages from common public sources

For example: nuget.org, npmjs.com

Cancel Create

Figure 7-5. *Creating feeds*

As we discussed in this lesson, NuGet packages are a useful and reliable way to release your software as packages. Further, they can be used to share the common code with your development teams.

Lesson 7.03: Using NuGet Packages in Builds

You can use NuGet packages that you have created on your own or publicly available NuGet packages in your build pipelines. For this purpose, you can use the NuGet restore task. But it is advisable to set the NuGet version to be used using a NuGet restore task to make sure the correct version of NuGet exe is used for restore operations in your builds. See Figure 7-6.

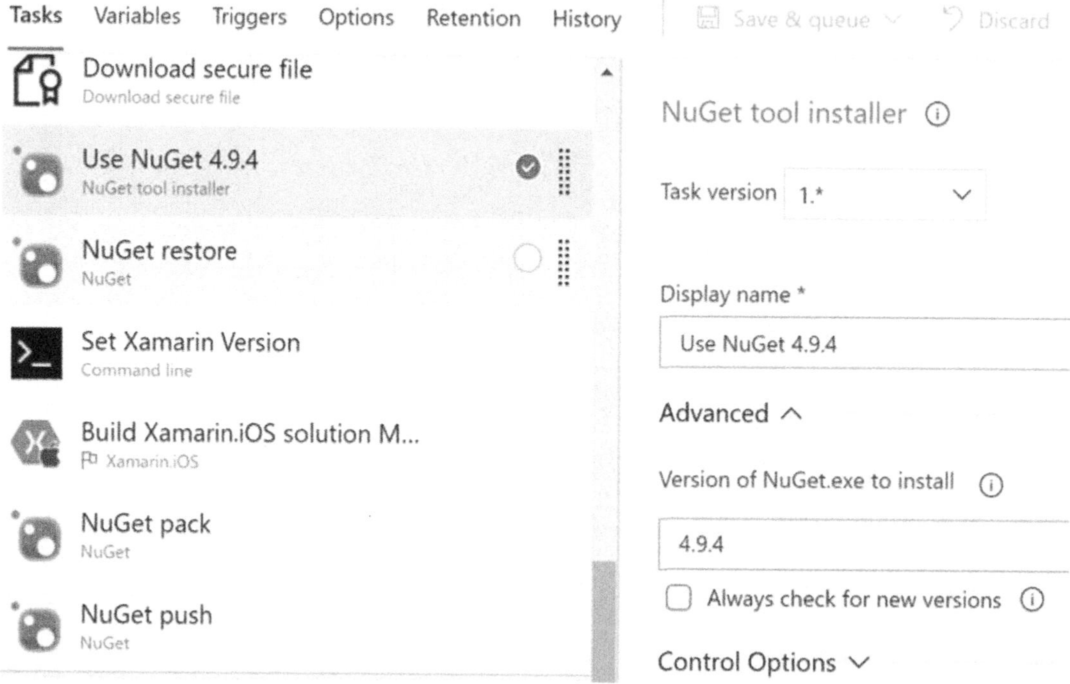

Figure 7-6. *Set NuGet version*

Then you can use the NuGet restore task and specify the feed you want to read from if it is an internal feed from a team project. See Figure 7-7.

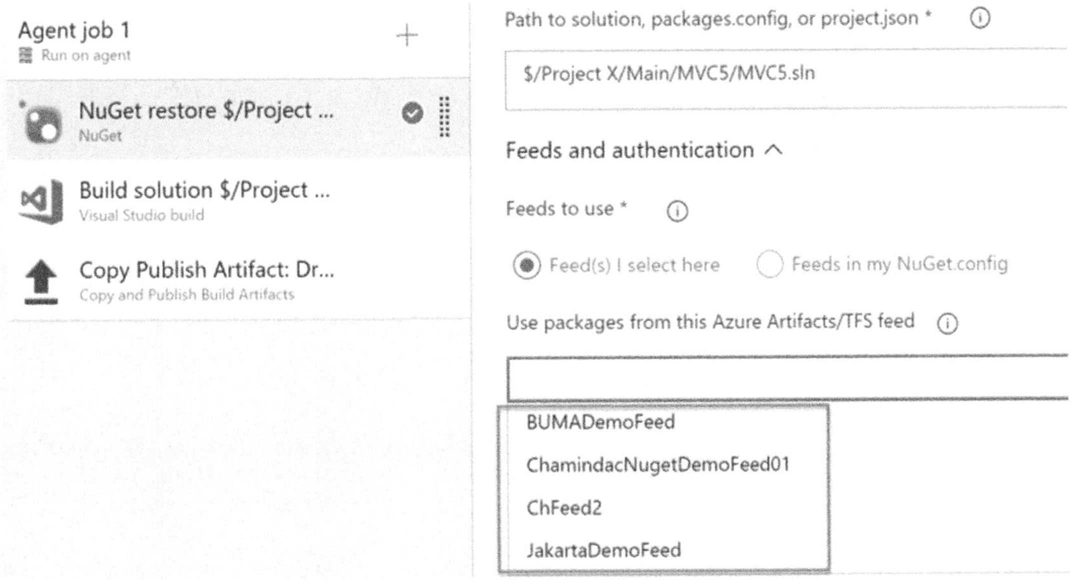

Figure 7-7. NuGet feeds

Or the option is there to use a NuGet.cong file, which can specify the external feed references. The link `https://docs.microsoft.com/en-us/nuget/reference/nuget-config-file` provides detailed reference information on NuGet.config files.

Even the dotnet restore task supports specifying the internal feeds, public NuGet gallery, or a NuGet.config file to locate the feeds to download packages in a build.

We discussed how we can utilize NuGet packages in build in this lesson.

Summary

In this chapter, we looked at the usage and capabilities of artifact publishing with Azure build pipelines. We also looked at different publish options for artifacts and a detailed discussion of the artifacts as NuGet packages, including reusing the NuGet packages in the build pipelines.

In the next chapter, we focus on creating YAML-based build pipelines, which will allow us to keep our pipelines version controlled as code.

CHAPTER 8

Creating and Using YAML Build Pipelines

We discussed Azure DevOps classic build pipelines in previous chapters. You should now have a good understanding of the features of classic builds and the usage of build pipelines. Azure DevOps has two types of pipelines available with it: classic build and release pipelines and YAML pipelines. In this chapter, let's discuss the YAML build pipelines, which enable us to keep the pipelines as code.

Lesson 8.01: Getting Started with YAML Pipelines

YAML pipelines are the Azure DevOps pipelines created with use of the YAML script, which provides all the triggers, pipeline tasks, etc., as code. Hence, an entire build pipeline is managed as one script without using any UI. The knowledge you have gained in the previous chapters on the classic build pipelines will make it easier for you to learn and work with YAML pipelines. However, compared to classic build pipelines, you need more knowledge of scripting to implement YAML build pipelines.

When creating an Azure DevOps YAML pipeline, it provides you with a list of source repos to select where your code may exist. See Figure 8-1.

C. Chandrasekara and P. Herath, *Hands-on Azure Pipelines*, https://doi.org/10.1007/978-1-4842-5902-3_8

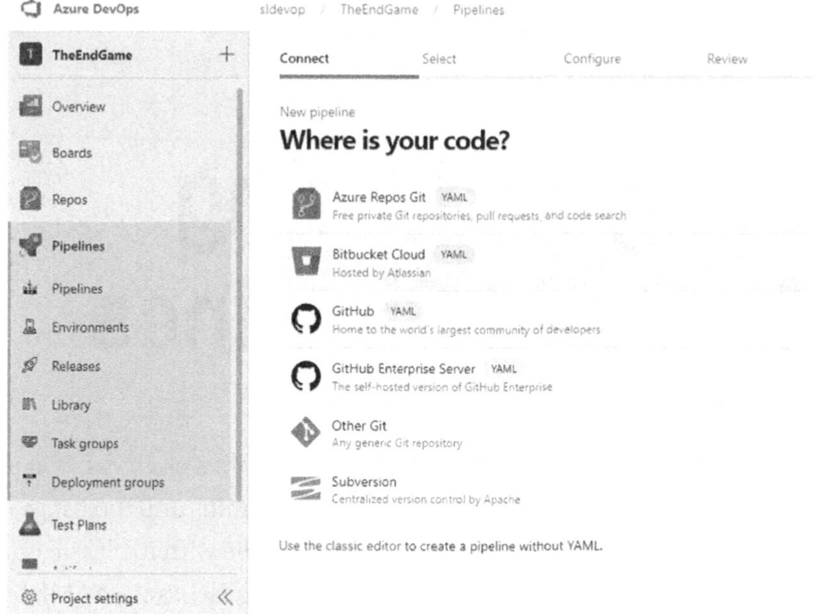

Figure 8-1. *Select the source control*

In the next step, it allows you to select the repository. As an example, if you select Azure Git as the source repo, all the Azure Git Repos in the project will be listed down to select in the second step. See Figure 8-2.

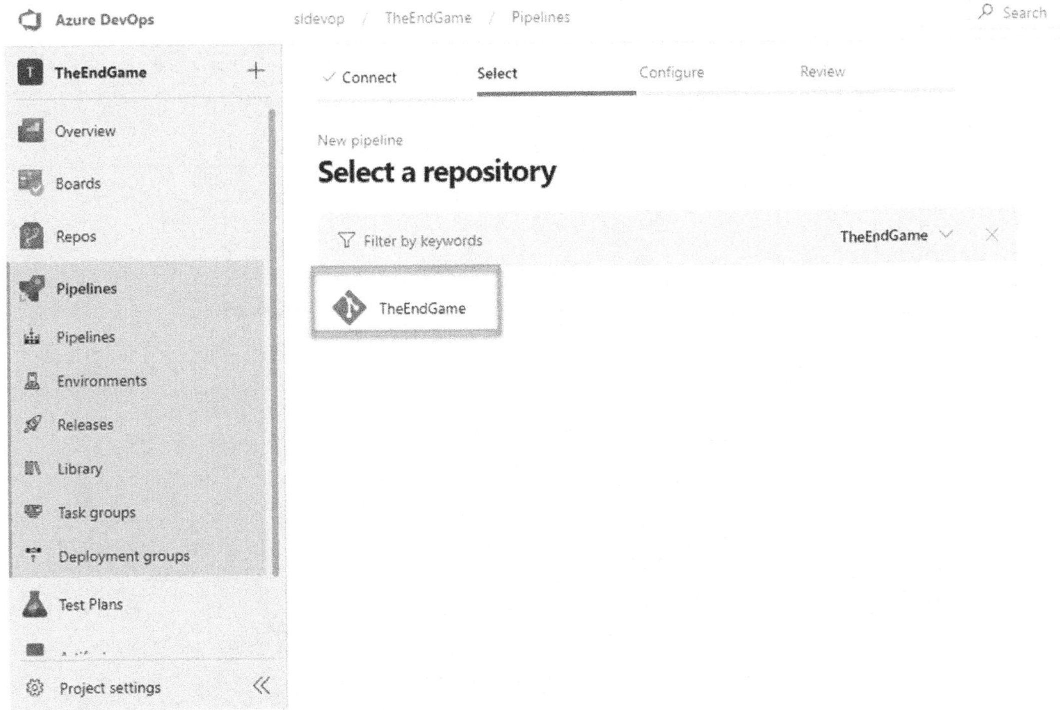

Figure 8-2. Select the repository

The next step allows users to select the technology that the pipeline is going to configure. As an example, if you need to configure a .NET Core Application, you need to select the .NET Core Framework in the list. See Figure 8-3.

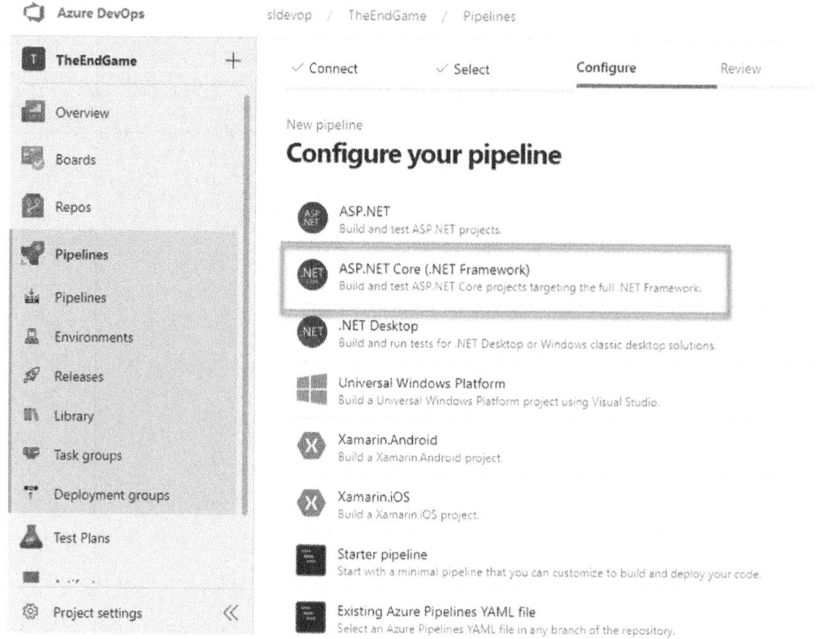

Figure 8-3. *Select the framework to configure pipeline*

At the end of the process, it will create a YAML pipeline according to the values selected when creating the pipeline. You can modify this YAML script to add or remove tasks, variables, triggers, and pools. See Figure 8-4.

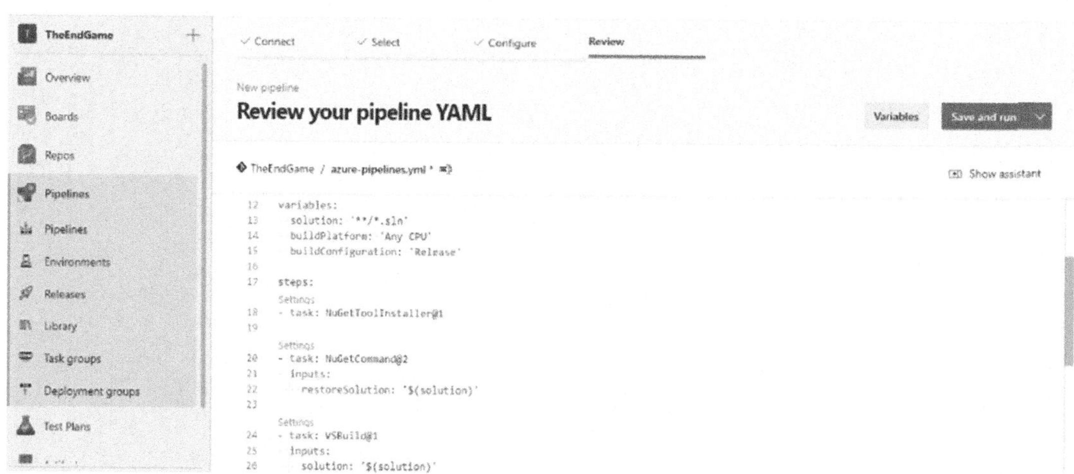

Figure 8-4. *YAML script*

Rather than using this pipeline-creating process explained above, you can write your own YAML scripts from scratch and keep them in the source repo. Those YAML scripts can be converted to YAML build pipelines by creating a classic build pipeline. In classic build pipelines, there is a template to configure the pipeline as code. See Figure 8-5.

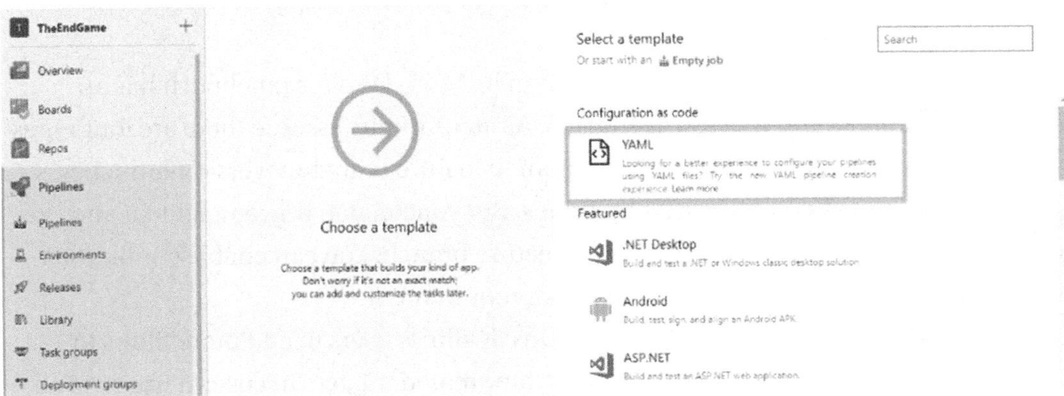

Figure 8-5. *YAML template in classic build*

Select that template and create a build pipeline using your own YAML build pipeline.

So far, we have discussed how to create YAML build pipelines in Azure DevOps. Let's see how YAML build pipelines are used. When it compares to a classic build pipeline created with UI components, YAML pipelines are created using a script. Hence, it is easy to update the pipelines using a one-script file. The most important benefit we get by using YAML pipelines is that the user can version control the build, which helps to track the changes made to the pipelines. As an example, you get a requirement to integrate sonar analyze tasks to the pipeline. If you use the YAML pipelines, you can create a feature branch out of the stable branch of your repo as a feature branch and update the YAML file in the feature branch. Then you can test the pipeline and merge it to the stable branch, as you do with normal source code.

In this lesson, we looked at basic steps of getting started with Azure DevOps YAML pipelines.

Lesson 8.02: Set Up Pipeline Triggers and Filters

As we have discussed in previous chapters, an automated pipeline can be set up to trigger automatically once you push a code change to the repo. You were able to set up automation triggers and filters for classic builds using visual tools as explained in the previous chapters. This lesson discusses the YAML pipeline triggers and filters that can be done in a codified manner.

When enabling the continuous integration in Azure DevOps pipeline, it has an option to add filters and specify the triggers. As an example, assume there are four types of branches in the Azure DevOps project named feature branches, version branches, development branches, and master branches. But you need to trigger a build if and only when the code change is pushed to a feature branch. You can enable continuous integration with branch filters to achieve that requirement.

Also, in the branch filters of Azure DevOps, it allows users to add more filters to the paths of code, which helps to specify the automated triggers in custom ways. As an example, assume an Azure DevOps branch trigger that has been set up to trigger once a code change pushes to a feature branch. Additionally, there is a requirement that the build should be triggered if and only if a change has been made to the code inside a specific folder. So, you can achieve that requirement by using a path filter feature available in the Azure DevOps YAML pipelines.

Let's try to identify the use of triggers with another example. When you develop a solution using microservices architecture, each component of the application should be able to be deployed separately. Assume multiple Azure function apps have been implemented while developing a microservice-based application. So, it is required to create a build and release pipeline for each function app separately. If you enable continuous integration in the build pipeline and add only a branch filter, this build will trigger for every push made to the selected branch. It makes unnecessary traffic for the build agents as it builds all microservice builds, even if only one is changed, and it is a waste of time of resources. By adding a path filter you can solve this issue. Therefore, you can specify a trigger for a given microservice build to build when only a code change is pushed to the relevant microservice code folder path.

Following a YAML sample script will help you to learn how to set triggers. It is set up to trigger a build once the change happens to the master or develop branch or any version branch or any feature branch. If you want to trigger a build for a specific branch, you can give the branch a name with the "include" keyword as shown below. If you do not want to trigger a build for a given branch, you can give the branch a name with the "exclude" keyword in the YAML script. Also, the meaning of the path filter in the following YAML triggers a build on the push of a code change to the UserRegistration Folder inside the Functions folder.

```
trigger:
  branches:
    include:
    - master
    - develop
    - version/*
    - feature/*
  paths:
    include:
    - Functions/UserRegistration
variables:
  BuildConfiguration: 'Release'
  FunctionPath: 'Functions/ UserRegistration'
  NuspecName: 'TestPro.Services.UserRegistration.nuspec'
pool:
  vmImage: 'windows-latest'
name: $(Build.SourceBranchName).$(Build.BuildId)
steps:
- template: ../Templates/BuildNumber.yml
- template: ../Templates/CoreFunctionBuild.yml
  parameters:
    BuildConfiguration: $(BuildConfiguration)
    FunctionPath: $(FunctionPath)
    NuspecName: $(NuspecName)
```

In addition to setting up triggers with branch and path filters, you can even use tag filters. Tag filters let you trigger pipelines based on the tags applied to the Git commits. You can also set it to exclude tags as well. There is an option to set a batch as true or false to enable the changes to be batched and executed while a pipeline is actively running. See the example below.

```
trigger:
  batch: true
```

Similar to code push triggers, you can set up pull request triggers in YAML pipelines with branch and path filters. A sample implementation is shown below and is similar to continuous integration triggers. Pull request triggers can also include and exclude branches and paths.

```
pr:
  branches:
    include:
    - master
    - develop
    - version/*
    - feature/*
  paths:
    include:
    - Functions/UserRegistration
```

To disable pull request triggers, you can use the syntax below; however, this would not affect the continuous integration triggers.

```
pr: none
```

There is an auto-cancel Boolean option that is by default true, which will make an in-progress pull request build be cancelled automatically if there are more changes pushed to the same pull request.

```
pr:
  autoCancel: false
```

Further, you have the ability to set scheduled triggers with filters in YAML pipelines. Cron syntax is used to set the triggers in UTC time. As shown in the sample below, you can set multiple schedules. The always Boolean value setting to true allows you to set if the scheduled build should run even if there is no change to code is pushed after the last run. The default value for the always Boolean is false.

```
schedules:
- cron: "0 0 * * *"
  displayName: Daily midnight build
  branches:
    include:
    - master
    - version/*
    exclude:
    - releases/ancient/*
- cron: "0 12 * * 0"
  displayName: Weekly Sunday build
  branches:
    include:
    - version/*
  always: true
```

This lesson explained the use of triggers of the Azure DevOps pipelines and the use of filters. Also, we were able to identify the usage of the filters and triggers by implementation examples.

Lesson 8.03: Using Variables with YAML

When setting up a build pipeline, various types of values need to be provided to build pipeline tasks. We have discussed the use of Azure DevOps variable groups and variables in previous chapters and how to work with variables when using classic builds. This lesson will discuss how to use variable values with the YAML build pipelines.

In the YAML script, variables can be defined with the “variables” keyword. In the variables section, provide a variable name and value. After that, these values can be used in the pipeline tasks. Since the variables are defined only one place, it is easy to change the variables of the script. See Figure 8-6.

```
variables:
  buildPlatform: 'Any CPU'
  buildConfiguration: 'Release'

steps:
Settings
- task: NuGetToolInstaller@1

Settings
- task: NuGetCommand@2
  inputs:
    restoreSolution: '$(Solution)'

Settings
- task: VSTest@2
  inputs:
    platform: '$(buildPlatform)'
    configuration: '$(buildConfiguration)'
```

***Figure 8-6.** YAML variables used in tasks*

While you maintain your builds as YAML, you might need to define the variables with different access levels. A YAML script can be written with mainly three types of variables. You can define global variables that can be used in multiple jobs and stages. Also, you can define variables that can be used inside the specified job. As an example, if you want to build one agent job with a debug configuration and another with a release configuration, you can define job-level variables. There is another type of variable available that can be used not only in the jobs but also as the agent variables. Sometimes we need to access environment variables to perform various actions in the pipelines.

You can use two syntaxes to define variables. The first syntax is shown in Figure 8-6. In the second syntax, you can define the name and value for a variable in two lines as shown in the example below.

```
variables:
- name: MY_VARIABLE
  value: some value
- name: MY_VARIABLE2
  value: some value2
```

In previous lessons we learned about variable groups and how to use them. As you are already aware, variable groups allow users to keep variable values that are shared between more pipelines. Variable groups can be referred in YAML pipelines using the syntax shown below.

```
variables:
- name: MY_VARIABLE
  value: some value
- group: my-variable-group-1
- group: my-variable-group-2
```

You can use the variables from the variable group in your pipeline tasks with two syntaxes: macro style and runtime expression style. Say you have a myvar variable specified in the variable group, the usage of it would be as shown below in the pipeline.

```
variables:
- group: my-variable-group

steps:
- script: echo $(myvar) # uses macro syntax
- script: echo $[variables.myvar] # runtime expression
```

Another question you might have is how to keep secret values while working with YAML pipelines. As you already know, YAML variables are defined in the script and we can't provide encrypted values in the YAML script. Hence, if you want to use any secret value, it needs to be defined as a pipeline variable using a web UI instead of defining it as a YAML variable or you can keep it in a variable group.

We discussed the usage and syntax of using variables in YAML pipelines in this lesson.

Lesson 8.04: Jobs and Stages in Pipeline

Jobs are used to define pipeline execution phases. A job can be defined with steps/tasks to perform required actions.

When you have a pipeline with a single job, you do not have to specify the job keyword, but you do have to specify the steps of the pipeline similar to that shown below.

```
pool:
  vmImage: 'ubuntu-16.04'
steps:
- bash: echo "Hello world"
```

Similar to classic build pipelines, you can define multiple jobs in a single pipeline if required.

```
jobs:
- job: A
  steps:
  - bash: echo "A"

- job: B
  steps:
  - bash: echo "B"
```

In a job you can define which agent is to be used as shown here.

```
jobs:
- job: myJob
  timeoutInMinutes: 10
  pool:
    vmImage: 'ubuntu-16.04'
  steps:
  - bash: echo "Hello world"
```

You can define stages in your pipeline similar to the stages in release pipelines, which we are going to discuss in Chapters 9 and 10 with classic release pipelines. In each stage, you can use multiple jobs if required.

```
stages:
- stage: MyBuild
  jobs:
  - job: BuildJob
    steps:
    - script: echo My Build steps!
```

```
- stage: MyTest
  jobs:
  - job: TestingOnWindows
    steps:
    - script: echo Testing on Windows!
  - job: TestingOnLinux
    steps:
    - script: echo Testing on Linux!
- stage: MyDeploy
  jobs:
  - job: DeployJob
    steps:
    - script: echo Deploying the code!
```

When you are defining jobs, you can define the conditions and dependencies to other jobs in the pipeline.

```
jobs:
- job: FirstJob
  steps:
  - script: exit 1

- job: SecondJob
  dependsOn: FirstJob
  condition: failed()
  steps:
  - script: echo this will run when FirstJob fails

- job: THirdJob
  dependsOn:
  - FirstJob
  - SecondJob
  condition: succeeded('SecondJob')
  steps:
  - script: echo this will run when SecondJob runs and succeeds
```

Jobs can run as agent pool jobs that run on an agent of a pool; or server jobs, which run on Azure DevOps server or container jobs. An agent pool job can demand agent capabilities such as an operating system.

```
pool:
  name: myPrivateAgents
  demands:
  - agent.os -equals Windows_NT
  - anotherCapability -equals capabilityvalue
```

For server jobs you can specify the pool as the server.

```
jobs:
- job: myserverjob
  pool: server
```

Container jobs will run on hosted agents. For example, the following YAML pipeline obtains the Ubuntu container image with version:16.04 from DockerHub and runs it on a hosted Linux VM agent, and the steps are getting executed in the container instance created with the container image.

```
pool:
  vmImage: 'ubuntu-16.04'

container: ubuntu:16.04

steps:
- script: printenv
```

You can define YAML pipelines with jobs set to check out as none to prevent code checkout to facilitate implementing deployment pipelines. The syntax below is defined to execute a deployment job without checking out the repo and downloading the latest artifacts from the specified build pipeline, for example, a build pipeline with ID 15 in this example.

```
- job: Deploy
  pool:
    vmImage: 'ubuntu-16.04'
```

```
  steps:
  - checkout: none
  - task: DownloadPipelineArtifact@2
  inputs:
    source: 'specific'
    project: 'mysampleproj'
    pipeline: 15
    runVersion: 'latest'
```

In a deployment job, you can use agent pools to target your deployment machines. Additionally, it is possible to use the environment as virtual machines or Kubernetes to do the deployments.

```
jobs:
- deployment: VMDeploy
  displayName: web
  environment:
    name:  VMenv
    resourceType: VirtualMachine
    tags: web1
```

As we discussed in this lesson, with YAML pipeline jobs, which can be even used in multiples stages of the pipeline, they can be used to implement build pipelines as well as deployment pipelines.

Lesson 8.05: Steps and Tasks in Job

In a job, you can define steps with tasks to define actions for execution. There are multiple types of steps that can be defined as steps in a YAML pipeline.

The command-line tasks can be defined in a pipeline as scripts.

```
steps:
- script: echo Hello world!
  displayName: hellosample
```

Shell script tasks can be defined within steps to execute bash commands. pwsh allows you to define PowerShell Core tasks that can execute in Windows, macOS, or Linux. However, if you use PowerShell as a task in a step, it can be only run on the Windows platform.

```
steps:
- powershell: echo Hello $(name)
  displayName: Say hello name
  name: chaminda
```

With all these step tasks, you can use the failOnStderr Boolean to define whether the execution should fail the pipeline on script or command-line execution failures.

```
steps:
- pwsh: echo Hello $(name)
  displayName: Say hello name
  name: chaminda
  workingDirectory: $(build.sourcesDirectory)
  failOnStderr: true
```

Checkout is another step action you can define to allow checking out of source control repos. Setting this to none will prevent the checkout action as we mentioned in the previous lesson. Checkout set to self will check out the repo where the current YAML pipeline code is existing. However, you can define other repos and check them out if required in your pipeline steps using a checkout task. You can see the usage of a GitHub repo and an Azure Git repo in the example below with checkout.

```
resources:
  repositories:
  - repository: MyRepoNameToUseInChekoutStep
    type: github
    endpoint: MyGitHubServiceConnection
    name: Chamindac/myrepo

trigger:
- master
```

```
pool:
  vmImage: 'ubuntu-latest'

steps:
- checkout: self
- checkout: MyRepoNameToUseInChekoutStep
- checkout: git://MyTeamProject/myazuregitrepo
```

Tasks are a catalogue of tasks available for pipelines, which we discussed in classic builds. You can find a list of all available tasks in the link `https://docs.microsoft.com/en-us/azure/devops/pipelines/tasks/?view=azure-devops` and find out a YAML snippet for each of them. All the tasks are predefined and useful so that you can implement your pipelines quickly. Tasks such as Query Work Items and Invoke HTTP REST API can be used to implement gating with the YAML-based deployment pipelines, using server jobs (agentless), which we will describe in the usage of classic release pipelines lessons in Chapters 9 and 10.

In this lesson, we explored a couple of available tasks in pipelines specified in their own names such as script and pwsh, as well as catalogues of tasks available by default to implement your pipeline needs.

Lesson 8.06: Using Templates

In Chapter 6, we discussed using tasks groups to implement common steps. Similarly, with YAML pipelines, you can serve the same purpose by sharing the steps to multiple pipelines using templates.

There are four kinds of templates available in Azure YAML pipelines. Stage, Job, Step, and Variable are those template types, which make more sense to you now as you have gone through each of these types in previous lessons of this chapter.

Following is a usage of a stage template, and the parameter named name is defined with its default value as empty string.

```
# File: stages/mystagetemplate.yml

parameters:
  name: ''
```

```
stages:
- stage: Print_${{ parameters.name }}
  jobs:
  - job: ${{ parameters.name }}_Windows
    pool:
      vmImage: vs2017-win2016
    steps:
    - script: echo hello ${{ parameters.name }}
  - job: ${{ parameters.name }}_Mac
    pool:
      vmImage: macos-10.14
    steps:
    - script: echo hello ${{ parameters.name }}
```

The above stage template can be used in a pipeline as shown below. Notice how the parameter values are passed.

```
stages:
- template: stages/mystagetemplate.yml
  parameters:
    name: Chaminda

- template: stages/mystagetemplate.yml
  parameters:
    name: Pushpa
```

In a similar way, you can define job and step templates as well and use them in the pipelines.

A job template is below.

```
# File: jobs/myjobtemplate.yml

parameters:
  name: ''
  pool: ''
  sign: false
```

```
jobs:
- job: ${{ parameters.name }}
  pool: ${{ parameters.pool }}
  steps:
  - script: echo hello
```

The job template can be used as shown here.

```
jobs:
- template: jobs/myjobtemplate.yml
  parameters:
    name: macOS
    pool:
      vmImage: 'macOS-10.14'

- template: jobs/myjobtemplate.yml
  parameters:
    name: Linux
    pool:
      vmImage: 'ubuntu-16.04'
```

Step would be also having a similar syntax, and the only difference would be instead of job content, it would be step content and the parameterization to match the step needs.

Variable templates can be defined to keep the variables shared. The variable names and values can be defined in the template as shown below.

```
# File: variables/mybuildvartemplate.yml
variables:
- name: vmImage
  value: vs2017-win2016
- name: buildplatform
  value: x64
- name: buildconfiguration
  value: release
```

Then the variable template can be used in pipelines with the following syntax.

```
variables:
- template: variables/mybuildvartemplate.yml
pool:
  vmImage: ${{ variables.vmImage }}
steps:
- script: build x ${{ variables.buildplatform }} ${{ variables.
buildconfiguration }}
```

In this lesson, we explored the usage of templates to share stages, jobs, steps, and variables as templates and usage of the templates in YAML pipelines.

Summary

In this chapter, we have focused on gaining an understanding of the YAML pipeline implementation to support pipelines as code, which allows us to version control and trace changes easily with our source code for the pipelines we implement. Various options available to define YAML-based pipelines to support build, test, and deployment needs are explored in the chapter. With this knowledge, you will be able to codify your pipelines and version control them, side by side, with your application code.

In the next chapter, we discuss classic release pipelines implementation options and features. Once you discover available features in classic release pipelines, you may use that knowledge to try and implement the same requirements catered by classic pipelines, with YAML pipelines as well, since you now have a solid understanding of YAML pipeline syntax.

CHAPTER 9

Azure Release Pipelines – Service Connections, Templates, Artifacts, Stages, and Environments

Over the last few chapters, we discussed the features and options to set up build pipelines. The build pipelines let you build the source code and create deployable packages with built binaries, check for vulnerabilities in source code with code analysis tools, and run unit tests. Additionally, you can run deployment actions in the build pipelines, especially when it comes to YAML pipelines, and the implementation of deployments is also set up with YAML build pipelines.

The release pipelines in Azure DevOps come with various features enabling you to deploy to almost all targets and platforms available. In this chapter we are going to explore a few of the available features in Azure DevOps related to deployment pipelines, so that you will be able to understand the usage of the features to implement automated software deliveries, even to production targets.

Lesson 9.01: Service Connections

Generally, there can be various deployment targets on different platforms in a given software. There can be cloud targets as well as on-premise targets. Further, the targets can be cloud platform resources or infrastructure on cloud. To support deploying to such a variety of platforms, it is required to make connections to such resources.

C. Chandrasekara and P. Herath, *Hands-on Azure Pipelines*, https://doi.org/10.1007/978-1-4842-5902-3_9

In other words, an endpoint in a given resource should be authenticated, and a connection should be made to the endpoint as a service connection from Azure DevOps, in order to allow the pipelines to interact with the resource.

As an example, we can consider an Azure subscription or a resource group. A service principle in Azure allows accessibility to Azure resources. Using the service principle, you can make an Azure service connection in Azure DevOps. See Figure 9-1.

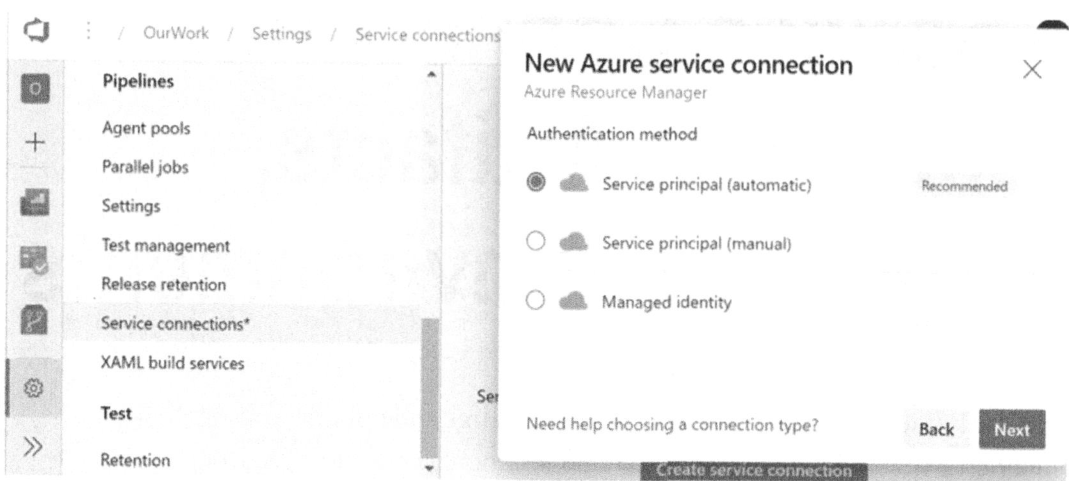

Figure 9-1. *Azure Service Connection*

There is a wide variety of service connections that you can make from Azure DevOps. They involve cloud service targets such as Azure, AWS, code repos such as Bitbucket and GitHub, different types of deployment tools chefs, Octopus, and so many other targets connecting code quality tools.

The service connections to source control repos such as GitHub and Bitbucket allow you to connect different source control repos to Azure pipelines. You can build code available in such repos by lining them with a service connection.

Some of the service connection types are getting installed with the marketplace extensions for Azure DevOps. For example, to link the SonarQube server, you need to install the SonarQube extensions. Once the extension is added, the pipelines can be set up to trigger code analysis for your source code in source control repos. Another example would be service connections targeting Amazon Web Services (AWS), allowing deployments to AWS. See Figure 9-2.

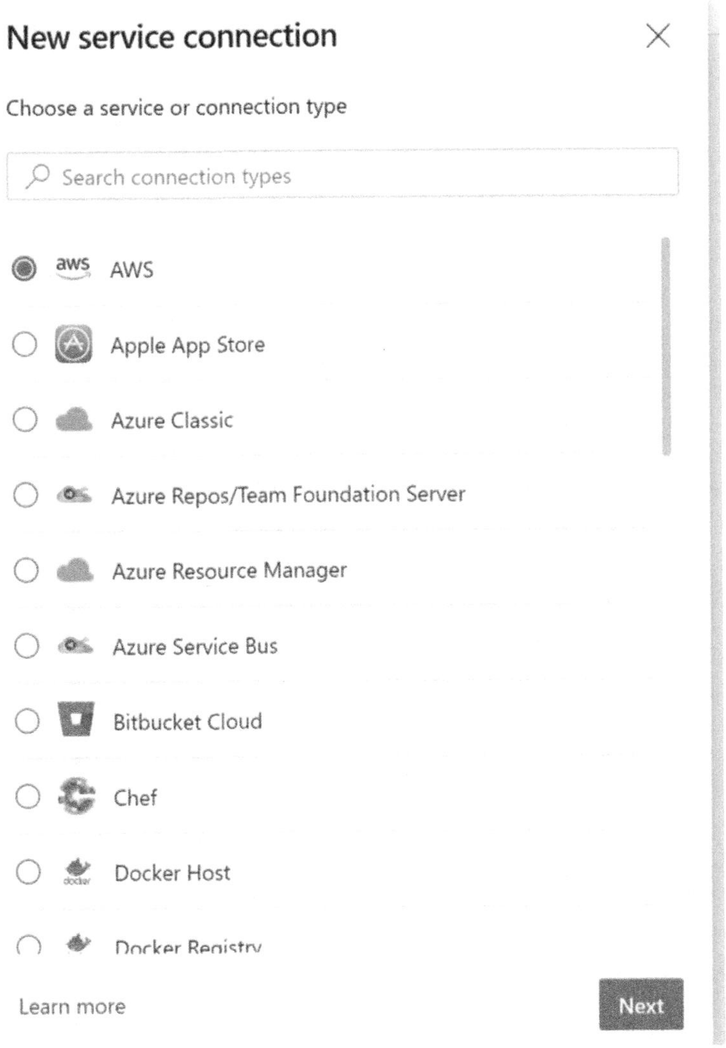

New service connection

Choose a service or connection type

Search connection types

AWS

Apple App Store

Azure Classic

Azure Repos/Team Foundation Server

Azure Resource Manager

Azure Service Bus

Bitbucket Cloud

Chef

Docker Host

Docker Registry

Learn more

Next

Figure 9-2. *Different types of service connections*

In this lesson, we explored the service connections and usage of them to facilitate external resource connections with Azure DevOps.

Lesson 9.02: Using Templates

Templates are pre-created as a set of pipeline tasks grouped together, serving a given purpose. These templates are set up with commonly used variables as well to get you quickly deploying to the desired targets. See Figure 9-3.

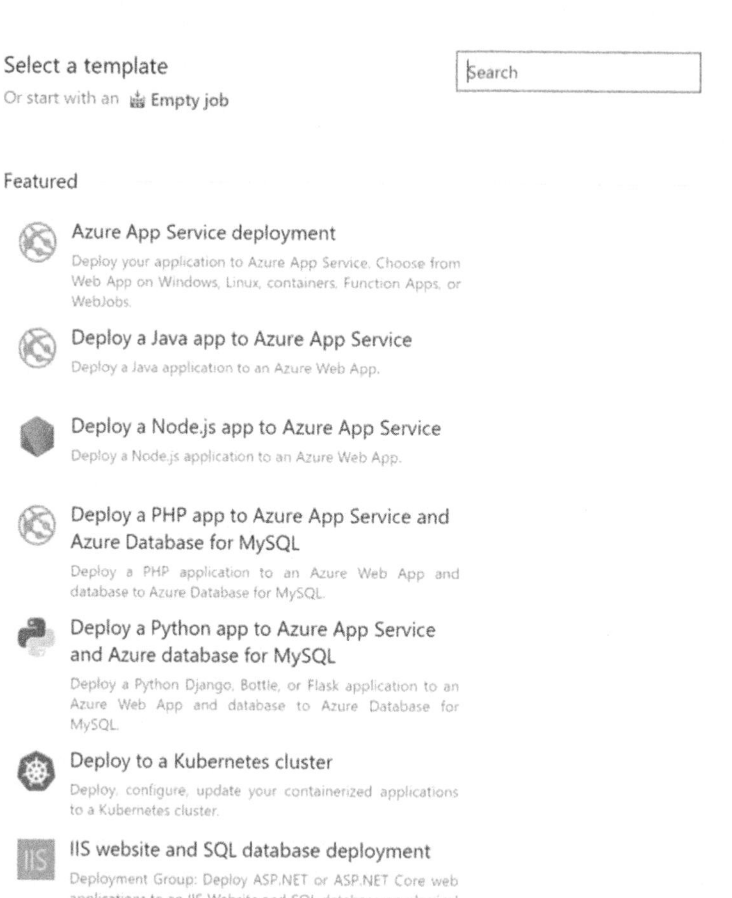

Figure 9-3. *Release Templates*

As an example, if you apply the Azure Machine Learning model deployment template as your pipeline template, it would create the two steps required to deploy a machine learning mode. You can select the Azure subscription created as a service connection and get quickly started with machine learning model deployments using this template. See Figure 9-4.

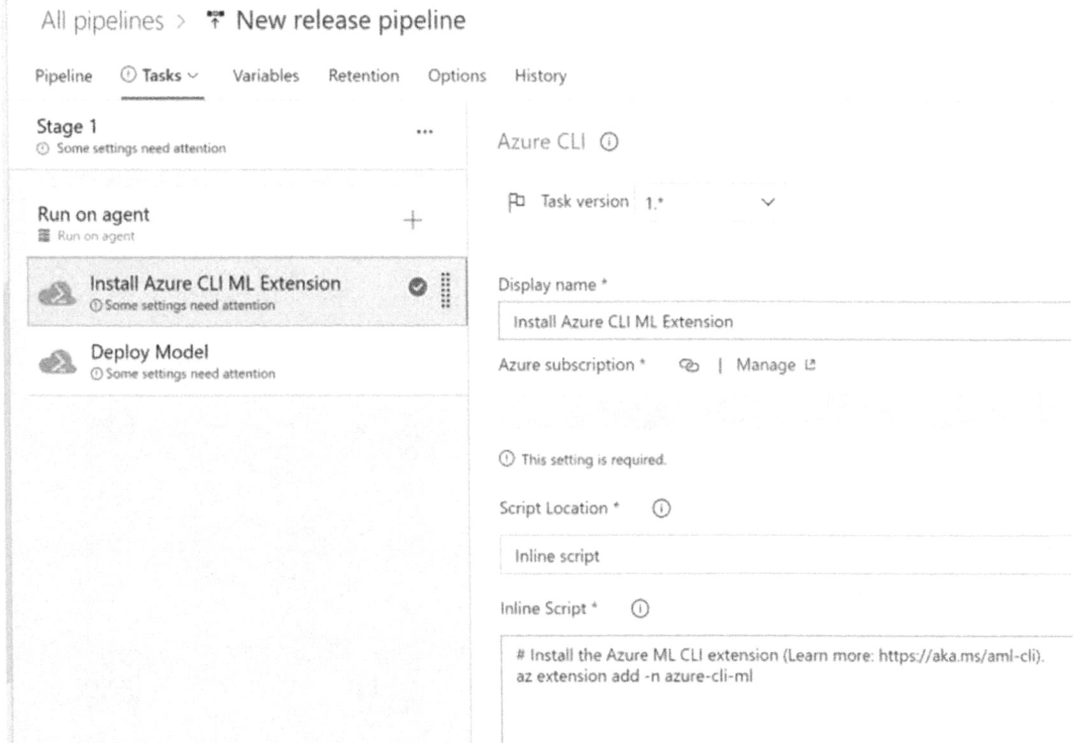

***Figure 9-4.** ML Model Deploy Template*

The main usage of the template is to get you started with a given type of application and target deployment done quickly. If you are a beginner at setting up release pipelines, the templates will assist you in getting familiarized with release pipelines in a shorter time, minimizing the learning effort. You can get the additional templates installed by setting up the extensions from the Visual Studio Marketplace.

We discussed the usage of templates in this lesson, which will help you to get started quickly with release pipelines.

Lesson 9.03: Artifacts for Release

As we discussed in Chapter 7 of this book, the build pipelines are supposed to generate deployable binary packages called artifacts. These artifacts can be consumed in the release pipelines to get their content downloaded to a target and deploy as necessary.

There are a number of artifacts types supported in Azure release pipelines. See Figure 9-5.

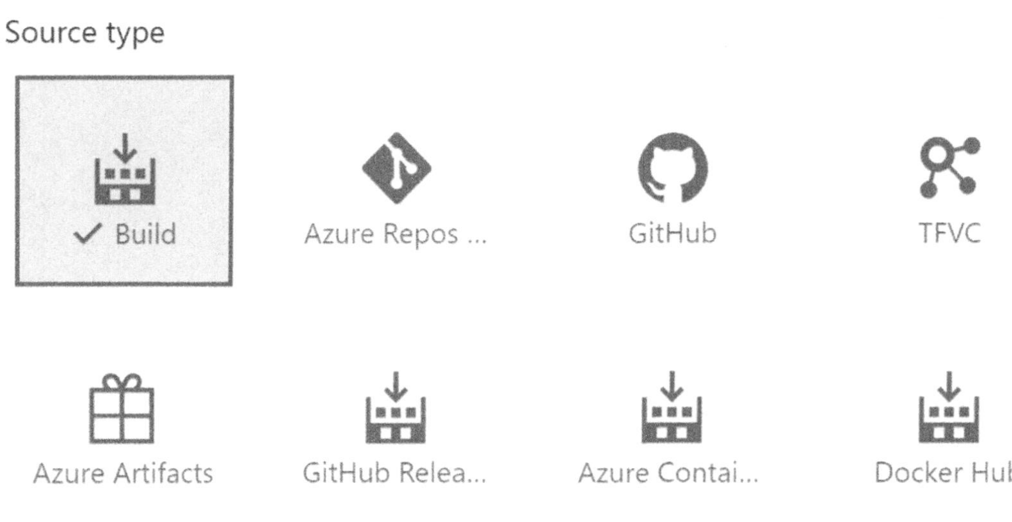

Figure 9-5. *Artifact types*

If you have published your artifacts in the build itself as a published drop folder, you can use the build as an artifact type for your build. It is even useful for you to set the build as an artifact type that published the artifacts by other means such as an artifact feed in the release if you want to set up continuous triggering of the release, once a build is competed.

Azure repos can be used as another artifact type. Code or other files such as YAML deployment support files can be used in release steps. Sometimes even Python-based code files for deployment and testing after deployment required for machine learning can be stored in Azure repos and used in release pipelines to perform deployments and testing steps. A similar purpose can be achieved by using GitHub and Team Foundation Version Control repos as artifacts in release pipelines.

Azure artifacts, as explained in Chapter 7, can be used to store artifacts generated such as NuGet packages, in the artifact feeds. The artifact feeds can be consumed in the release, and packages can be downloaded and used in deployment agents to deploy to required targets.

Azure container repositories and docker hub as artifacts let you use docker images available in them to be used in release pipelines. Further, the Jenkins pipeline can be integrated as an artifact source so that you can use the output of Jenkins pipelines in the release pipelines.

Once the artifacts are added, you can set up a trigger for the pipeline based on new artifact availability, which allows continuous deployments. When using builds you can add additional exclude or include branch filters for the trigger. When a repo is used, it can set up a trigger based on pull request, with a target branch filter, and you can use branch filters to trigger for commits. See Figure 9-6.

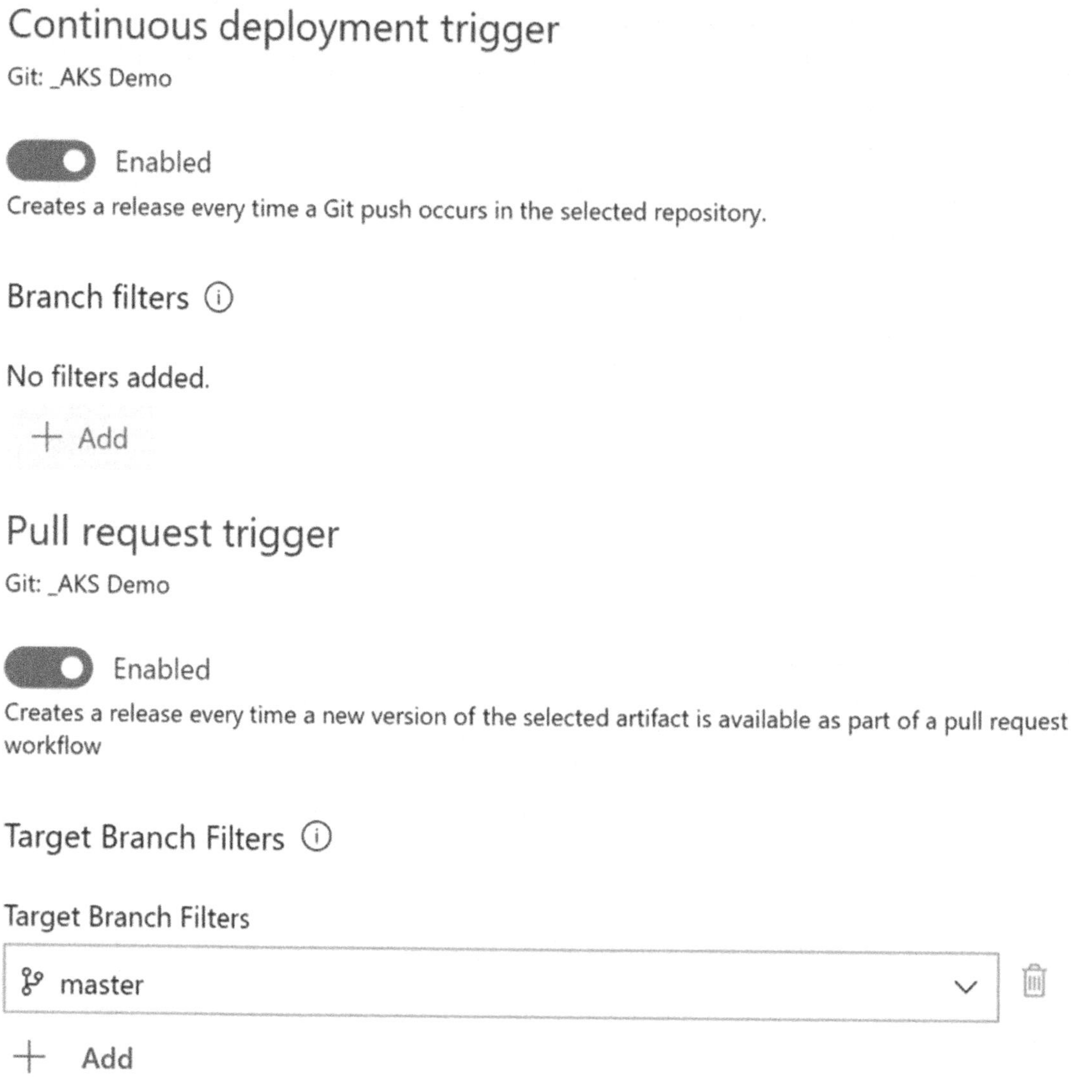

Continuous deployment trigger

Git: _AKS Demo

Creates a release every time a Git push occurs in the selected repository.

Branch filters ⓘ

No filters added.

+ Add

Pull request trigger

Git: _AKS Demo

Creates a release every time a new version of the selected artifact is available as part of a pull request workflow

Target Branch Filters ⓘ

Target Branch Filters

master

+ Add

Figure 9-6. *Repo artifact triggers*

In this lesson, we discussed the different types of artifacts that can be used in release pipelines, which enable you to trigger release pipelines based on new artifact availability.

Lesson 9.04: Release Stages

Release stages can be used to control the flow of a release pipeline. You may treat them as your deployment environment representation in the pipeline. Stages in the pipeline provide you the flexibility to define your desired workflow of software delivery. In this lesson, let's explore the capabilities and usage of release stages to manage the delivery of your software project to the desired targets. See Figure 9-7.

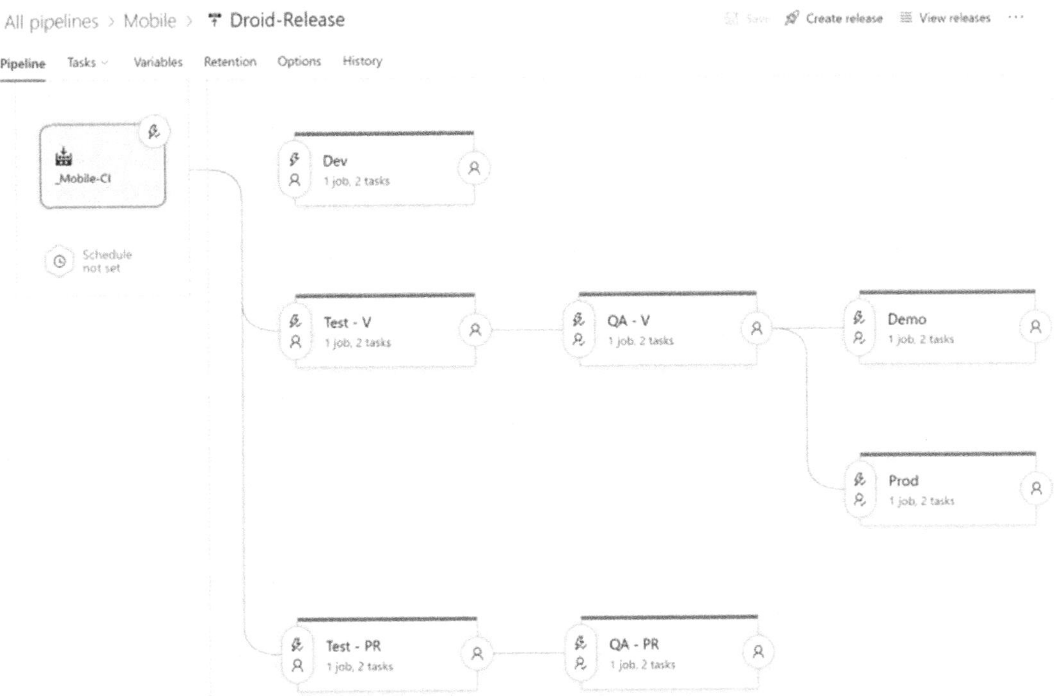

Figure 9-7. *Release pipeline flow*

A stage can be set up with three type of triggers. Manual trigger requires you to trigger the stage manually by clicking deploy manually after creating the release from the release pipeline. After stage lets you define previous stage(s) so that the current stage gets triggered only when all previous stages are completed. After release will trigger a stage once the release is created for the pipeline, by the means of manual creation or continuous deployment trigger set at connected artifacts. See Figure 9-8. Further, you set scheduled releases for a given stage. Artifact filters let you filter branches, exclude or include patterns, or set up other artifact conditions. Pull request deployment enabling will allow the release based on pull requests to be deployed to the given stage; however, it is advisable to keep this disabled for production stages.

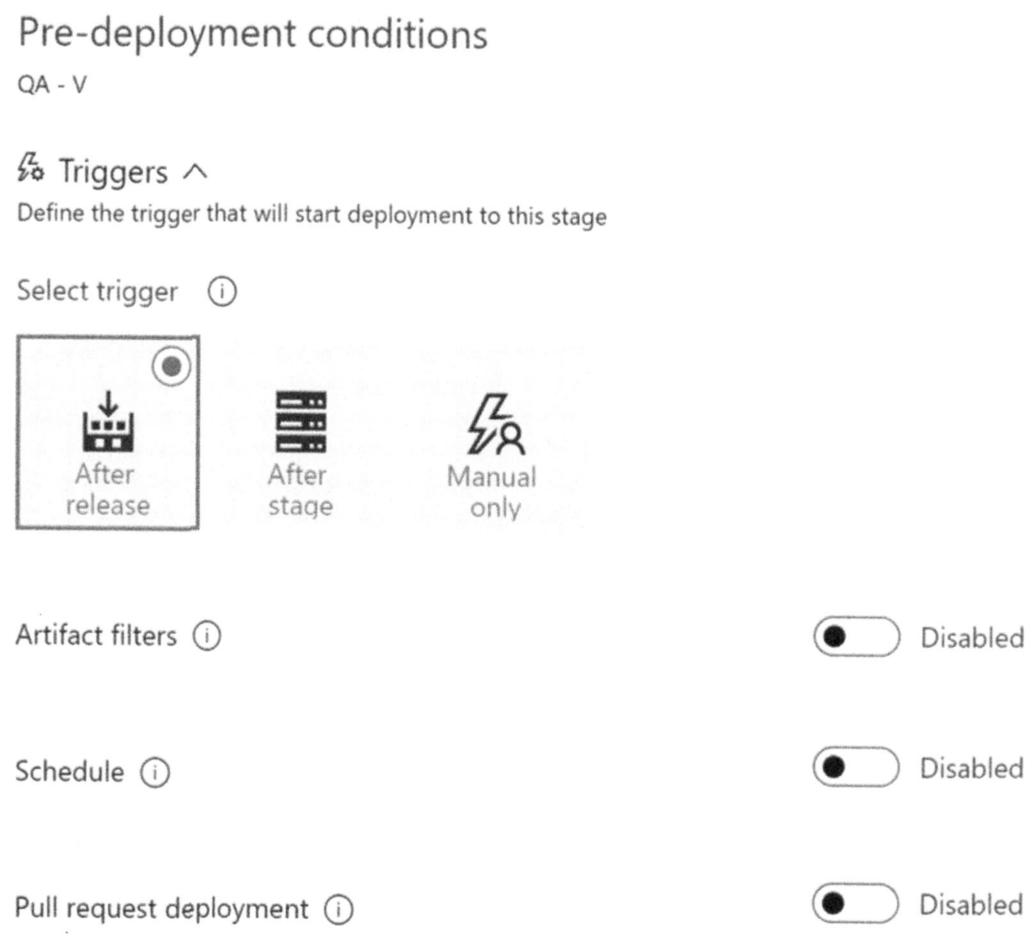

Figure 9-8. *Stage triggers*

A stage can be set up with pre-deployment approvals. As the approvers, you can add individuals or groups and set a timeout for approval. Setting up approval will send an alert email to the approvers when the stage is triggered. The approvers can approve or reject a deployment to a given stage. However, approving the deployment can be scheduled with a delay time if required. This approval for pre-deployment can be effectively used to protect required environments such as production or demo. Further, it can be utilized to prevent any deployments to a stage such as quality assurance while one version of the application is being tested, so that it prevents the components of the application in the quality assurance stage getting accidentally overwritten, until the QA team decides to take in the new release for testing. See Figure 9-9 for pre-deployment approval settings. Post-deployment approvals can be set up as well similar to pre-deployment approvals to denote that a stage deployed application is verified and considered if it passes the required, mandatory working conditions of the given application. See Figure 9-9.

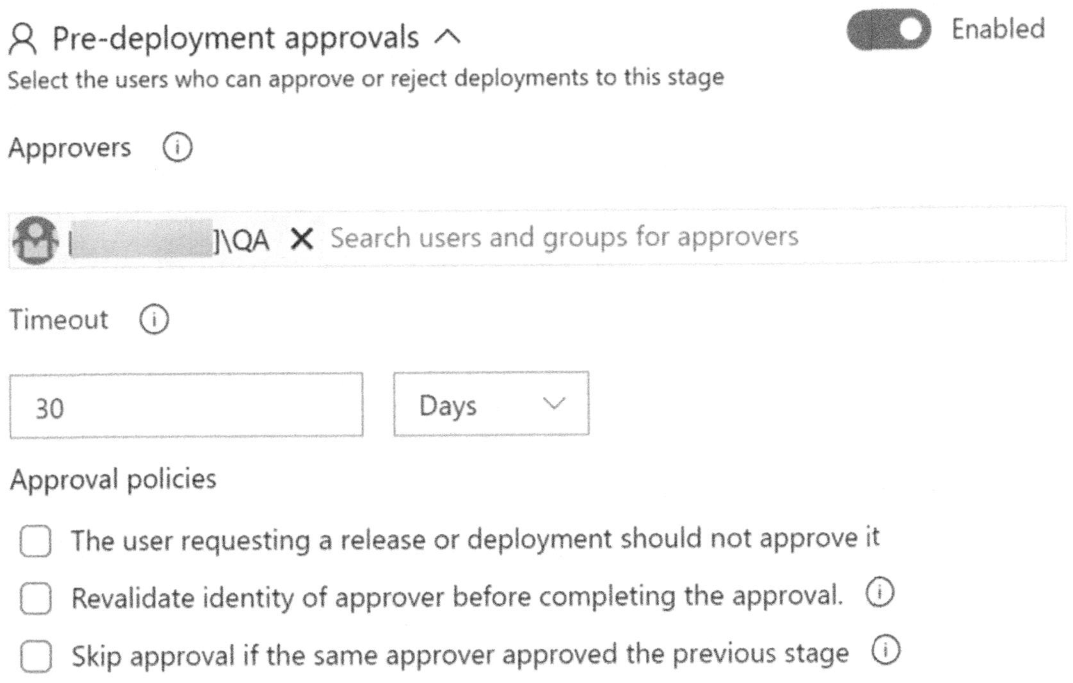

Pre-deployment approvals
Enabled
Select the users who can approve or reject deployments to this stage
Approvers
]\QA Search users and groups for approvers
Timeout
30
Days
Approval policies
The user requesting a release or deployment should not approve it
Revalidate identity of approver before completing the approval.
Skip approval if the same approver approved the previous stage

Figure 9-9. *Pre-deployment approvals*

Another pre-deployment setting that can be applied to a stage is gates, in Azure pipelines. Gates let you invoke third-party calls and wait for desired outcomes before proceeding with a particular stage. In other words, gates are for performing a gatekeeper job before a given stage is deployed. For example, a query work item gate may evaluate, if any critical bugs are in an unresolved state before letting a release to deploy any stage beyond the QA stage. See Figure 9-10.

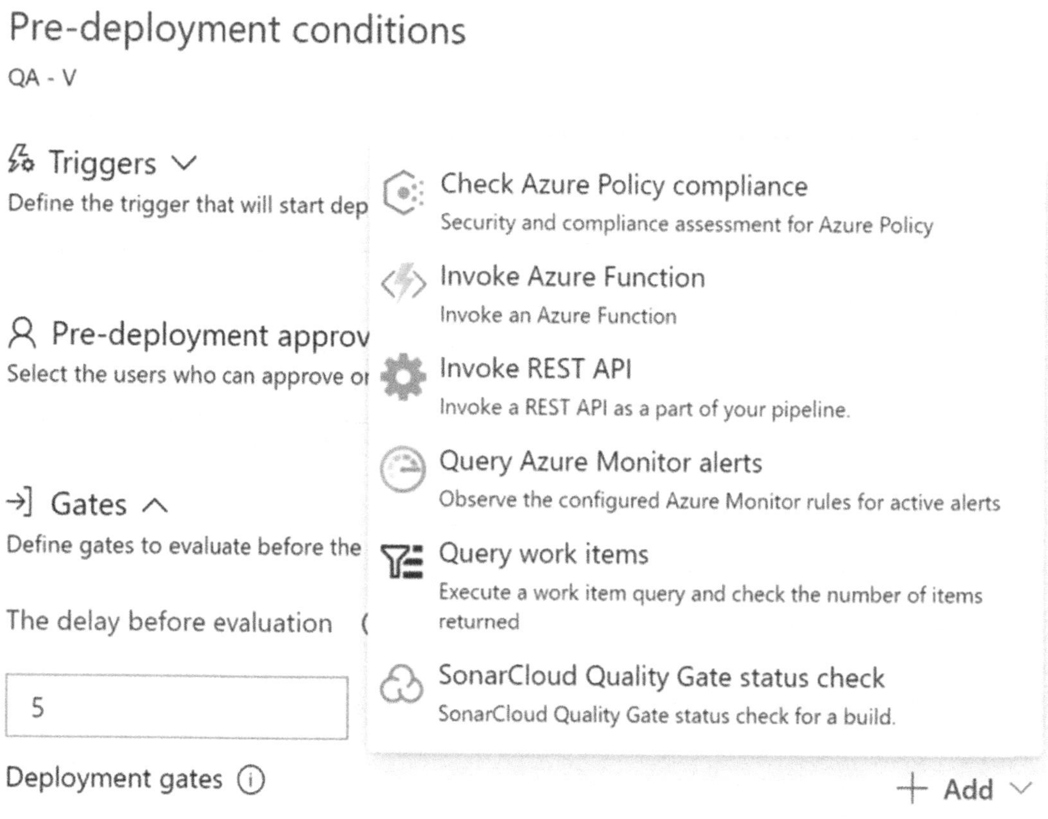

Figure 9-10. *Gates*

A deployment queue setting for a stage lets you define the behavior when multiple releases are queued for a given stage. You can define if parallel deployments are allowed to a given stage, but this is a highly unlikely scenario. When multiple releases that are queued deploy, all in a sequence can be used. Or you can set up to only deploy the latest release and discard the other previous deploy requests. See Figure 9-11.

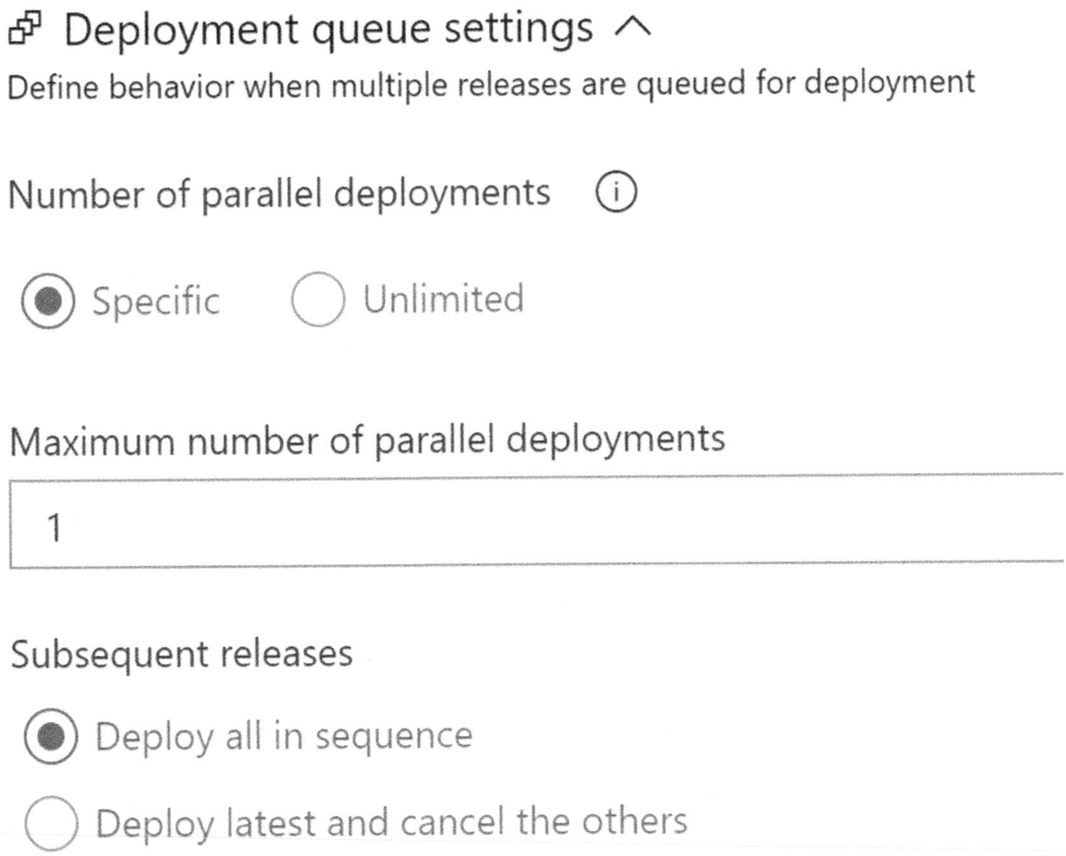

Deployment queue settings

Define behavior when multiple releases are queued for deployment

Number of parallel deployments

Specific Unlimited

Maximum number of parallel deployments

1

Subsequent releases

Deploy all in sequence

Deploy latest and cancel the others

Figure 9-11. *Deployment queue settings*

In post-deployment, as discussed previously in this lesson, the approvals can be set up to denote the application works fine in the stage, after the deployment to the stage, letting it trigger any next stages. Additionally, you can add gates as well to a post-deployment stage. Further, you have the option to set up a redeployment trigger when a deployment stage is failed, so that it deploys previous successful deployments of the current stage again to the stage. See Figure 9-12.

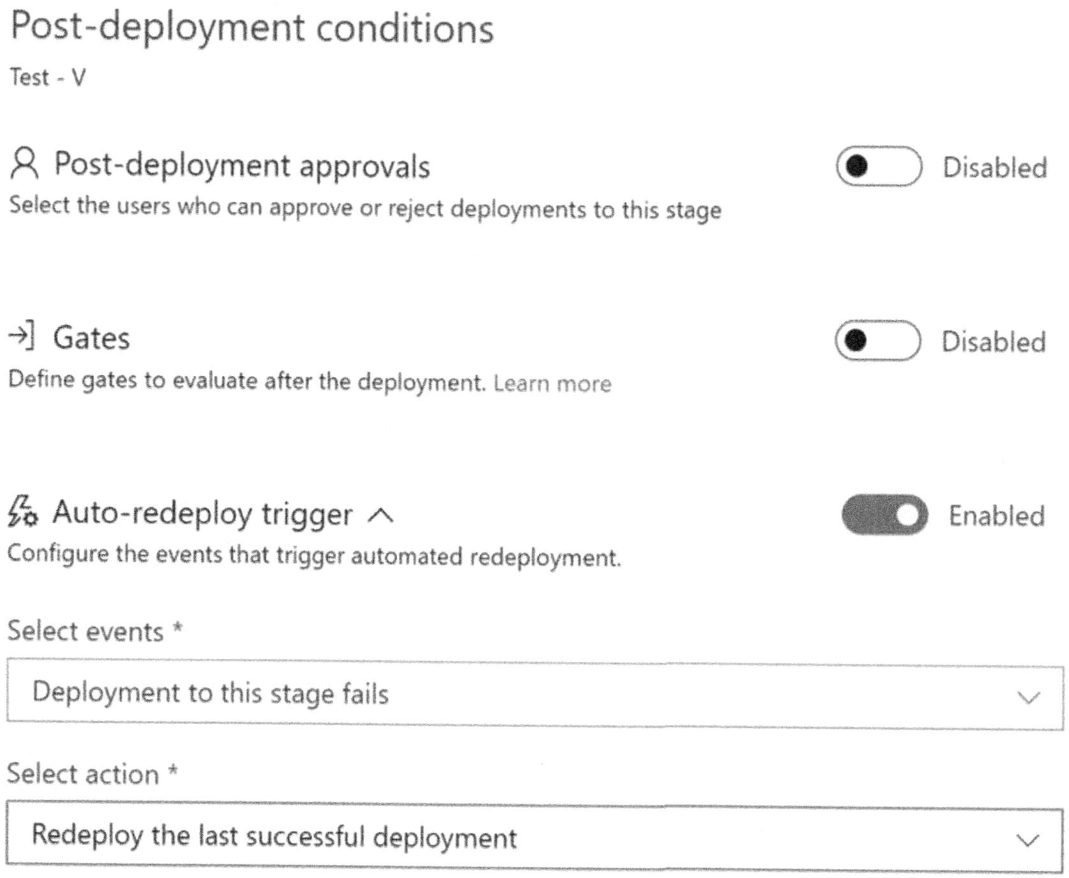

Figure 9-12. *Redeploy trigger*

You have the faculty of cloning a stage to create another stage, which allows you to easily create the release workflow. In a stage, you can add agent phases, deployment group phases, and agentless phases that will be explained in more detail in Chapter 10. Similar to build pipelines, you can add tasks to the release stage to define the steps to be executed as deployment and automated testing actions. See Figure 9-13.

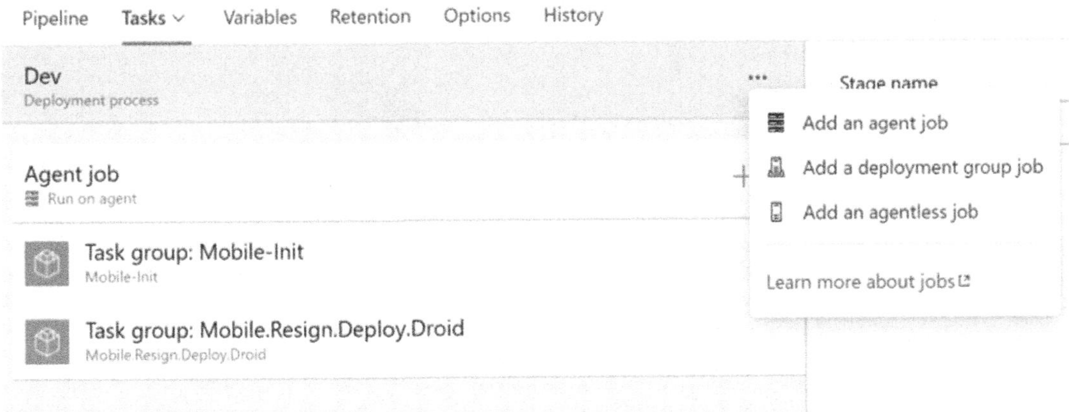

Figure 9-13. *Stage*

We discussed several features available in pre- and post-stages to facilitate a release workflow in this lesson.

Lesson 9.05: Environments

A collection of resources that can be used as targets for deployments can be set up as an environment in Azure DevOps. An environment may contain a Kubernetes cluster, set of virtual machines, or resources such as Azure web app or functions apps as examples.

You can create an environment with virtual machines, Kubernetes, or no resources. When you create a no resources environment, you can add resources later to the environment. See Figure 9-14.

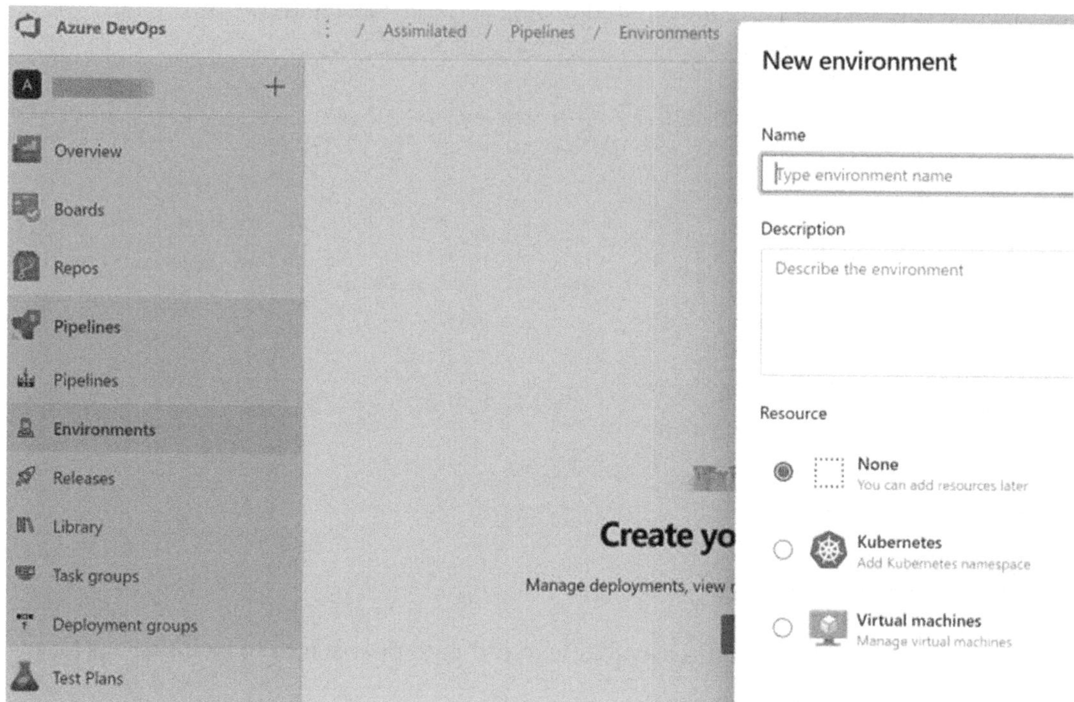

Figure 9-14. *Environment*

For an environment, you can set up permissions based on the roles of reader, user, and administrator, where administrators will be able to manage, users will be able to use the environment in pipelines, and readers will only be able to view.

The environment can be added with checks, which is a bit similar to gates. The checks even include approver evaluation of artifacts as well. See Figure 9-15.

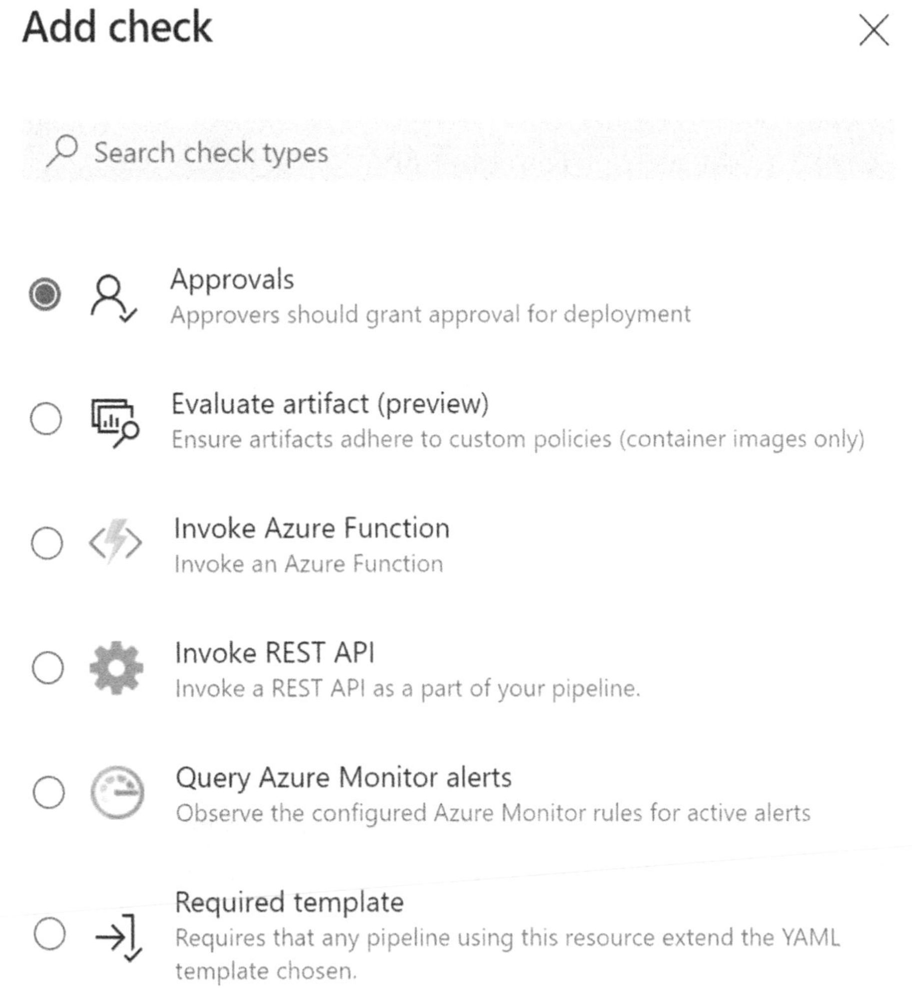

***Figure 9-15.** Environment checks*

YAML pipelines can use the environments as targets for deployment actions. See Figure 9-16.

YAML

```yaml
- stage: deploy
  jobs:
  - deployment: DeployWeb
    displayName: deploy Web App
    pool:
      vmImage: 'Ubuntu-latest'
    # creates an environment if it doesn't exist
    environment: 'smarthotel-dev'
    strategy:
      runOnce:
        deploy:
          steps:
          - script: echo Hello world
```

Figure 9-16. *Using environment in YAML*

Environments facilitate the approval-based workflow implementation for YAML pipelines, similar to the stages available in the classic release pipelines.

In this lesson we have identified the usage and available options in environments to use in YAML pipelines.

Summary

An initial introduction to release pipelines was given in this chapter, highlighting the capabilities of service connections and usage of templates to get started with release pipelines easily. Then we discussed the usage of artifacts in a release pipeline and setting up the artifacts-based triggers to enable continuous deployments. The release stage capabilities to implement a release workflow was also talked about in detail, explaining the usage of each option available. Additionally, we explored the environments, which are allowing the setup of deployment targets for YAML pipelines, similar to stages in the classic release pipelines.

In the next chapter, we discuss the phases available in the release pipeline stage to allow you to gain the required knowledge to successfully implement release workflows. Further, we will explore the other options and features such as variables, usage of release definition history, and exporting and importing options of release pipelines.

CHAPTER 10

Azure Release Pipelines – Jobs, Deployment Groups, Variables, and Other Options

In the previous chapter, we discussed a couple of important features related to release pipelines. The service connections allowing various deployment targets with release management were described. Further, we explored usage of templates available for release pipeline implementation, stages in release pipelines to implement release workflow, and a way to set up triggers, approvals, and gates. The new feature environment was also discussed to understand its usage.

As a continuation from the previous chapter, we will explore agent jobs, deployment group jobs, and agentless job phases and their usage. Then we briefly discuss variables and their usage in release pipelines, which is more or less similar to usage of variables in build pipelines.

Lesson 10.01: Agent Jobs

Agent jobs require an installed Azure DevOps agent to execute the job. Agent machines can be hosted agent machines or on-premise machines depending on the targets of deployment, which we discuss in this lesson.

C. Chandrasekara and P. Herath, *Hands-on Azure Pipelines*, https://doi.org/10.1007/978-1-4842-5902-3_10

Depending on the execution, steps technology requirements of the agent defer. The requirements of an agent can be demanded as demands of an agent phase. For example, if your deployment steps involve Azure CLI, to deploy to Azure target, your agent machine needs to have the Azure CLI available. Demands in the agent phase are used for these types of technology demands. See Figure 10-1.

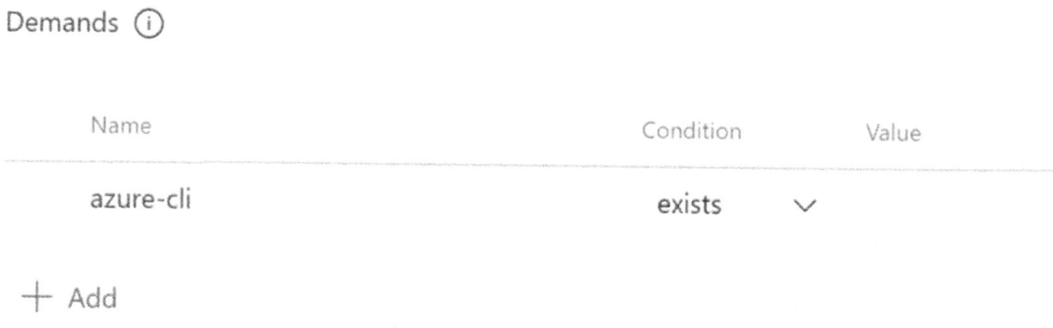

Figure 10-1. *Agent Demands*

If you are deploying to a cloud target such as Azure or AWS, you can use Microsoft hosted agents to execute deployment actions. However, if you are deploying to an on-premise target or a more secure Azure target such as Azure App Service Environment, you might need to set up your own deployment agent machine. Most of the time the on-premise environment would be behind a corporate firewall, and the hosted agents will not have a line of sight to execute deployments against such targets. Similar to that, in an Azure App Service Environment (ASE), access to even platform services would be allowed only within the defined virtual network in Azure ASE. Hence, you need to set up a virtual machine configured as an Azure DevOps agent, inside the Azure ASE virtual network, which can access the platform services in an Azure ASE.

There are parallelism options similar to build pipelines that allow you to run the job steps in a single agent, or multiple configurations as specified in multipliers. When running on multiple configurations, you can specify the number of agents limit. You can run the same set of tasks in multiple agents as well with a multi-agent option. See Figure 10-2. These options would be useful if you want to deploy to different targets based on if a configuration specified may be to enable deployment on the debug configuration to diagnose some issues while having a release configuration target as well.

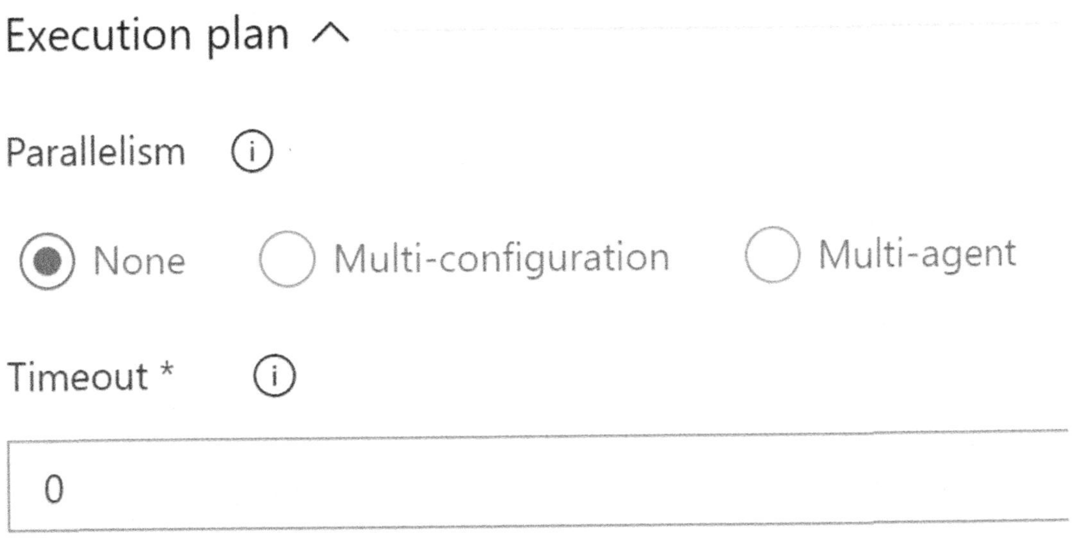

Execution plan

Parallelism

None Multi-configuration Multi-agent

Timeout *

0

Figure 10-2. *Parallelism*

You can selectively set to download or skip downloading artifacts in an agent step. See Figure 10-3. For example, if you have a separate agent job to run test automations, you may not need to download artifacts other than automated test scripts that need to be executed. Hence, you can skip the deployment files and only download the artifact related to the test execution.

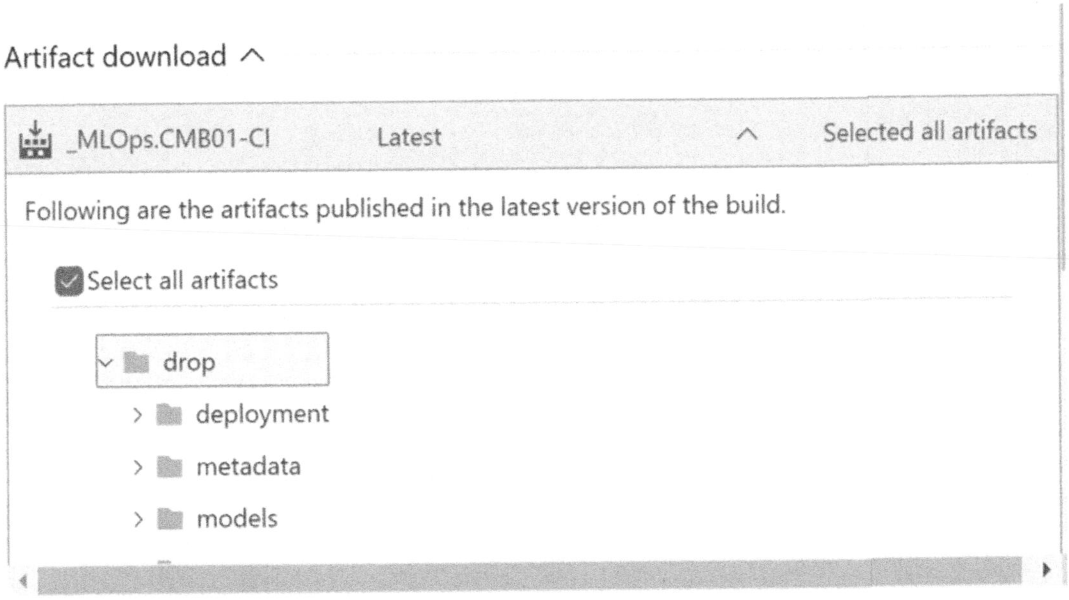

Artifact download

_MLOps.CMB01-CI Latest Selected all artifacts

Following are the artifacts published in the latest version of the build.

Select all artifacts

drop

deployment

metadata

models

Figure 10-3. *Artifacts*

You can set the Allow scripts to access the OAuth token in an agent phase so that any script task in an agent job can use the system access token to access a REST API of Azure DevOps.

There are two timeout settings available for agent jobs. A timeout defines how much time a job can be executed in the agent. A job cancellation timeout defines how much time a job is given to complete when a cancellation request is made before the server terminates the job.

The execution options allow you to define the conditions of how the job may get started. See Figure 10-4. You may want to set up a rollback procedure in case the deployment fails, which is defined in the previous agent job. In that scenario, you can set it to execute on a previous job failure in the current agent job and define the tasks for rollback. In a situation where you want to execute automation tests after a successful deployment job, you may set up one agent job to do the deployment upon successful execution of that job to execute the functional tests on the subsequent job with the condition that the previous job is successful. However, unlike the build agent jobs, the execution happens in release agent jobs in the defined sequence, and there is no option to define dependencies as in build agent jobs, which are not required as execution happens in the sequence the jobs are set up in the release pipeline.

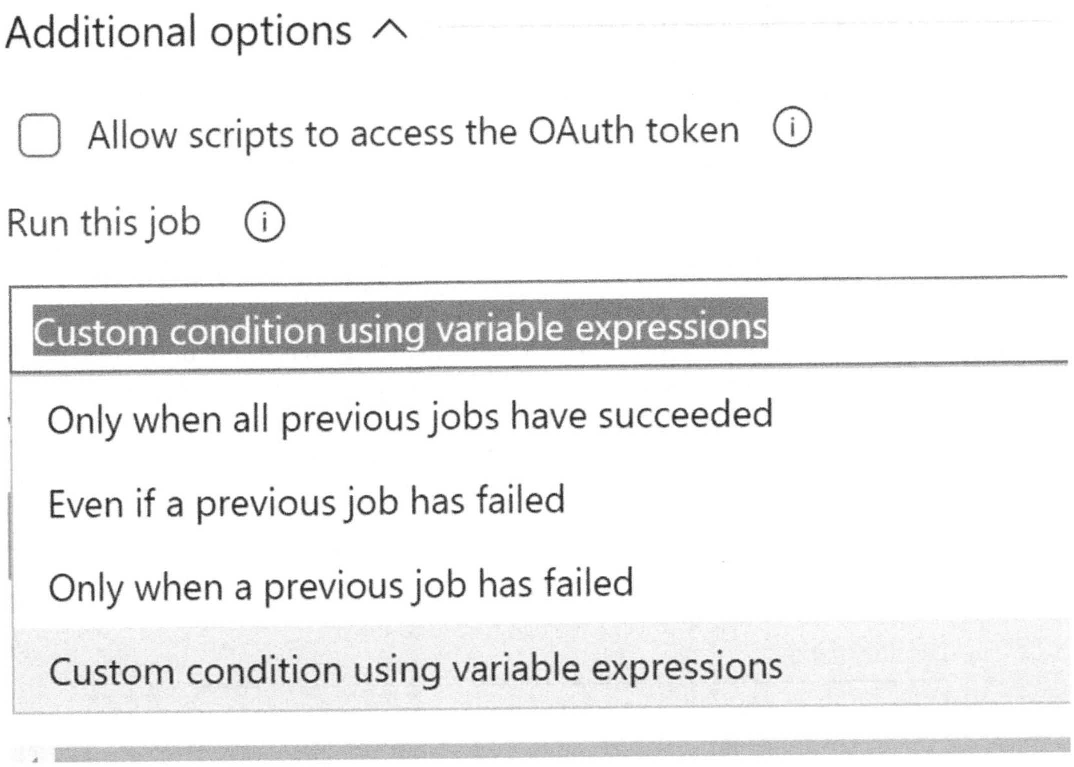

Additional options

Allow scripts to access the OAuth token

Run this job

Custom condition using variable expressions

Only when all previous jobs have succeeded

Even if a previous job has failed

Only when a previous job has failed

Custom condition using variable expressions

Figure 10-4. *OAuth token and Job run conditions*

You can use many tasks available by default in Azure DevOps as well as tasks getting added with the marketplace extensions in Agent jobs to execute the required deployment steps. These deployment steps may involve setting up infrastructure of a given environment target, deploy your applications, and even executing functional and integration tests. In the marketplace for Azure DevOps, you can find tasks supporting various platforms and almost all actions you are required to do. If a task cannot be found, you can implement them on your own, which we will discuss in more detail in Chapter 11. You can group your tasks as task groups to reuse them in multiple agent jobs, and we talked about task groups in Chapter 2.

In this lesson, we discussed using agent jobs in release pipelines.

Lesson 10.02: Deployment Group Jobs

Deployment group jobs are meant to execute on defined deployment groups. We have talked about deployment groups and deployment pools and how they can be added with target machines with roles in Chapter 2 of this book.

In release pipelines, you can use deployment groups defined in team projects in the deployment group jobs. You can use the roles defined in deployment group targets as required tags for a given deployment group phase. For example, any machines with a role set to WebSvr can be identified as Web Servers using the tags in the deployment group job, which need to be deployed with web server deployment steps of your application. See Figure 10-5.

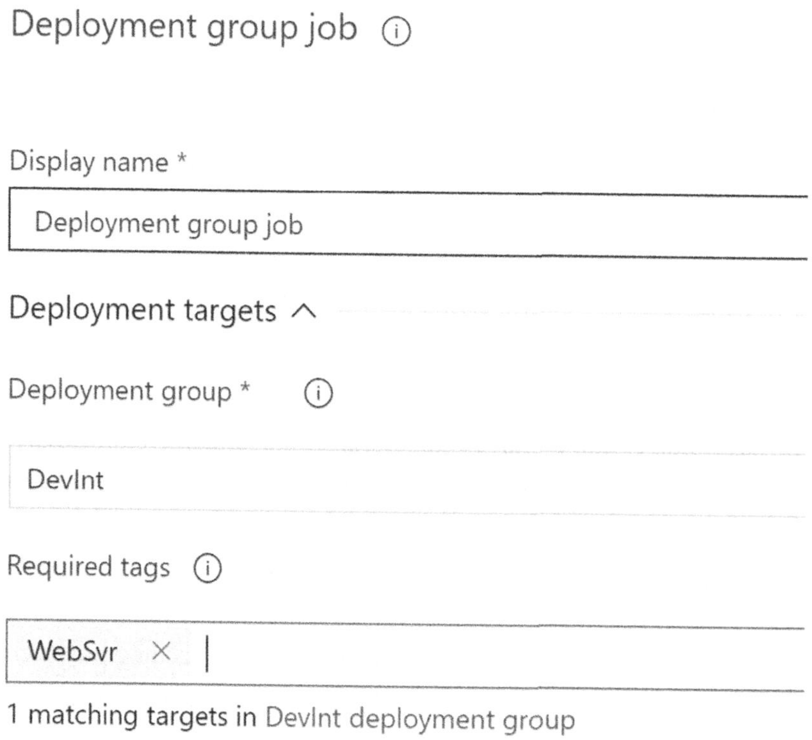

Deployment group job
Display name *
Deployment group job
Deployment targets
Deployment group *
DevInt
Required tags
WebSvr
1 matching targets in DevInt deployment group

Figure 10-5. *Deployment group tags*

Similar to an agent job, the deployment group job also has a timeout and job cancellation timeout settings that you can use to determine how much time a job can be executed before timing out and how much time is allowed to complete the job once a cancellation request is made before terminating, respectively.

Targets to deploy in parallel settings define how many targets the deployment actions execute in parallel when more than one target in the deployment group is available based on the selected tags and defined roles in the targets of the deployment group. This enables you to deploy to your load balanced multiple web servers, etc., in parallel. Timeout 0 means infinite time out and the timeout is defined in minutes. See Figure 10-6.

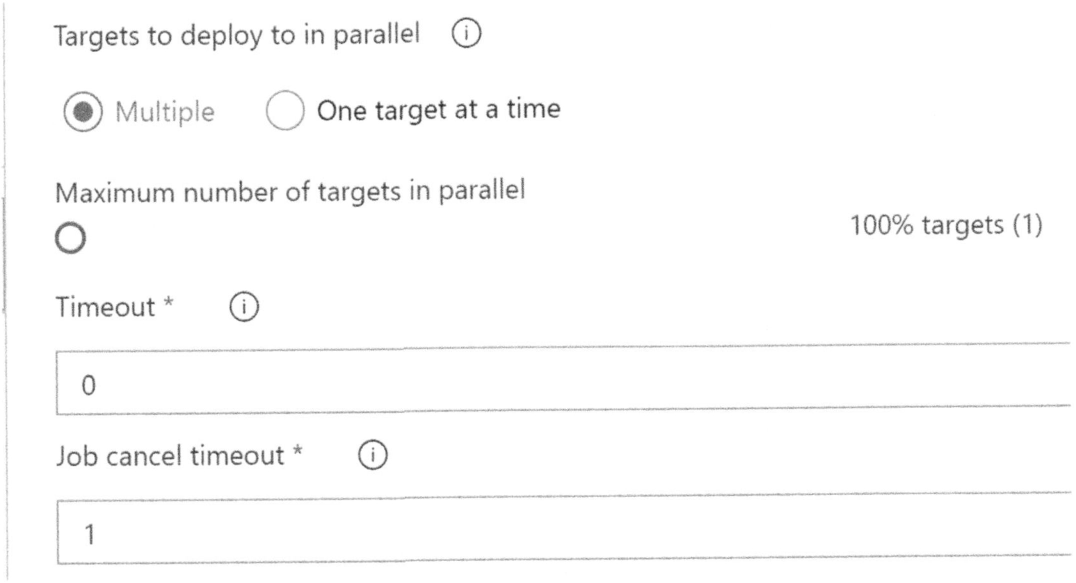

Targets to deploy to in parallel

Multiple One target at a time

Maximum number of targets in parallel

100% targets (1)

Timeout *

0

Job cancel timeout *

1

Figure 10-6. *Target parallel settings and timeouts*

Similar to agent jobs in the deployment groups, you can also define which of the artifacts are to be downloaded in a given job. OAuth token access and execution of jobs based on conditions can be also set similarly to agent jobs. These features can be used to define rollback and test execution scenarios with deployment groups as we have explained with agent jobs in the previous lesson. When using test executions, the role in such a machine can be a test client role based on a tag such as TestClient.

The tasks can be used in deployment group phases similar to agent jobs to achieve deployments based on their target roles. Even in the marketplace tasks, task groups can be utilized as required.

In this lesson, we explored the options available in the deployment group jobs to set up release pipelines in Azure DevOps.

Lesson 10.03: Agentless Jobs

Agentless jobs are useful to execute steps that do not require a machine to perform the steps that are being executed. There are a limited number of steps that can be executed on an agentless job. See Figure 10-7.

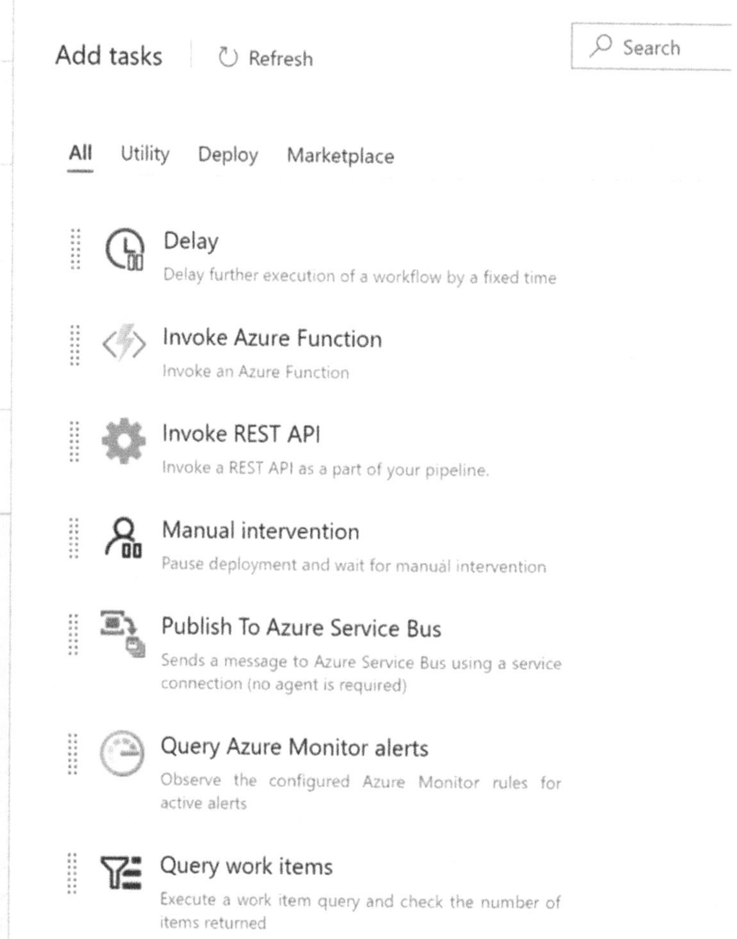

Figure 10-7. *Agentless job steps*

You can use delay steps to wait for a given time after a given agent or deployment group job, using an agentless phase. Once the delay time is passed, the next agent or deployment group job can be executed. This type of delay would be useful in scenarios such as when you are provisioning infrastructure on cloud platform targets. There might be time requirements once infrastructure commands are executed on such cloud platforms to provision the required platform resources. Therefore, the delay task could be used to wait on such a required time.

Similar to gates applied between stages of a pipeline, in pre- and post-deploy stages, you can utilize the agentless phase to implement such gating between agent or deployment group jobs or by using tasks such as Invoke Azure Function, Invoke REST API, Query Azure Monitor Alerts, and Query Work Item tasks. For more information about gating, refer to Chapter 9.

The manual intervention task can be used to implement an approval, a rejection step in between the agent, or the deployment group jobs. These approvals can be useful in scenarios such as where you want to manually perform an action before executing the next steps of the pipeline.

In agentless jobs, there are minimal sets of settings compared to the agent or deployment group jobs. See Figure 10-8. The agentless job can be executed for multiple configurations as specified in multipliers. A timeout can be specified to execute the agentless phase. The run conditions allow you to define if the agentless phase should be executed based on previous step success or failure; or using a custom condition, which help you to determine whether you need to execute an agentless job based on the pipeline execution flow.

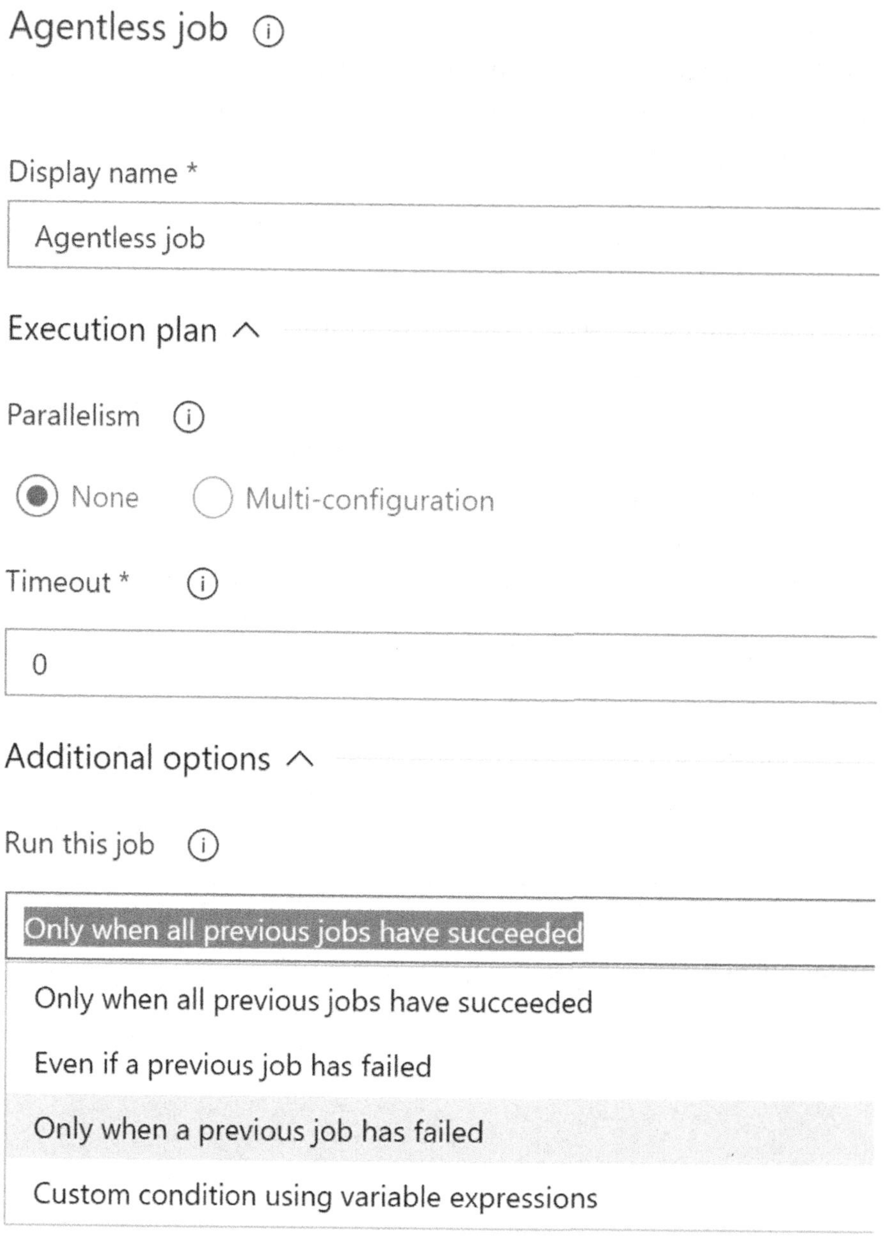

Figure 10-8. *Agentless job settings*

In this lesson, we discussed the agentless phase and usage of the agentless steps in release pipelines.

Lesson 10.04: Variables

Release pipelines similar to build pipelines contain the variables. In the variables tab of release pipelines, you can define the key and value pairs. The sensitive information contained in variables can be defined as secrets, and such variable values are not visible once marked as sensitive. See Figure 10-9.

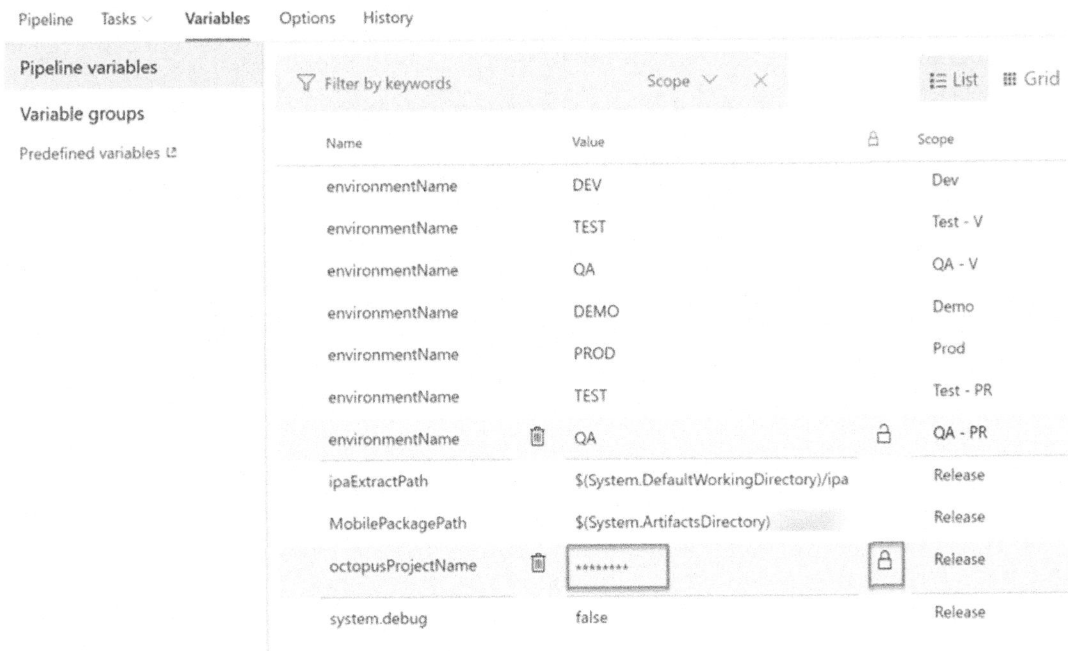

Figure 10-9. Sensitive variables

The variables in a release pipeline can be scoped to the release or to a stage as shown in Figure 10-9. The same variable can contain a different value for each stage. For each variable in the release pipeline, you can set it to settable at release time, which allows the values of those variables to be set at the time of the release creation. See Figure 10-10.

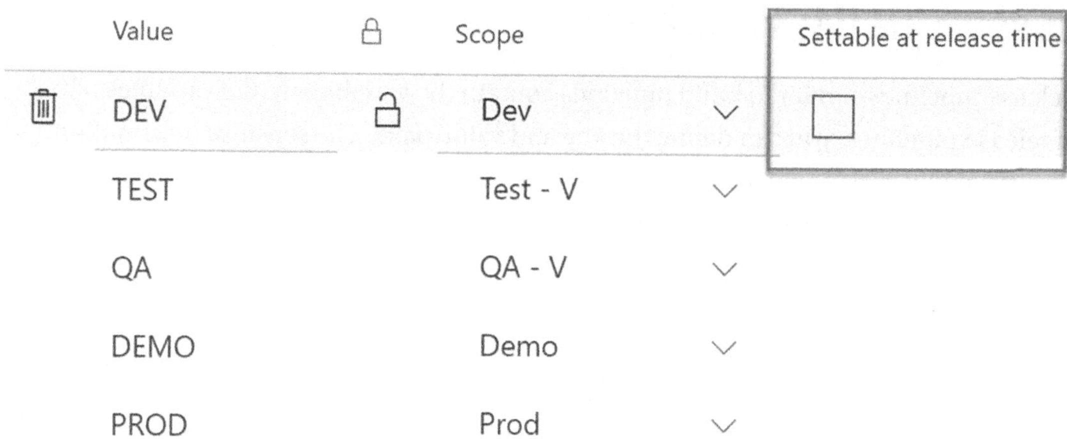

***Figure 10-10.** Settable at release time*

Variable groups, as explained in Chapter 2, can be used to keep shared variables for multiple release pipelines, or even to share variables with the build pipelines. Such variable groups can be utilized in release pipelines with the scope of release or with a stage(s) scope. See Figure 10-11.

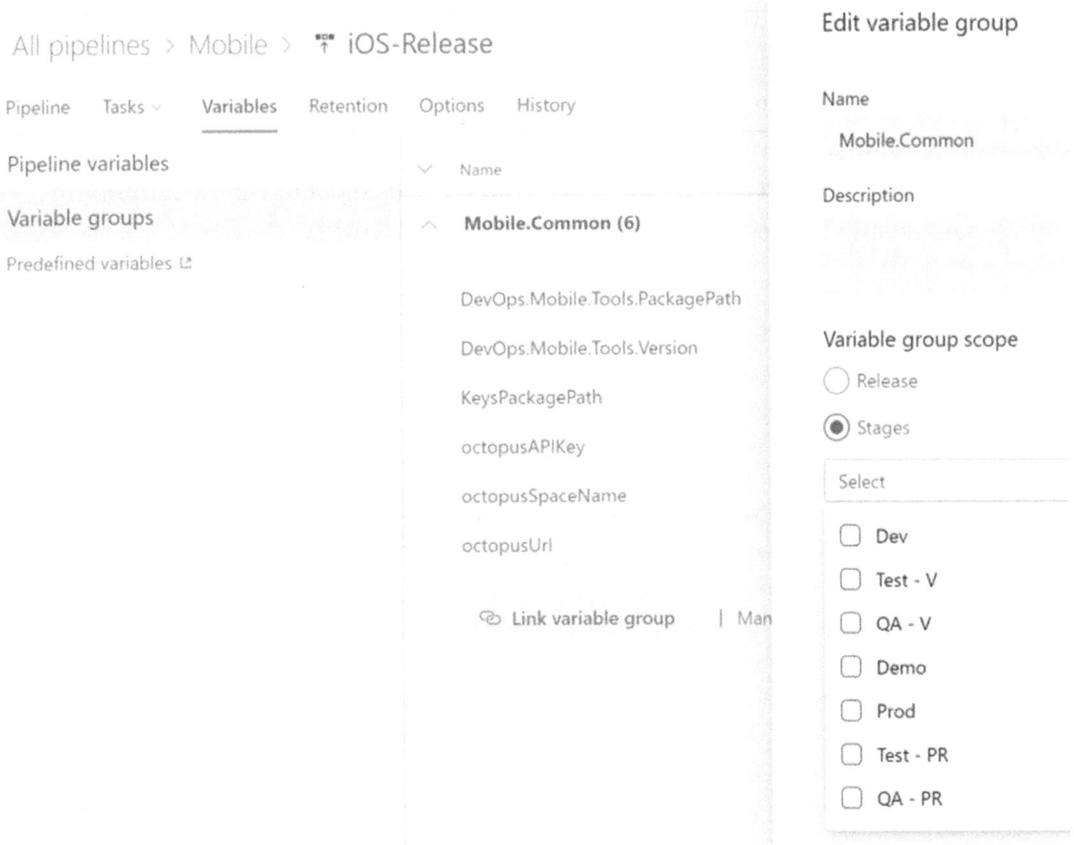

Figure 10-11. *Variable groups in release pipelines*

Variables can be reused using a $(variablename) in another variable as it automatically resolves. This is useful to repeating values in multiple variables and makes sure variables are containing unique values, and changing one place is only required to change variable values.

In this lesson, we discussed variables and their usage in release pipelines.

Lesson 10.05: Other Useful Features

Release pipelines have a couple of other useful features: in the retentions tab, options tab, history, tab and in a release menu such as import, export options.

In the retentions tab, you can set release retention settings. There is a link to set up project defaults as well for retentions. You can set the number of days to retain a release and the minimum number of releases that should be retained regardless of the retain dates setting. Days to retain specifies the number of days a release would be kept. Regardless of the number of days, the number of releases specified in the minimum number of releases to keep will be preserved. See Figure 10-12.

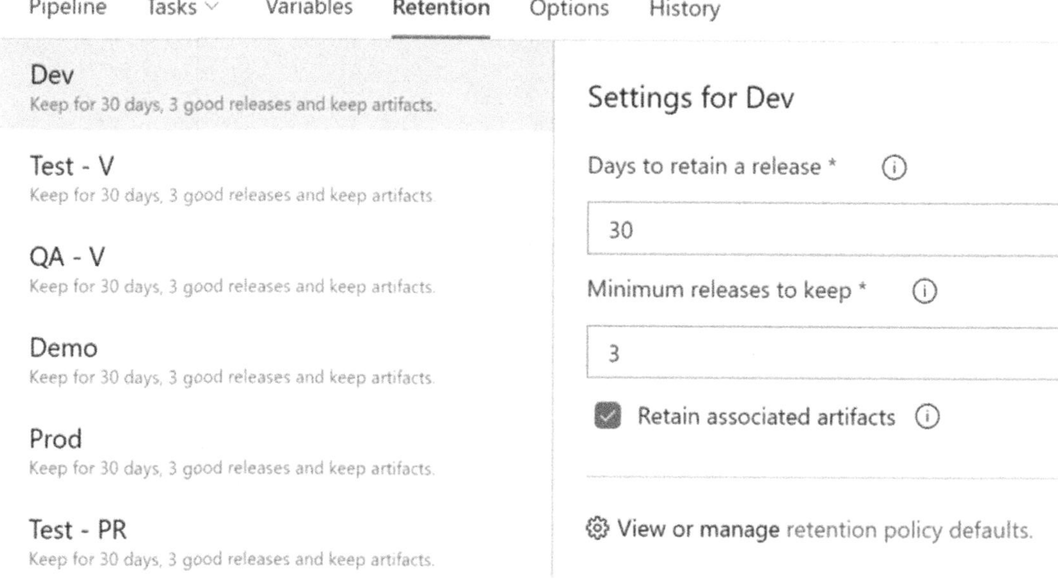

Figure 10-12. *Retention*

You can set the release number format and add a description to the release definition. The release number can be used with a build number with a revision to give more meaning to the full release number as an example. See Figure 10-13.

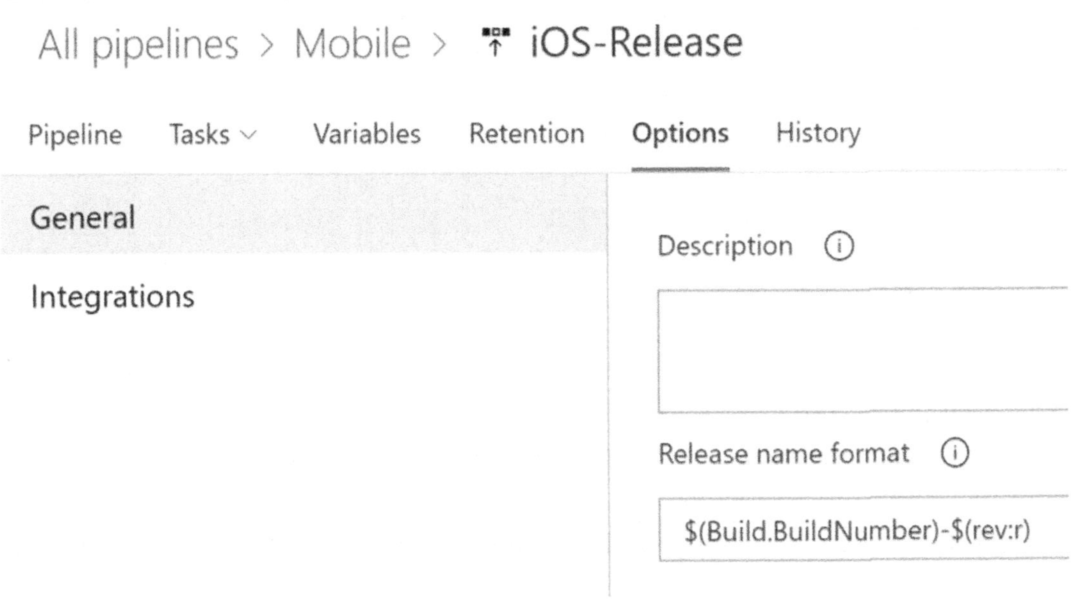

Figure 10-13. Release number

The options tab has integration options for the release pipeline to integrate with the repositories, boards, and external service Jira as well. See Figure 10-14.

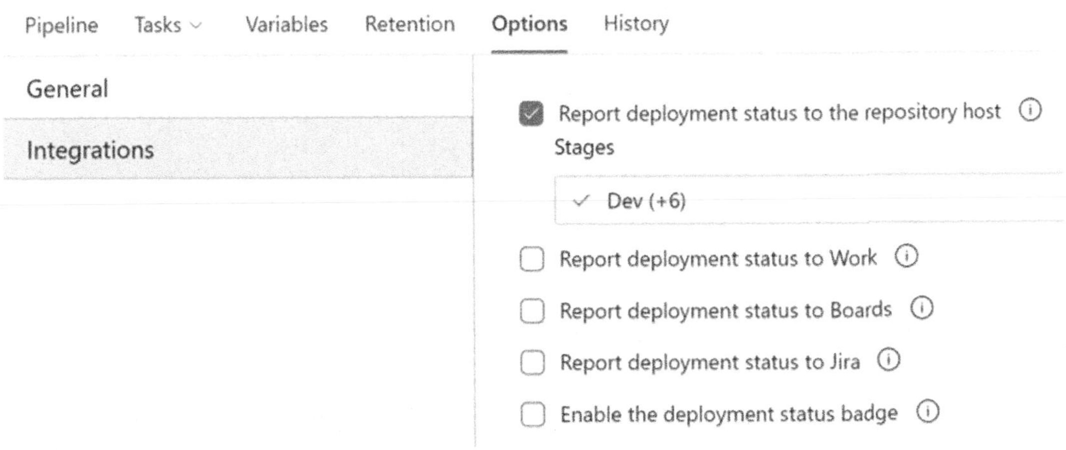

Figure 10-14. Integrations

The history of the release pipeline provides information about revisions in the release pipeline where you can make comparisons of versions as well as revert to a given version if required.

In this lesson, we discussed a few of the useful options available with release pipelines.

Summary

In this chapter, we explored agent jobs, deployment group jobs, and agentless jobs and their usage in detail. Additionally, we looked at a few other features such as variables, options, integrations, retention settings, and histories of release pipelines and their usage.

In the next chapter, we explore the REST API and the command-line interface features and the usage of them.

CHAPTER 11

REST API, Command Line, and Extension Development

Over the last few chapters, we talked about build and release pipelines in Azure DevOps. We have looked at the classic as well as YAML pipelines. For the pipeline capabilities we discussed, there is REST API support for us to handle many actions programmatically. Further, the command-line interface (CLI) for Azure DevOps is providing several commands, which can be used for programmatic management of build and releases.

Programmatic access to the build and release pipelines is useful to generate reports, manipulate pipelines behavior, or even implement extensibility to pipelines. In this chapter, let's look at how we can utilize the REST API and CLI and what the prerequisites are. Next, we discuss how to build extensions using programmatic access to the build and release pipelines.

Lesson 11.01: Using Build and Release REST APIs

REST API for the Azure DevOps build is provided with several APIs. You perform operations such as run a build, update build definition, get details about a build, tag a build, and many more with the REST API.

C. Chandrasekara and P. Herath, *Hands-on Azure Pipelines*, https://doi.org/10.1007/978-1-4842-5902-3_11

A REST API request/response pair can be identified with five components as listed below.

- **Request URI**

  `VERB https://{instance}[/{team-project}]/_apis[/{area}]/{resource}?api-version={version}`

  where `instance` defines the Azure DevOps organization or Azure DevOps server as `dev.azure.com/{organization}` or `{server:port}/tfs/{collection}` respectively.

  The resource path should be in the form of `_apis/{area}/{resource}`for example, `_apis/build/builds`. The API version should be defined to denote the version of the REST API to use in the format of `{major}.{minor}[-{stage}[.{resource-version}]]`for example, `api-version=5.0` or `api-version=5.0-preview` or `api-version=5.0-preview.1`

- **HTTPS Request Header**

  A mandatory request header/verb/operation such as GET, POST, PUT, PATCH, or HEAD. Optionally you can provide an authorization header as a bearer token.

- **Message Request Body**

  To support the POST, PUT operations, you can provide a body such as JSON with the content type specified as application/json.

- **Response Message Header**

  HTTP response code with 2xx for success and 4xxx, 5xx for errors. Optionally a response header such as Content-type to support request/response.

- **Response Message Body**

  JSON or XML response body.

The authorization header to access the REST API should be provided with each request. You can use a Personal Access Token (PAT) generated in Azure DevOps with the required scope of access (We have described PAT in more detail in the Hands-On Azure Boards book).

To create the required authorization header in PowerShell, you can use the code segment below.

```
$AzureDevOpsPAT = "yourazuredevopsPAT"
$User="";

$base64AuthInfo = [Convert]::ToBase64String([Text.Encoding]::ASCII.
GetBytes(("{0}:{1}" -f $User,$AzureDevOpsPAT)));
$header = @{Authorization=("Basic {0}" -f $base64AuthInfo)};
```

Then you can use the header in the invoking request as shown here.

```
$Url = 'https://dev.azure.com/'+ $OrganizationName + '/' + $teamProjectName +
            '/_apis/git/policy/configurations?repositoryId=' + $repository.
            id + '&refName=refs/heads/' + $fromBranch + '&api-version=5.1-
            preview.1';

$policies = Invoke-RestMethod -Uri $Url -Method Get -ContentType
application/json -Headers $header
```

The usage of REST API to implement functionality, which is not available out of the box in Azure DevOps, is something worth discussing. For example, take a scenario where you are using build policies to protect your version (release) branches. If you want to copy over branch protection build policies in one version branch to another, there is no out-of-the-box way to do it. You have to manually create the branch protection build policies in a new branch. However, you may use REST API and implement a PowerShell script by getting the policies of one branch and applying it to another.

One other example would be that you may want to generate a release note out of your builds' associated changes and work items, at the time of releasing to a given target. The release to the given target has to consider previous releases done to the target and then check all in-between releases and builds from the last release to the target to identify all the changes coming in with the current release. REST API would come in handy in this situation for you to implement the required functionally in PowerShell and execute it in the release pipeline itself to generate a release note.

Let's have a quick look how you can queue a build using the REST API to understand how it works.

```
POST https://dev.azure.com/{organization}/{project}/_apis/build/builds?api-
version=5.1
```

You have to provide the body for this post request for the REST API. The json body provided should contain the build definition id as a minimum requirement. Additionally, you can provide more information such as the source branch. Note that build definition id 48 is hard-coded below, and it can be parameterized.

```
{
        "definition": {
            "id": 48
        },
        "sourceBranch": "master"}
```

A sample script for this type of a request can be identified as shown below.

```
$AzureDevOpsPAT = "yourPAT"
$OrganizationName = "yourAzureDevOpsOrgname"
$teamProjectName = 'yourteamprojectname'

$User="";

$base64AuthInfo = [Convert]::ToBase64String([Text.Encoding]::ASCII.
GetBytes(("{0}:{1}" -f $User,$AzureDevOpsPAT)));
$header = @{Authorization=("Basic {0}" -f $base64AuthInfo)};

$Url = 'https://dev.azure.com/'+ $OrganizationName + '/' + $teamProjectName
+ '/_apis/build/builds?api-version=5.1'

$body = '{
        "definition": {
            "id": 48
        },
        "sourceBranch": "master",
    }';

$BuildQResponse = Invoke-RestMethod -Uri $Url -Method Post -ContentType
application/json -Headers $header -Body $body

$BuildQResponse
```

In this lesson, we discussed the possibilities of using REST API for perform actions on build and release. Further, a couple of useful scenarios explained where REST API can be used and we had a look at a sample to understand how it works with PowerShell.

Lesson 11.02: Using the Azure Pipeline CLI

Similar to the REST API, we can use the Azure DevOps CLI for programmatic access and perform actions on Azure pipelines. Azure DevOps CLI is an extension to the Azure CLI. As a prerequisite, you need to have Azure CLI installed.

You can check currently installed extensions to Azure CLI by executing `az --version` in a PowerShell window or in a command prompt. See Figure 11-1.

```
PS C:\WINDOWS\system32> az --version
azure-cli                         2.0.76 *

command-modules-nspkg              2.0.3
core                              2.0.76 *
nspkg                              3.0.4
telemetry                          1.0.4

Python location 'C:\Program Files (x86)\Microsoft SDKs\Azure\CLI2\python.exe'
Extensions directory 'C:\Users\chami\.azure\cliextensions'

Python (Windows) 3.6.6 (v3.6.6:4cf1f54eb7, Jun 27 2018, 02:47:15) [MSC v.1900 32 bit (Intel)]

Legal docs and information: aka.ms/AzureCliLegal


You have 2 updates available. Consider updating your CLI installation.
PS C:\WINDOWS\system32>
```

Figure 11-1. *Installed az extensions*

To set up the az devops extension, you can execute the `az extension add --name azure-devops` in a PowerShell, Command Prompt, or Terminal window. See Figure 11-2.

```
PS C:\WINDOWS\system32> az extension add --name azure-devops
PS C:\WINDOWS\system32> az --version
azure-cli                          2.0.76 *

command-modules-nspkg               2.0.3
core                               2.0.76 *
nspkg                               3.0.4
telemetry                           1.0.4

Extensions:
azure-devops                       0.17.0
```

Figure 11-2. *Install az devops extension*

To understand the available commands in az devops extension, execute `az devops --help`. You can see there are several commands available. Out of that let's focus on the pipeline commands. See Figure 11-3.

```
PS C:\WINDOWS\system32> az devops --help

Group
    az devops : Manage Azure DevOps organization level operations.
        Related Groups
        az pipelines: Manage Azure Pipelines
        az boards: Manage Azure Boards
        az repos: Manage Azure Repos
        az artifacts: Manage Azure Artifacts.

Subgroups:
    admin            : Manage administration operations.
    extension        : Manage extensions.
    project          : Manage team projects.
    security         : Manage security related operations.
    service-endpoint : Manage service endpoints/connections.
    team             : Manage teams.
    user             : Manage users.
    wiki             : Manage wikis.

Commands:
    configure        : Configure the Azure DevOps CLI or view your configuration.
    invoke           : This command will invoke request for any DevOps area and resource. Please use
                       only json output as the response of this command is not fixed. Helpful docs -
                       https://docs.microsoft.com/en-us/rest/api/azure/devops/.
    login            : Set the credential (PAT) to use for a particular organization.
    logout           : Clear the credential for all or a particular organization.
```

Figure 11-3. *az devops commands*

You have to execute the `az devops login --org orgname` and then provide the PAT as the token when prompted to get the CLI authenticated with the Azure DevOps organization. You can also set the environment variable using `$env:AZURE_DEVOPS_EXT_PAT = 'yourPAT'` in Windows and using `export AZURE_DEVOPS_EXT_PAT=yourPAT` in Linux or macOS, and log on. See Figure 11-4.

```
PS C:\WINDOWS\system32> az devops login --org https://dev.azure.com/chamindac
Token:
PS C:\WINDOWS\system32>
```

Figure 11-4. *Login to Azure DevOps with CLI*

Let's take the same example as with REST APPI and try to queue a build to see how it can be done with CLI. To understand the build queue command, you can run an `az pipelines build queue -help,` and it will give all the help information. To queue a build, you can run a command, for example, `az pipelines build queue -p 'Project X' --definition-id 48` and the build will be queued. See Figure 11-5.

```
PS C:\WINDOWS\system32> az pipelines build queue -p 'Project X' --definition-id 48
{
  "buildNumber": "1103",
  "buildNumberRevision": null,
  "controller": null,
  "definition": {
    "createdDate": null,
    "drafts": [],
    "id": 48,
    "name": "MVC5.Rel",
    "path": "\\WebAppBuilds",
    "project": {
      "abbreviation": null,
      "defaultTeamImageUrl": null,
      "description": null,
      "id": "0f1db1ab-7e58-4c72-b5b2-81b3da8c93b6",
      "lastUpdateTime": "2019-01-12T08:33:59.087Z",
      "name": "Project X",
```

Figure 11-5. *Queue build with CLI*

You can use the CLI inside PowerShell scripts or batch scripts and then use them as steps in pipelines or for other purposes.

In this lesson, we discussed how the Azure DevOps CLI can be used for programmatic access to Azure pipelines.

Lesson 11.03: Developing and Distributing Extensions

You can develop extensions for Azure pipelines if the existing out-of-the-box functionality or available extensions in the marketplace are not satisfying your required action for the pipeline.

You have options to set up pipeline extensions with typescript based or PowerShell based ones. However, only windows agents are able to run PowerShell-based tasks. It is advisable to use typescript for developing pipeline extensions if you intend to run it on all agent platforms.

You need to run an `npm init` in a folder from PowerShell or in a Terminal window to get the npm initialization done for the extension. Provide required information when prompted, and the initial package.json will be created in the folder. See Figure 11-6.

```
About to write to C:\temp\extsample\package.json:

{
  "name": "extsample",
  "version": "1.0.0",
  "description": "",
  "main": "index.js",
  "scripts": {
    "test": "echo \"Error: no test specified\" && exit 1"
  },
  "author": "chamindac",
  "license": "ISC"
}


Is this OK? (yes)
PS C:\temp\extsample>
```

Figure 11-6. *npm init to create package.json*

Then you can run npm install azure-pipelines-task-lib -save to add the task library to create pipeline tasks. See Figure 11-7. This installs required node modules to your extensions folder.

```
PS C:\temp\extsample> npm install azure-pipelines-task-lib --save
npm        created a lockfile as package-lock.json. You should commit this file.
npm WARN extsample@1.0.0 No description
npm WARN extsample@1.0.0 No repository field.

+ azure-pipelines-task-lib@2.9.3
added 10 packages from 16 contributors and audited 10 packages in 6.02s
found 0 vulnerabilities

PS C:\temp\extsample>
```

Figure 11-7. *Add pipeline task lib*

Then you need to add typescript typings by executing the following commands.

```
npm install @types/node --save-dev
npm install @types/q --save-dev
```

Run the `tsc -init` to make sure typescripts are compiled to javascripts when the extension is built. If typescript is not already set up in your machine, you need to install it globally with the `npm install -g typescript` command.

With this all necessary structure to develop, your extension is created in the folder. Next, you need to add the task json to the extension task folder. You can use the template shown below and replace the {{placeholder}} with the required values. This template is available in the Microsoft documentation, and it is advisable to copy the latest one from the documentation. Inputs in the below file content are intended for the sample task, and you may have to use inputs depending on your task requirements.

```
{
    "$schema": "https://raw.githubusercontent.com/Microsoft/azure-
    pipelines-task-lib/master/tasks.schema.json",
    "id": "{{taskguid}}",
    "name": "{{taskname}}",
    "friendlyName": "{{taskfriendlyname}}",
    "description": "{{taskdescription}}",
    "helpMarkDown": "",
```

```
    "category": "Utility",
    "author": "{{taskauthor}}",
    "version": {
        "Major": 0,
        "Minor": 1,
        "Patch": 0
    },
    "instanceNameFormat": "Echo $(samplestring)",
    "inputs": [
        {
            "name": "samplestring",
            "type": "string",
            "label": "Sample String",
            "defaultValue": "",
            "required": true,
            "helpMarkDown": "A sample string"
        }
    ],
    "execution": {
        "Node10": {
            "target": "index.js"
        }
    }
}
```

Replaceable values in the above task json file can be updated similarly to what is below.

```
    "id": "bdf70ab0-8600-45fd-98d4-834e22030ff6",
    "name": "chamindacdemotask",
    "friendlyName": "My Demo Task",
    "description": "Demo Task",
    "helpMarkDown": "",
    "category": "Utility",
    "author": "chamindac",
```

Then we can create an intex.ts (typescript file) with the content below to enable functionality of the demo/sample task.

```
import tl = require('azure-pipelines-task-lib/task');

async function run() {
    try {
        const inputString: string | undefined = tl.getInput
        ('samplestring', true);
        if (inputString == 'bad') {
            tl.setResult(tl.TaskResult.Failed, 'Bad input was given');
            return;
        }
        console.log('Hello', inputString);
    }
    catch (err) {
        tl.setResult(tl.TaskResult.Failed, err.message);
    }
}

run();
```

Then you can execute `tsc` from the extension folder to compile the typescript as a javascript. Now if you run node `index.js`, it will test the extension locally; however, it will fail since no input is provided. See Figure 11-8.

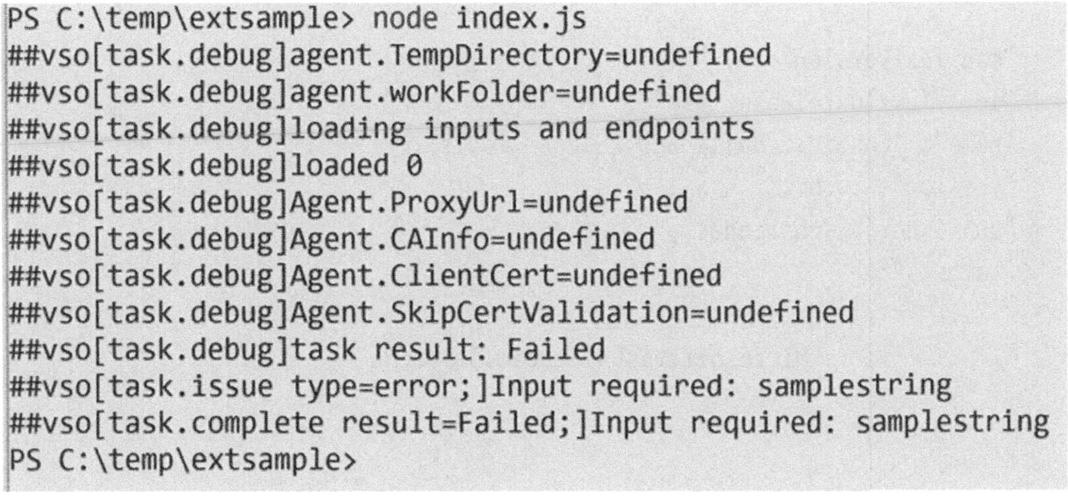

```
PS C:\temp\extsample> node index.js
##vso[task.debug]agent.TempDirectory=undefined
##vso[task.debug]agent.workFolder=undefined
##vso[task.debug]loading inputs and endpoints
##vso[task.debug]loaded 0
##vso[task.debug]Agent.ProxyUrl=undefined
##vso[task.debug]Agent.CAInfo=undefined
##vso[task.debug]Agent.ClientCert=undefined
##vso[task.debug]Agent.SkipCertValidation=undefined
##vso[task.debug]task result: Failed
##vso[task.issue type=error;]Input required: samplestring
##vso[task.complete result=Failed;]Input required: samplestring
PS C:\temp\extsample>
```

Figure 11-8. *Test the extension task*

You can provide an input string with `$env:INPUT_SAMPLESTRING="Chaminda"` and test it as well to check the successful execution. See Figure 11-9.

```
PS C:\temp\extsample> $env:INPUT_SAMPLESTRING="Chaminda"
PS C:\temp\extsample> node index.js
##vso[task.debug]agent.TempDirectory=undefined
##vso[task.debug]agent.workFolder=undefined
##vso[task.debug]loading inputs and endpoints
##vso[task.debug]loading INPUT_SAMPLESTRING
##vso[task.debug]loaded 1
##vso[task.debug]Agent.ProxyUrl=undefined
##vso[task.debug]Agent.CAInfo=undefined
##vso[task.debug]Agent.ClientCert=undefined
##vso[task.debug]Agent.SkipCertValidation=undefined
##vso[task.debug]samplestring=Chaminda
Hello Chaminda
PS C:\temp\extsample>
```

Figure 11-9. *Test function providing input parameter value*

To deploy the extension, you need to package it. But before packaging it, you need to create a manifest file for it. For the example we used, you can create a file named vss-extension.json and add the content below.

```
{
    "manifestVersion": 1,
    "id": "build-release-task",
    "name": "Chamidac Build and Release Tools",
    "version": "0.0.1",
    "publisher": "chamindac",
    "targets": [
        {
            "id": "Microsoft.VisualStudio.Services"
        }
    ],
```

```
    "description": "Tools for building/releasing with chamindac. Includes
    one build/release task.",
    "categories": [
        "Azure Pipelines"
    ],
    "icons": {
        "default": "images/extension-icon.png"
    },
    "files": [
        {
            "path": "buildAndReleaseTask"
        }
    ],
    "contributions": [
        {
            "id": "custom-build-release-task",
            "type": "ms.vss-distributed-task.task",
            "targets": [
                "ms.vss-distributed-task.tasks"
            ],
            "properties": {
                "name": "buildAndReleaseTask"
            }
        }
    ]
}
```

To package your extension you need to have tfx CLI, which can be installed with the `npm i -g tfx-cli` command. You have to create a folder named `buildAndReleaseTask` in the extension folder and move all the files and folders except the `vss-extension.json` file. You can add more folders in the extension and add more tasks to create an extension with multiple tasks. Then from the extension folder, run `tfx extension create --manifest-globs vss-extension.json` command to package the extension.

To create a publisher you have to sign into `https://marketplace.visualstudio.com/manage` and set up your publisher profile. Then you can publish your extension, sharing to your organization with the `tfx extension publish --manifest-globs vss-extension.json --share-with https://dev.azure.com/yourorgname` command.

Once published, your extension can be shared to other organizations or shared publicly. See Figure 11-10.

Figure 11-10. *Extensions*

In this lesson, we discussed how to build an extension for Azure pipelines.

Summary

We discussed programmatic access to Azure pipelines using the REST API and command-line interface in this chapter. Further, we have talked about basic steps required to build an extension for pipelines.

In the next chapter, we look at test automation integration options with Azure pipelines.

CHAPTER 12

Integrating Tests to Pipelines

Testing is a very important aspect of the software delivery process. A couple of testing types can be easily automated and get integrated with the build and release pipelines in order to assure the quality of the delivered software projects or products.

In this chapter, we are going to look at the types of testing that can be automated and the features and components that we can use to effectively run test automations with pipelines.

Lesson 12.01: Running Unit Tests with Pipelines

It is important to validate the code of your application with unit tests to ensure the code is working as expected. Unit tests are implemented to test the code that is written by the developers using the test-driven development approaches (TDD) and behavioral driven development (BDD).

Build pipelines can be used to execute unit tests written with many types of unit testing tools. The general practice is to build the code and then execute the unit tests and package the code as deployable binaries. To execute the test with build pipelines, you can find several tasks available. See Figure 12-1.

C. Chandrasekara and P. Herath, *Hands-on Azure Pipelines*, https://doi.org/10.1007/978-1-4842-5902-3_12

All Build Utility Test Package Deploy Tool Marketplace
structure-test) to validate the structure of an image based on four categories of tests - command tests, file existence tests, file content tests and metadata tests

Publish code coverage results
Publish Cobertura or JaCoCo code coverage results from a build

Publish Test Results
Publish test results to Azure Pipelines

Python Unit Test
Runs unit tests against your Python 3 code base

Visual Studio Test
Run unit and functional tests (Selenium, Appium, Coded UI test, etc.) using the Visual Studio Test (VsTest) runner. Test frameworks that have a Visual Studio test adapter such as MsTest, xUnit, NUnit, Chutzpah (for JavaScript tests using QUnit, Mocha and Jasmine), etc. can be run. Tests can be distributed on multiple agents using this task (version 2).

Figure 12-1. *Test tasks*

Using a Visual Studio Test task, you can execute multiple types of tests developed with test frameworks such as MSTest, xUnit, NUnit, etc. The task allows you to distribute your test across multiple agents to run them efficiently, while using a multiple agents configuration in the agent job.

There are other tasks such as the dotnet command-line task, allowing you to run a dotnet test to execute the tests developed with .NET Core. The command-line tasks can be used to execute tasks such as machine learning code unit test runs. See Figure 12-2.

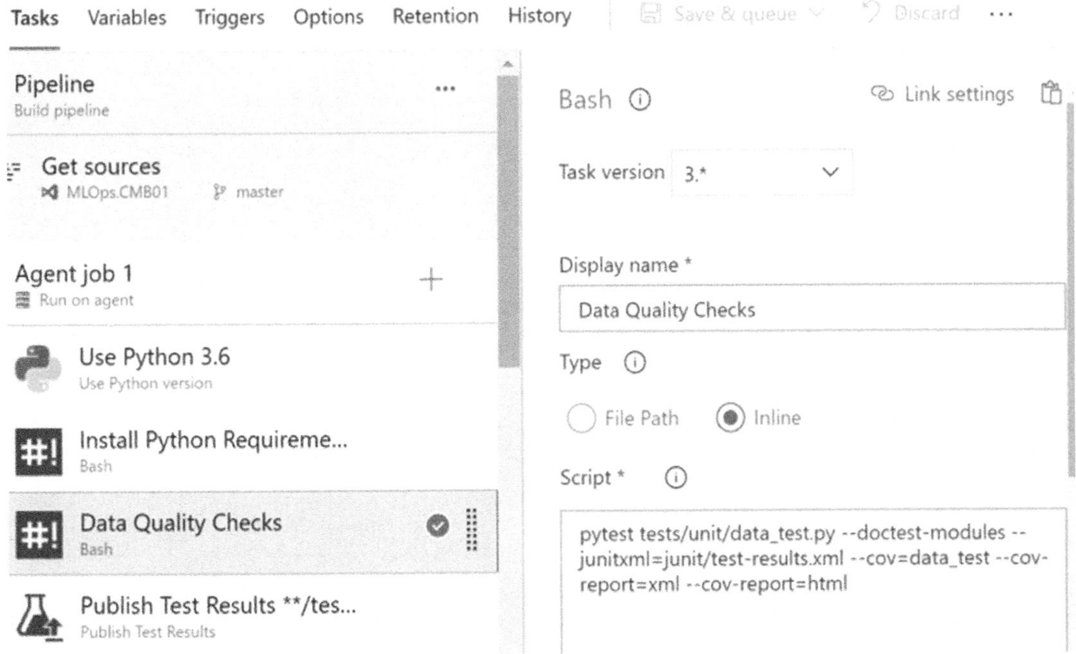

Figure 12-2. *Running Python tests*

When tests are run from the VS Test task or dotnet test, the results of the test run get published to the pipeline automatically. However, if you are executing tests using command lines, such as Python tests, the output of the test result may need to be published to the pipeline so that the results are shown in the test tab of the executed build. To publish tests results, you can use the Publish Test Results task and specify the result output file and the format of test results of the test execution so that it will be published to the pipeline. See Figure 12-3.

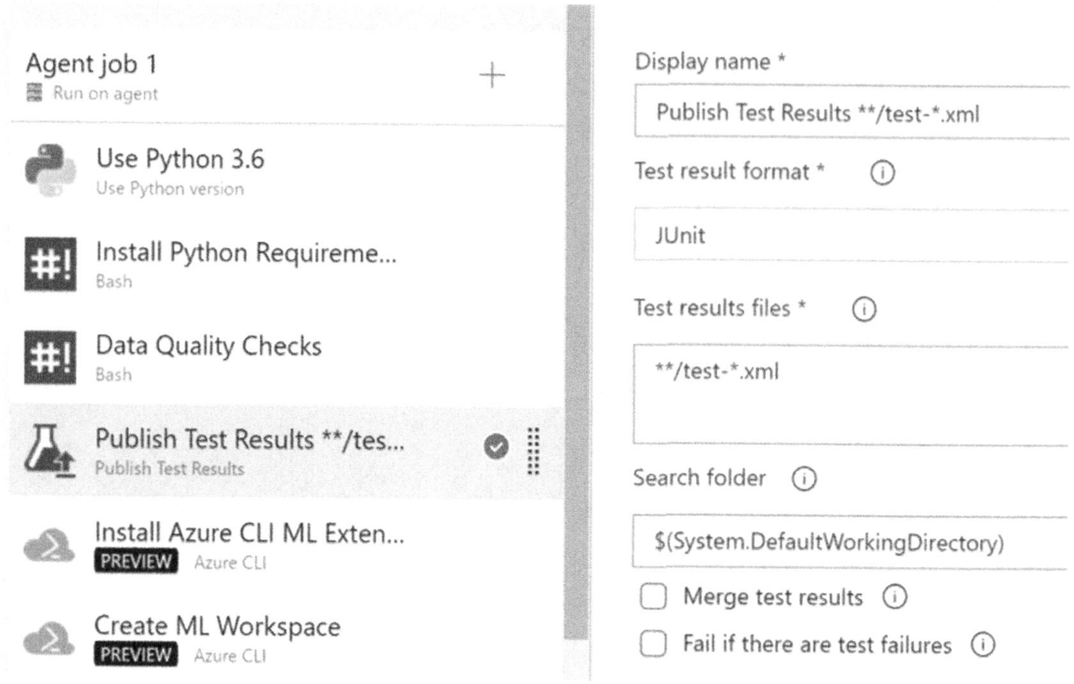

Figure 12-3. Publish test results

In this lesson, we discussed how we can utilize tasks available for pipelines to set up unit test execution with build pipelines.

Lesson 12.02: Running Functional Tests with Pipelines

Integration and functional tests are used to test deployed applications. They might be implemented as API-level testing or User Interface testing using different test frameworks. Selenium is one of the main test frameworks widely used with .Net and other languages. There are other test frameworks such as Cypress, which is also facilitating scenario-based functional UI test implementation.

The implemented automated functional testing to test an application should be executed after a deployment to a given target to make sure the target application is working as expected. Automation and running the automated functional tests with deployment pipelines enable teams to run most of their tests, for each release, so that higher quality in delivered applications can be achieved.

A functional test based on Selenium requires you to run the agent in interactive mode to execute the testing. We talked about setting up agents in Chapter 3 of this book. However, Cypress framework UI tests can be executed with non-interactive agents as well.

To execute Selenium-based tests, you can utilize an agent setup in a virtual or physical machine as an interactive agent. Such an agent should be prepared for test execution with the Visual Studio Test Platform Installer task. See Figure 12-4.

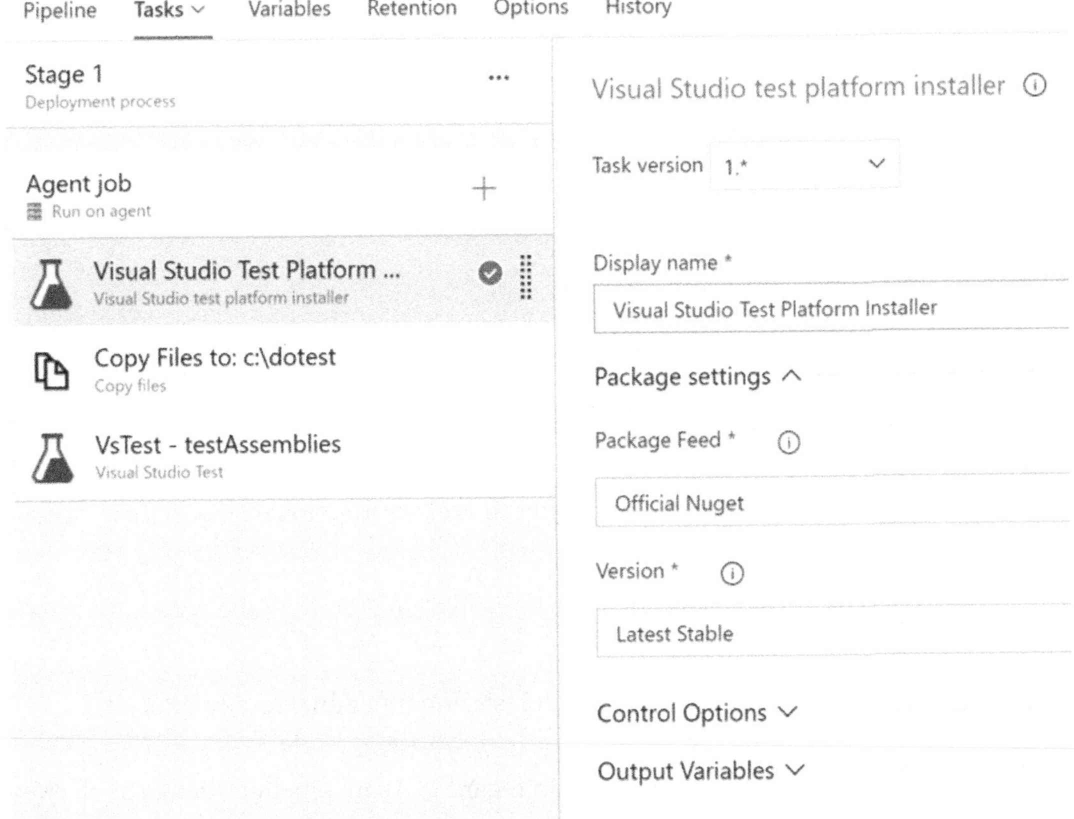

Figure 12-4. *VS Test Platform Installer*

Then you can use the VS Test task to execute the tests written with Selenium using C#. If you have developed the tests in Java, you can use Maven tasks to execute the tests in the release pipelines.

The test execution may require you to use virtual machines as test clients, especially when you need to run an interactive agent. You may need to set up multiple test client machines to efficiently distribute and run your functional tests. However, keeping these virtual machines continuously running in a cloud platform such as Azure would be costly. To minimize the costs, you can set up to an on-demand start for the machines, just before test execution; and once the test execution is done, shut down the test clients so the charges on the cloud platform will be minimized. See Figure 12-5.

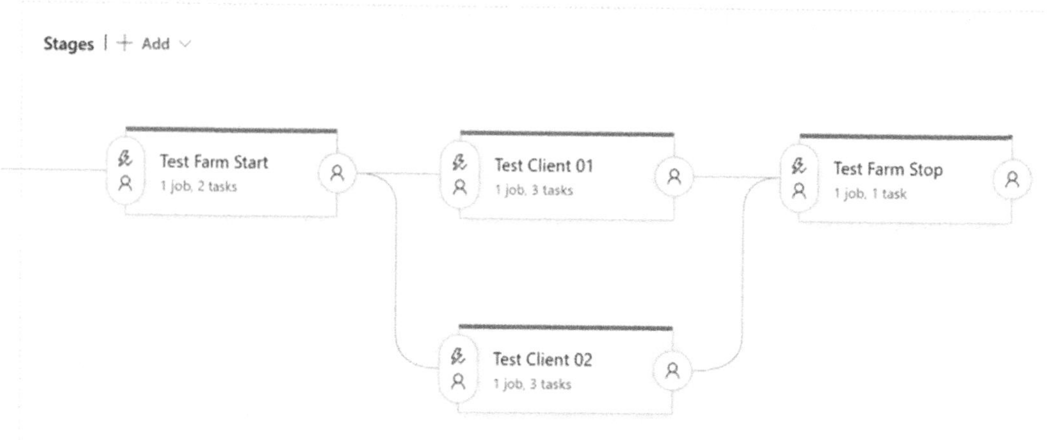

Figure 12-5. *Test client start and stop on demand*

We discussed the usage of release pipelines to execute functional tests in this lesson.

Summary

In this chapter, we discussed the usage of unit tests and functional test execution to ensure quality of the delivered applications.

We talked about several important facts in regard to Azure pipelines in this book. We have gone through why we need to implement continuous integration and delivery with the introductory chapter. Then we explored how the agent pools and agents and even the deployment setup. Next, we discussed classic build pipelines in detail in the next couple of chapters. The YAML pipelines were also discussed to enable you to understand the usage of pipelines as code. In addition to that, we discussed release pipelines usage and implementation and usage of test execution in release and build pipelines. Overall, the book has given you essential insights into implementing and using Azure pipelines, to enable you to deploy software applications with a rapid cadence while not compromising the quality of the applications delivered.

Index

C. Chandrasekara and P. Herath, *Hands-on Azure Pipelines*, https://doi.org/10.1007/978-1-4842-5902-3

S

T, U

V, W, X

Y, Z

Made in the USA
Middletown, DE
08 October 2021